John Clare

New Approaches

John Clare

New Approaches

Edited by John Goodridge and Simon Kövesi

The John Clare Society

2000

Published by the John Clare Society, 2000

The John Clare Society
The Stables,
1A West St, Helpston,
Peterborough PE6 7DU

http://human.ntu.ac.uk/clare

Copyright (c) John Goodridge, Simon Kövesi,
and the other contributors as listed on the contents page.

Typeset by Simon Kövesi

Printed by Bell and Bain, Glasgow

ISBN 0 9522541 6 6

First edition, 2000

The front cover image is Andy Goldsworthy's photograph of his sculpted oak-tree ball, reproduced from *Andy Goldsworthy* (Viking, 1990), by kind permission of the artist. Goldsworthy's own note beneath the image is 'Large, fallen oak tree / used leaves with branches still attached / for supporting structure inside ball / JENNY NOBLE'S GILL, DUMFRIESSHIRE / 15 SEPTEMBER 1985'

For Ronald Blythe

CONTENTS

ACKNOWLEDGEMENTS

We would like to thank our respective universities, the Nottingham Trent University and the University of Dundee, as well as the John Clare Society and the Margaret Grainger Memorial Trust, for supporting this publication and the research that led to it. Thanks are also due to Rodney Lines, the Chairman of the John Clare Society, for his valuable help from an early stage in the project, to Marilyn Gaull for her generous support and advice, and to Iain Sim (University of Glasgow) and Simon Scott (University of Dundee) for technical assistance. We are especially grateful to Dr Greg Crossan (Massey University), who very kindly and at short notice read through these essays for us, applying scholarly wisdom and generosity in equal measure. We would also like to thank the delegates of the Nottingham Trent University Clare Conference in 1998, which formed the basis for this selection of essays.

The illustration on p. 91 is reproduced by kind permission of the British Library, and the illustration from NMS 6 on p. 160 is reproduced by kind permission of Northamptonshire Libraries and Information Service. We are grateful to Terry Bracher at Northamptonshire Central Library for his help.

John Goodridge and Simon Kövesi
john.goodridge@ntu.ac.uk
kovesi@hotmail.com

ABBREVIATIONS

Books

AUTOBIOGRAPHICAL WRITINGS *John Clare, Autobiographical Writings*, ed. by Eric Robinson (Oxford: Oxford University Press, 1983, paperback edition 1986).

BY HIMSELF *John Clare By Himself*, ed. by Eric Robinson and David Powell (Ashington and Manchester: Mid-NAG and Carcanet, 1996).

CRITICAL HERITAGE *Clare: The Critical Heritage*, ed. by Mark Storey (London: Routledge & Kegan Paul, 1973).

EARLY POEMS (I-II) *The Early Poems of John Clare*, ed. by Eric Robinson, David Powell and Margaret Grainger (two volumes, Oxford: Clarendon Press, 1989).

HAUGHTON, CONTEXT Hugh Haughton, Adam Phillips, and Geoffrey Summerfield (eds.), *John Clare in Context* (Cambridge: Cambridge University Press, 1994).

JCSJ *The John Clare Society Journal* (1982-).

LATER POEMS *The Later Poems of John Clare*, ed. by Eric Robinson, David Powell and Margaret Grainger (two volumes, Oxford: Clarendon Press, 1984).

LETTERS *The Letters of John Clare*, ed. by Mark Storey (Oxford: Clarendon Press, 1985).

MIDDLE PERIOD *John Clare, Poems of the Middle Period 1822-1837*, ed. by Eric Robinson, David Powell, and P.M.S. Dawson (Oxford: Clarendon Press), volumes I-II (1996), volumes III-IV (1998).

NATURAL HISTORY *The Natural History Prose Writings of John Clare*, ed. by Margaret Grainger (Oxford: Clarendon Press, 1983).

PROSE *The Prose of John Clare*, ed. by J.W. and Anne Tibble (London: Routledge & Kegan Paul, 1951, reprinted 1970).

SHEPHERD'S CALENDAR *John Clare, The Shepherd's Calendar*, ed. by Eric Robinson, Geoffrey Summerfield, and David Powell (Oxford: Oxford University Press, revised edition, 1993).

Manuscripts

Eg.   British Library, Egerton Manuscript.

NMS   Northampton Manuscript, held at Northamptonshire Central Library.

PMS   Peterborough Manuscript, held at Peterborough Museum and Art Gallery.

General

Manuscripts are normally cited using folio (f.) numbers. Deleted material is indicated by angle brackets, editorial interpolations by square brackets. Letters are given in the form *sender-recipient*, date. Clare's poem *Child Harold* may be distinguished from Byron's *Childe Harold* by its variant spelling.

NOTES ON CONTRIBUTORS

JONATHAN BATE is Leverhulme Research Professor at the University of Liverpool and a Fellow of the British Academy. The most recent of his many books is *The Song of the Earth* (Picador UK and Harvard University Press USA, 2000). He is writing a biography of Clare, due for completion at the end of 2001.

PAUL CHIRICO is a Research Fellow at Jesus College, Cambridge. He is working on an edition of Clare's 'fugitive' publications, and a study of the publishing trade in the early nineteenth century.

STEPHEN COLCLOUGH is a Research Fellow with the Book History and Bibliography Research Group in the Department of Literature at the Open University. He has published articles on Clare, and on the history of reading practices in the Romantic period.

RICHARD CRONIN is a Reader in English at the University of Glasgow. His most recent book is *The Politics of Romantic Poetry: In Search of the Pure Commonwealth* (Macmillan, 2000).

P.M.S. DAWSON is a Senior Lecturer in English at the University of Manchester, and an Editor of the Oxford Clare.

JOHN GOODRIDGE is a Reader in English at the Nottingham Trent University. His most recent books are *The Same Stars Shine: The Great War Diary and Letters of Corporal Ernest Goodridge* (Loughborough: Teamprint, 2000), and *John Dyer, Selected Poetry and Prose* (Nottingham: Trent Editions, 2000).

MINA GORJI is working on a PhD on John Clare's Intertextual Language, at Lady Margaret Hall, Oxford.

BOB HEYES has published a number of essays and reviews in the field of Clare studies. He recently completed a PhD at Birkbeck College, University of London, entitled '"Looking to Futurity": John Clare and Provincial Culture'.

BRIDGET KEEGAN is an Associate Professor of English at Creighton University. She has recently edited, with Jim McKusick, *Literature and Nature: Four Centuries of English and American Nature Writing* (Prentice-Hall, 2000). She is currently at work on Volume 2 (1740-1780) of the forthcoming *English Labouring-Class Poets 1700-1900*, and a monograph entitled *Poets Born and Made: The English Self-taught Tradition*.

SIMON KÖVESI is a Teaching Fellow at the University of Dundee. He is editing a series of paperback selections of Clare's verse, which started with *Love Poems* (1999) and *Flower Poems* (2000). He is the Editor of *The John Clare Page* on the Internet, Assistant Editor of the *John Clare Society Journal*, and is working on a book entitled *John Clare and Femininity*.

VALERIE PEDLAR works for the Open University in the North-West, and has contributed to the OU's forthcoming course on the Nineteenth-Century novel. She has published in the *John Clare Society Journal* and is working on a book on madness and masculinity in nineteenth-century fiction.

CATHY TAYLOR recently completed a PhD at the University of York, on 'The Resurrection of *Child Harold*: A Transcription of Nor, MS6 and a Reconsideration of John Clare's *Child Harold* and Related Writings'.

ALAN VARDY is Assistant Professor of English at Hunter College, City University of New York. He is currently completing a monograph on Clare: *John Clare and the Making of a Peasant Poet: Class, Aesthetics, Politics, Poetry*.

INTRODUCTION

John Goodridge and Simon Kövesi

These are interesting times for Clare scholars and enthusiasts. On the one hand, our poet moves inexorably into the cultural and critical mainstream, canonised in Poet's Corner and the National Curriculum,[1] quoted approvingly in government reports on the environment,[2] and vigorously argued over in the scholarly and broadsheet press, as the demand for his writings becomes more urgent, and as new editions and selections emerge at an increasing rate.[3] On the other hand, literary studies has itself moved sharply away from the idea of canonising 'great writers'. Literary canonisation is a process which places much emphasis on the lone, Romantic genius, and the purity of his inspired text. But perhaps the most influential idea in recent Romantic studies, embodied especially in the work of Jerome McGann and Jack Stillinger,[4] has been that literature is above all a social product, whose meaning derives as much from the cultural circumstances of its production and reception as from more ethereal (and inherently Romantic) notions of transcendent genius. At the same time there has been a tremendous growth of interest in the *un*canonised: marginal and neglected writers, particularly women writers, and writers from what has become known as the self-taught tradition. The rise of new disciplines, particularly postcolonial, gender and heritage studies, has given focus to this quickening interest, and done much to determine the ways in which the rediscovered writers are perceived.

These developments may be traced in recent Clare Studies. The three bicentenary essay collections on Clare,[5] all published in 1994, developed ideas of Clare as a resistant, transgressive, trespassing figure, postcolonial *avant la lettre*. The view of Clare as a merely transparent and innocent eye was strongly questioned, and the 'peasant poet' tradition, from which this conception had sprung, was subjected to new scrutiny: just what is, and what was, the self-taught tradition? The project of comparing Clare with his Romantic contemporaries, seemingly stalled by the 'huge Wordsworthian shadow' Harold Bloom had seen looming over Clare in 1961[6] (and perhaps also by the daunting prospect of 'canonisation'), was successfully re-launched in several essays. Clare's mental illness and incarceration were re-examined from perspectives that encompassed for the first time 1960s 'anti-psychiatry' as well as more traditional approaches. John Clare may or may not have been mad: putting him in an asylum for twenty-three years certainly helped to make him so. And the poets (notably Seamus Heaney, Tom Paulin, Andrew Motion, R.S. Thomas and Ted Hughes) reclaimed their ancient kinship with Clare, in prose and verse.[7] Other recent developments in Clare Studies have included a number of theoretically charged essays,[8] joining the more familiar folkloric and historical research on Clare. Although P.M.S. Dawson notes that Clare's 'unusually undogmatic' personality, reflected in his writings, tends to resist single lines of interpretation,[9] there have been some interesting attempts to read Clare in terms of our contemporary theories and concerns: as an ecological thinker, for example,[10] or as a figure who might be read as a vital link between Romanticism and postmodernism.[11]

The present collection of essays, written predominantly by new scholars or by senior scholars who have developed an interest in Clare in recent years, takes up some of these burgeoning themes, and offers some important new ideas and approaches. There is an intense interest here in the nature of Clare as a 'peasant poet': how he was presented to the world by his publishers and patrons; how he presented and created himself as a poet; and how he is presented by modern editors and by biographers. Thus the collection begins with Jonathan Bate's incisive critique of current biographical presentations of Clare, which reads, tests, and establishes some of the strengths and weaknesses of the various accounts.[12] Bate finds some surprising strengths in what has been regarded as the most fanciful of the biographies, and some corresponding blind spots in one of the most respected, forcing us to think afresh about the ways in which a life might be written, and what information a biography can offer. Valerie Pedlar's essay considers Clare's self-presentation in his autobiographical writings, raising important issues about the ways in which these writings have been posthumously edited and presented, and adding to an increasingly impressive body of recent work on the editing of Clare.[13]

More sociable models of literary production are beginning to alter significantly the way that Clare is perceived. He has almost always been seen as an isolated figure, a Wordsworthian solitary, 'poor Clare', set alone in a cultural wilderness with only his love of the natural world to sustain him. Clare certainly presented himself in this light often enough, complaining of the ignorance and narrowness of Helpston society, and declaring plainly in one of the Northborough sonnets that: 'I hate the very noise of troublous man / Who did & does me all the harm he can'.[14] But major work over the past two decades on Clare's roots in popular and folk culture, has done something to alleviate this sense of Romantic isolation.[15] Two essays in particular in the present collection, by Mina Gorji and Bob Heyes, go rather further, setting Clare firmly within literary culture, and offering models of literary communities—real or imagined—in which to situate the poet. For Bob Heyes, who has made a major study of the archive of letters to Clare in the British Library, Clare drew on a range of opinions in developing and honing his poetical talent. Clare's parents, routinely dismissed by modern critics as illiterates, play along with their son's deception that they are hearing someone else's work being recited each night, and respond thoughtfully: 'Aye, boy, if you coud write so, you woud do.' Clare's Stamford publisher Edward Drury, often represented as a sharp and unscrupulous operator (most wittily by Roger Sales, who dubbed him 'Fast Eddie' Drury), is recast as a further kindly helper in the process of publication, as are some of Clare's other local friends. John Taylor, Clare's London publisher, upon whom Clare scholars have heaped much opprobrium,[16] is also presented as someone who helped rather than hindered Clare. Heyes's revisionist essay suggests that there is further work to be done on these issues. Mina Gorji's model of a literary community is equally valuable, though more schematic. Gorji neatly dovetails what we might call Clare's 'fantasy team' of favourite seventeenth-century poetical friends, with the *London Magazine* circle who shared Clare's love of these poets. This in turn casts light on the theme of Clare's self-creation as a poet, and on the means by which he was able to draw together literary and folk culture.

Bridget Keegan, who has been working intensively on the self-taught tradition, identifies in her essay an important sub-stratum of this tradition, that of the Chattertonian 'marvellous boy', in whom youthfulness and spontaneous creativity are intertwined. Though much has been written about Clare as a 'peasant poet', from Taylor's Introductions to the first two volumes, to the early reviews and onwards, it is only recently that the tradition has been subjected to rigorous critical scrutiny. Keegan contributes to this process:

in looking at the idea of a 'boy' she offers also a culturally-gendered reading of Clare.[17]

There has been much debate about Clare's politics in recent years, particularly over the question of his radicalism or conservatism (perhaps typically of Clare, evidence may be drawn from his writings in support of either position). This debate will be considerably refreshed by the recent selection of his political writings, *A Champion for the Poor,*[18] and Stephen Colclough opens another new approach in the exploration of this area. His essay, which recovers a lost political poem, draws our attention to the 'voice of labour' in Clare's poetry. One suspects that some of the political debate about Clare is underscored by a vestigial need to preserve the poet's cultural innocence (perhaps in turn enhancing the value of our role as modern 'recoverers' of that innocence). But the more we learn about Clare, the more deeply 'encultured' he seems. One aspect of this is his intense relationship with the soil beneath his feet, and Paul Chirico draws on this in his essay. Clare dug lime, dug up what he called 'antiquities', dug gardens and perhaps also enclosure ditches. His favourite eighteenth-century poem was Gray's 'Elegy in a Country Churchyard'; and he was intensely aware of the fertility of the earth, as both a burial place and a quickener of life, and so as a marker of time itself. Chirico uses the discovery of archaeological relics as an image of the landscape yielding information, and draws us into the politics of Clare's senses of both geography and history.[19]

Alan Vardy contributes to what is now quite a substantial body of detailed information about the way in which Clare's first two volumes were presented and received, the 'moment', as it were, of Clare's emergence into the limelight.[20] Vardy offers a rigorously contextualised reading of the way Taylor presented Clare: offering a familiar image of 'natural genius' for the critics and reviewers to follow (as, on the whole, they obligingly did). We are to some extent drawn back from the more sympathetic portrayal of Taylor offered by Heyes (and before him by Tim Chilcott and Zachary Leader), in order to be shown what Vardy calls the 'powerful cultural forces' surrounding Clare. Taylor's relationship with Clare, it seems, will continue to stimulate wide scholarly debate.

Moving in quite different directions, Richard Cronin and Paul Dawson bring to Clare Studies their wider experiences of studying both Clare's great contemporaries, and Romanticism in general. Both critics treat Clare's texts as profoundly literary, and are especially alert to the richness of form and language in Clare. Richard Cronin, uneasy with the sentimental stereotyping of Clare which may still often be found in Clare scholarship, finds the poet striving for a linguistic transcendence and purity, occupying an uneasy position, somewhere between strangeness and familiarity, but quite unlike the picturesque view of his language and landscape to which many of us (often quite unconsciously) subscribe. Paul Dawson uses 'The Skylark', and a Keatsian comparison, to offer a reassessment of Clare's position in relation to Romanticism. Fully aware that Romanticism ultimately exploits the natural world, Clare rejects this exploitation. His failed bird's-nesting boys in 'The Skylark' eloquently stand for his attitudes to Romanticism in this detailed reading of the poem.

Both Cronin and Dawson focus on Clare's most accomplished and important collection, *The Midsummer Cushion*, which was gathered together for publication in the early 1830s, but not published until 1979.[21] This was Clare's last serious attempt to get published as a poet (there were stray publications later), and there is a sense in which the poetry of 1841, which has attracted much attention recently,[22] moves completely beyond the dynamics of public presentation established by Clare and his publishers and patrons in 1820-1. Our last two essays address the two key poems of 1841 (recently dubbed by Tim Chilcott Clare's *annus mirabilis*[23]), *Child Harold* and 'Don Juan A Poem'. Cathy Taylor, who has recently completed a detailed study of the *Child Harold* manuscripts, discovers a rich intertextuality in this, the most complex of Clare's longer poems. Her intertextual reading, as one would expect, examines Clare alongside Byron, and adds to earlier comparative studies. But, much more surprisingly, she also discovers Tasso behind the poem, and here we get a real sense of the depth of Clare's poetical knowledge and engagement. His 'self-taught' or 'untaught' status, ironically, disguises a massive knowledge of poetry of all kinds and from all periods. The final essay in the volume, by Simon Kövesi, finds another kind of richness in the poetry of 1841, in the verbal exuberance of 'Don Juan A Poem'. Giving up on his hopes of poetical success, abandoning the systems of publication and patronage have, by this reading, paradoxically freed Clare to say whatever he likes. His rancid misogyny and political cynicism represent an excoriating satirical attack on the society that has first petted, then abandoned, and finally imprisoned and destroyed him.

These, then, are some of the critical issues and approaches that concern contemporary readers, critics and scholars of Clare, which can be investigated more thoroughly via John Goodridge's 'Chronological Survey of Clare Criticism, 1970-2000', which concludes this volume. At the time of writing, the future of Clare Studies in some ways hangs in the balance,[24] but there is little doubt that Clare now attracts more readers, critics, publishers and editors, teachers and students, than ever before. This collection of essays suggests that Clare engages with a remarkably broad spread of cultural and historical materials. He was a vibrantly idiosyncratic reader of both literature and life. If his vision is sometimes strange because of its idiosyncrasy, it is also strangely familiar, and peculiarly interesting to the modern reader. What centrally concerned Clare, increasingly concerns us all. As the first full edition of his poetry nears completion, there is an increasing desire to savour the richness of his *oeuvre*, to empathise with and understand him in his literary and cultural contexts, and to compare his ideas with our own.

NOTES

1. A memorial to Clare in Poets' Corner, Westminster Abbey, designed by John Skelton, was unveiled by the poet laureate Ted Hughes on 13 June 1989. An audio-cassette of the ceremony is available from the John Clare Society. For Clare in the National Curriculum see Jenny Green, 'John Clare (1793-1864)' in *Key Poets: Classic Poetry for the National Curriculum Key Stages 3 and 4* (London: Penguin, 1995), pp. 336-49; David Preen, 'John Clare's Claims in the National Curriculum', *The Use of English*, 50.1 (Autumn 1998), 1-11.
2. Thirteenth Report of the Select Committee on Environment, Transport and Regional Affairs, On the Protection of Field Boundaries, 12 November 1998, archived at <http://www.publications.parliament.uk/pa/cm199798/cmselect/cmenvtra/969/96906.htm>.
3. John Goodridge, 'Poor Clare', *The Guardian*, 22 July 2000, Weekend section, p. 3. See also the many articles and letters listed under 'Further Reading' for 1999 and 2000, below, and at <http://human.ntu.ac.uk/clare/copyright.htm>.
4. Jerome McGann, *The Beauty of Inflections: Literary Investigations in Historical Method and Theory* (Oxford: Clarendon Press, 1985); Jack Stillinger, *Multiple Authorship and the Myth of Solitary Genius* (New York: Oxford University Press, 1991).
5. Richard Foulkes (ed.), *John Clare: a Bicentenary Celebration* (Northampton:

University of Leicester, Department of Adult Education, 1994); John Goodridge (ed.), *The Independent Spirit: John Clare and the Self-Taught Tradition* (Helpston: The John Clare Society and the Margaret Grainger Memorial Trust, 1994); Hugh Haughton, Adam Phillips, and Geoffrey Summerfield (eds.), *John Clare in Context* (Cambridge: Cambridge University Press, 1994).

6. Harold Bloom, 'John Clare: The Wordsworthian Shadow', in his *The Visionary Company* (Garden City, NY: Doubleday, 1961), pp. 434-45. See also James C. McKusick, 'Beyond the Visionary Company: John Clare's Resistance to Romanticism' in Haughton, *Context*, pp. 221-37.

7. Seamus Heaney, 'John Clare: A Bi-centenary Lecture', in Haughton, *Context*, pp. 130-47, reprinted in his *The Redress of Poetry* (London: Faber, 1995), pp. 63-82, as 'John Clare's Prog'. Tom Paulin, 'Clare in Babylon', *Times Literary Supplement*, 20 June 1986, pp. 675-6, reprinted in his *Minotaur: Poetry and the Nation State* (London: Faber, 1992), pp. 47-55; 'John Clare: A Bicentennial Celebration', in Foulkes, *John Clare: A Bicentenary Celebration*, pp. 69-78; 'The Writing Lark: A Letter to John Clare', *JCSJ*, 17 (1998), 5-15. Andrew Motion, 'Find enclosed: John Clare', *Observer*, 5 September 1993, pp. 51-2; 'Bicentenary Thoughts', *JCSJ*, 12 (1993), 30. R.S. Thomas, 'Lunar', *JCSJ*, 12 (1993), 62, collected in his *No Truce with the Furies* (Newcastle upon Tyne: Bloodaxe Books, 1995), p. 12. We are unaware of any publication on Clare by Ted Hughes, but he was a Clare enthusiast, and his reading of 'The Nightingale's Nest' in Westminster Abbey (see note 1) is richly resonant. See also John Lucas (ed.), *For John Clare: An Anthology of Verse* (Helpston: The John Clare Society, 1997).

8. Good examples might include Lynne Pearce, 'John Clare's "Child Harold": a Polyphonic Reading', *Criticism*, 31 (2) (1989), 139-57; Juliet Sychrava, *Schiller to Derrida: Idealism in Aesthetics* (Cambridge: Cambridge University Press, 1989), esp. ch. 6 (pp. 196-219); Margaret Russett 'Like "Wedding Gowns or Money from the Mint": Clare's Borrowed Inheritance', *Romantic Circles Praxis Series*, number on Romanticism and the Law (March 1999), published online at: <http://www.rc.umd.edu/praxis/law/russett/mruss.htm>.

9. P.M.S. Dawson, 'John Clare', in *Literature of the Romantic Period: A Bibliographical Guide*, ed. by Michael O'Neill (Oxford: Clarendon Press, 1998), pp. 167-80.

10. See James McKusick, '"A language that is ever green"; the ecological vision of John Clare', *University of Toronto Quarterly*, 61 (Winter 1991-92), 30-52; Robert Pogue Harrison, *Forests: The Shadow of Civilization* (Chicago and London: University of Chicago Press, 1992), pp. 211-20; Richard Mabey, 'Guest Editorial: Clare and Ecology', Jonathan Bate, 'The Rights of Nature', and W. John Coletta, 'Ecological Aesthetics and the Natural History Poetry of

John Clare', all in *JCSJ*, 14 (1995), 5-6, 7-15 and 29-46.

11. Theresa M. Kelley, 'Postmodernism, Romanticism, and John Clare', in Thomas Pfau and Robert F. Gleckner (eds.), *Lessons of Romanticism: a Critical Companion* (Durham, NC and London: Duke University Press, 1998), pp. 157-70. See also, in the present collection, Valerie Pedlar's comments on the 'postmodern' presentation of Clare's autobiographical writings in recent editions.

12. Bate's essay follows on from and complements Greg Crossan's useful survey, 'The Nine *Lives* of John Clare', *JCSJ*, 5 (1986), 37-46.

13. See Mark Storey, 'Creeping into Print: editing the letters of John Clare', in *The Theory and Practice of Text Editing*, ed. by Ian Small and Marcus Walsh (Cambridge: Cambridge University Press, 1991), pp. 62-89; Zachary Leader, 'John Taylor and the Poems of Clare', in his *Revision and Romantic Authorship* (Oxford: Clarendon, 1996), pp. 206-61; Hugh Haughton, 'Review Essay: Revision and Romantic Authorship: the Case of Clare', *JCSJ*, 17 (1998), 65-73, also available at <http://human.ntu.ac.uk/clare/haughton.html>; Tim Chilcott '*Child Harold* or *Child Harolds*: The Editing of Clare's Texts', *JCSJ*, 19 (2000), 5-17, also available at <http://human.ntu.ac.uk/clare/chilcott.htm>.

14. *Clare-Taylor*, 8 February 1822, *Letters*, p. 230; John Clare, *Northborough Sonnets*, ed. by Eric Robinson, David Powell and P.M.S. Dawson (Ashington and Manchester: Mid-NAG and Carcanet, 1995), p. 55.

15. George Deacon, *John Clare and the Folk Tradition* (London: Sinclair Browne; New York: State Mutual Book and Periodical Service, 1983); David Blamires, 'Chapbooks, Fairytales and Children's Books in the Writings of John Clare', *JCSJ*, 15 (1996), 27-53; *JCSJ*, 16 (1997), 43-7.

16. See for example, the Introduction to *Shepherd's Calendar*, esp. pp. xv, xix.

17. See also Lynne Pearce, 'John Clare's *Child Harold*: the road not taken', in Susan Sellers, Linda Hutcheson and Paul Perron (eds.), *Feminist Criticism: Theory and Practice* (Toronto: University of Toronto Press, 1991), pp. 143-56; Helen Boden, 'Review Essay: Clare, Gender and Art', in Goodridge, *The Independent Spirit*, pp. 198-208.

18. John Clare, *A Champion for the Poor: Political Verse and Prose*, ed. by P.M.S. Dawson, Eric Robinson and David Powell (Ashington and Manchester: Mid-NAG and Carcanet, 2000). See also P.M.S. Dawson, 'John Clare—Radical?', *JCSJ*, 11 (1992), 17-27, 'Common Sense or Radicalism? Some Reflections on Clare's Politics', *Romanticism*, 2.1 (1996), 81-97, and 'Clare and the Ideology of "Common Sense"', *JCSJ*, 16 (1997), 71-78; John Lucas, 'Clare's Politics', in Haughton, *Context*, pp. 148-77.

19. See also Bob Heyes, '"Triumphs of Time": John Clare and the Uses of Antiquity', *JCSJ*, 16 (1997), 5-17.

20. See Tim Chilcott, *A Publisher and His Circle: The Life and Work of John Taylor, Keats's Publisher* (London and Boston: Routledge & Kegan Paul, 1972), pp. 86-128; Leader, 'Taylor and the Poems of Clare'; Matthew Smith, 'The "Peasant Poet" Replies: *Sketches in the Life of John Clare* as a Response to Taylor's Introduction to *Poems Descriptive'*, *JCSJ*, 15 (1996), 21-5.
21. Anne Tibble and R.K.R. Thornton (eds.), *John Clare, The Midsummer Cushion* (Ashington and Manchester: Mid-NAG and Carcanet, 1979).
22. See especially Tim Chilcott's edition of *John Clare, The Living Year 1841* (Nottingham: Trent Editions, 1999), and his essay on *Child Harold* (see note 13).
23. Chilcott, *The Living Year*, p. xvii.
24. A major dispute over the ownership of Clare's copyright dominates discussion of the poet at the time of writing: see note 3.

1. John Clare: Prologue to a New Life

Jonathan Bate

Another biography of Clare? Do we really need one? Of course we do. There are the obvious reasons: all the existing biographies are out of print and all are in different ways now dated. There is an audience hungry for new writing about Clare, and a much bigger potential audience who would be compelled by his life and work if only they knew about it—literary biography, as opposed to academic literary criticism, is the way to reach that audience.

Then there is the question of scholarly resources. Thanks to the extraordinary labours of Eric Robinson, David Powell and Paul Dawson the first complete edition of the poems is nearing completion. The biographer of the twenty-first century will be able to see the poetic career whole in a way that was impossible for those of the twentieth century—the Tibbles, June Wilson, Edward Storey—let alone for the pioneers of the years immediately after Clare's death, Frederick Martin (*The Life of John Clare*, London: Macmillan, 1865) and J. L. Cherry (*Life and Remains*, London: Frederick Warne, 1873). Even the most recent biography, Edward Storey's *A Right to Song: The Life of John Clare* (London: Methuen, 1982) was published before the rigorous re-editing of the key primary materials by Mark Storey (the *Letters*, 1985) and Robinson and Powell (the autobiographical writings, under the title *John Clare By Himself*, 1996).

And perhaps most importantly, there is the simultaneous nearness and farness of Clare. Great writers endure through time because different dimensions of their imagination are discovered and valued by different generations. By a process akin to Darwinian adaptation, their achievement adapts itself to new environments, new ages. Clare is a figure who haunts us because of our fascination with the marginal, the excluded, the silenced, the lost voices. We need such figures in order to question our own easy assumptions about class and sanity; in a deeper sense, we need his story as an admonition to our own self-confidence. Furthermore, his writings—in prose as well as poetry—are the authentic voice of a rural England that is

1

now lost. No one has written so powerfully of his bond with his native place, of the land and landscape, of birds and animals, of the rupture of environmental change. In a time of ecological crisis and heightened environmental awareness, Clare is being reclaimed as a kind of secular prophet. That work of reclamation will be well served by a biography which locates Clare firmly in the history of his own place and the wider history of the phenomenon of dis-place-ment, of psychological, communal and environmental alienation.

Although Clare is in important respects an eighteenth-century poet and in equally important ones a Victorian, he is properly regarded as one of the major English Romantics. The autobiographical impulse behind so much Romantic writing is another reason why biography is one of the essential ways of approaching him: we need to explore the intimate but sometimes deceptive relationship between the 'I' of the poems and the life itself, just as we do with Wordsworth's *Prelude*. As we need to ask in what respects Childe Harold is and is not Lord Byron, so we need to ask in what respects Lubin in 'The Village Minstrel' is and is not Clare. In this latter case we have a strong clue in an autobiographical fragment: 'the reason why I dislike it is that it does not describe the feelings of a ryhming peasant strongly or localy enough' (*By Himself*, pp. 113-14)—the vital word there being 'localy'.

There is, however, a crucial difference between Clare on the one hand, Wordsworth and Byron on the other. Whereas Wordsworth in *The Prelude* and *The Excursion*, Byron in his succession of poetic roles and personae, devoted their careers to the invention and reinvention of their own poetic self-image, Clare's image—as first 'peasant', then 'madman'—was not something of which he was in control. He colluded with the initial image: the pencil draft of one of his very earliest surviving letters, to the editor of the *Stamford Mercury*, seeking publication for a poem, is signed 'A Northamptonshire Pheasant' (Edward Drury kindly corrected this to 'A Northamptonshire Rustic'—*Letters*, p. 4). But the necessity of such collusion is an essential part of Clare's history. It was his only way of getting published. The story of his path to print and then away from it has some very modern resonances: Clare was 'created' in a manner not so very different from the way pop groups are often 'created' by the media for the market. And when the time came for a change of fashion, he was quickly forgotten, as pop groups often are.

The launch of the Northamptonshire Peasant Poet was carefully contrived to coincide with that of the *London Magazine*. January 1820. A new decade. The anticipation of a new king (George lll finally died at the end of the month). A new magazine. A new poetic phenomenon. The first article of substance in the first number of the *London* was Octavius Gilchrist's 'Some Account of John Clare, An Agricultural Labourer and Poet'. It began with the language of beginnings:

> 'A happy new year,' and the first number of a publication which has for its object to extend the influence of letters, and to aid the inquiries of science, may not be inaptly employed in introducing to the world a name, hitherto altogether unknown to literature, but which, if our estimate of genius be not more than commonly inaccurate, seems to merit a considerable portion of regard, while, at the same time, it stands in need of popular encouragement, and even protection. (*Critical Heritage*, p. 36)

It was Gilchrist who gave the public their first image of Clare the shy, tentative, frail, impoverished outsider. And it was Gilchrist who introduced that tone of condescension which characterises so many of the early accounts of him:

> Returning, a few days since, from the North of England, Mr Taylor became my guest for a day or two; and, the name of Clare being repeated, I expressed a wish to see the person of whose abilities my friend's correct judgment pronounced so favourably. Mr Taylor had seen Clare, for the first time, in the morning, and he doubted much if our invitation would be accepted by the rustic poet, who had now just returned from his day labour, shy, and reserved, and disarrayed, as he was. In a few minutes, however, Clare announced his arrival by a hesitating knock at the door,— 'between a single and a double rap,'—and immediately upon his introduction he dropped into a chair. Nothing could exceed the meekness, and simplicity, and diffidence with which he answered the various inquiries concerning his life and habits, which we mingled with subjects calculated or designed to put him much at his ease. Nothing, certainly, could less resemble splendour than the room into which Clare was shown; but there

was a carpet, upon which it is likely he never previously set foot; and wine, of which assuredly he had never tasted before. (*Critical Heritage*, p. 37)

Drury regarded this as a 'picturesqued' embellishment of the truth (NMS 43), but John Taylor the publisher considered Gilchrist's article 'calculated to be of essential service in promoting the sale of the Poems' (Eg. 2245, f. 27). It prepared the way for the edition of *Poems Descriptive of Rural Life and Scenery*, published on 16 January, which was itself carefully packaged with the soubriquet 'A Northamptonshire Peasant' on the title-page and a biographical introduction inside. Partly based on material provided by Drury, Taylor's narrative laid the ground for all subsequent readings and revisions of the life: the family's extreme poverty, the boyhood labour in the fields, the early morning purchase of Thomson's *Seasons* in Stamford, and so on.

From the point of view of the reading public, Clare's posthumous life began with his admission to High Beech in 1837. *The Rural Muse* of 1835 was the last volume published in his lifetime. From then on, his public persona was fragmented into occasional poems in provincial papers and a variety of reports from visitors, in which he was inspected and occasionally interrogated as if he were an alien. The mid-nineteenth-century term for a psychiatric doctor, we may recall, was 'alienist'.

Clare's story, then, is one of perpetual 're-fashioning'. First there was the peasant image projected by Gilchrist, Drury and Taylor. Later there were the diagnoses of the alienists, most notoriously that of Fenwick Skrimshire on the asylum commitment papers: 'After years addicted to Poetical prosings'. Then there were the reincarnations in biographies and editions: first, Frederick Martin's portrait of a tragic hero, brought down by the fatal flaw of drink; later, Arthur Symons's crucial revision, further developed by Edmund Blunden, in which madness supposedly liberated Clare into great poetry; and most recently, we have had the story, grounded on a theory of textual primitivism, of a man whose wings were trimmed by his editors, rather as Keats was supposedly killed by his critics. I say 'story' not to suggest that the Robinson and Powell version of truth to Clare—always go to the manuscript, never regularise or punctuate—is a fiction, but to suggest that in its own way it too is a re-fashioning, a *construction* which serves a particular purpose at a particular time.

Memory is selective. Even Clare's narrative of his own life constitutes a partial story, the 'truth' of which cannot be checked down to the last detail. According to the Tibbles, early in the first (1932) edition of their *John Clare: A Life*, Frederick Martin used the manuscripts and letters to which he had access 'as a novelist rather than as a biographer' (p. 12). The Tibbles' claim was that Martin offered 'romancings' whereas they had the facts. But Martin respected many facts, and the Tibbles were not without their romancings— not least the hackneyed romantic device of dividing Clare's life into four sequences under the titles 'Spring', 'Summer', 'Autumn' and 'Winter'. The distinction between the biographer's art and the novelist's is by no means so sharp as the Tibbles supposed: I have learnt some things about the life from John MacKenna's *Clare: A Novel* (1993), just as I have tried to teach some things about the life of William Hazlitt in my own novel *The Cure for Love*. Only the most unimaginative biographers and editors will claim that they have the 'truth' about Clare, whereas a novelist such as MacKenna, a dramatist such as Edward Bond (*The Fool*), or the many poets who have written 'to John Clare', have only romancings. After all, for Clare himself the most important truths were those of the poetry, not the autobiographical sketches.

I certainly do not want to deny that Martin was responsible for many fallacies about Clare's life. To take one example: as recently as 1982 Edward Storey included in his biography a sequence based on Martin concerning a certain Dr Smith of Peterborough who 'encouraged people to subscribe to *The Rural Muse* and would sometimes listen to Clare reading aloud a new poem which had just been written' (*A Right to Song*, p. 248). I would gladly be corrected, but as far as I can establish there is no evidence for the existence of Dr Smith of Peterborough; there is certainly no truth in the story, told by Martin and Storey, that Clare read the poem 'First Love's Recollections' to Smith in 1835 having just composed it after seeing Mary Joyce walk past the window—Clare sent this poem to Alaric Watts in 1825 for publication in his *Literary Souvenir*.

But provided he is approached with caution, Martin sometimes offers us more than his more responsible successors. Let us examine the poet's paternal grandparentage, as represented by the romancer Martin and the fact-bound Tibbles.

Some thirty years previous to the birth of John, there came into Helpston a big, swaggering fellow of no particular home, and, as far as could be ascertained, of no particular name: a wanderer over the earth, passing himself off, now for an Irishman, and now for a Scotchman. He had tramped over the greater part of Europe, alternately fighting and playing the fiddle; and being tired awhile of tramping, and footsore and thirsty withal, he resolved to settle for a few weeks, or months, at the quiet little village. The place of schoolmaster happened to be vacant, perhaps had been vacant for years; and the villagers were overjoyed when they heard that this noble stranger, able to play the fiddle, and to drink a gallon of beer at a sitting, would condescend to teach the A B C to their children. So 'Master Parker,' as the great unknown called himself for the nonce, was duly installed schoolmaster of Helpston. The event, taking place sometime about the commencement of the reign of King George the Third, marks the first dawn of the family history of John Clare.

The tramping schoolmaster had not been many days in the village before he made the acquaintance of a pretty young damsel, daughter of the parish-clerk. She came daily to wind the church clock, and for this purpose had to pass through the schoolroom, where sat Master Parker, teaching the A B C and playing the fiddle at intervals. He was as clever with his tongue as with his fiddlestick, the big schoolmaster; and while helping the sweet little maiden to wind the clock in the belfry, he told her wonderful tales of his doings in foreign lands, and of his travels through many countries. And now the old, old story, as ancient as the hills, was played over again once more. It was no very difficult task for the clever tramp to win the heart of the poor village girl; and the rest followed as may be imagined. When spring and summer was gone, and the cold wind came blowing over the fen, the poor little thing told her lover that she was in the way of becoming a mother, and, with tears in her eyes, entreated him to make her his wife. He promised to do so, the tramping schoolmaster; but early the next day he left the village, never to return. Then there was bitter lamentation in the cottage of the parish-clerk; and before the winter was gone, the poor man's daughter brought into the world a little boy, whom she gave her own family name, together with the prefixed one of the unworthy father. Such was the origin of Parker Clare.

Thus Frederick Martin (*The Life of John Clare*, 1865, pp. 3-4). Alternatively:

Parker Clare, born on January 14th, 1765, was 'one of fate's chancelings who drop into the world without the honour of matrimony'. His second name was that of his mother, doubtless the daughter of the 'John Clare, Clark' whose flowing signature in the Helpston parish registers is now all the trace that can be found of him. Parker was the name of the child's fiddler father, John Donald Parker, a Scotsman who stayed for a while at Helpston as schoolmaster. He disappeared at the inconvenient rumour of his child.

Thus the Tibbles (J. W. and Anne Tibble, *John Clare: A Life*, rev. edn., London: Michael Joseph, 1972, p. 5).

Both versions are based on the same source, Clare's own note about his grandfather:

my father was one of fates chance-lings who drop into the world without the honour of matrimony   he took the surname of his mother, who to commemorate the memory of a worthless father with more tenderness of love lorn feeling than he doubtless deservd, gave him his sirname at his christening, who was a Scotchman by birth and a schoolmaster by profession and in his stay at this and the neighboring villages went by the name of John Donald Parker   this I had from John Cue of Ufford, an old man who in his young days was a companion and confidential to my run-a-gate of a grandfather, for he left the village and my grandmother soon after the deplorable accident of misplaced love was revealed to him, but her love was not that frenzy which shortens the days of the victim of seduction, for she liv'd to the age of 86 and left this world of troubles Jan. 1. 1820 (*By Himself*, p. 2)

At first sight, the Tibbles are to be greatly preferred: they tell the bare facts, whereas Martin invents with all the gusto of a novelist (or perhaps a dramatist, given that the device of wooing a young woman by telling exotic tales of foreign adventures is lifted straight from *Othello*). But tone and implication are as important as facts. On closer inspection, there are problems with the Tibbles and strengths in Martin. The Tibbles, in a state of some embarrassment, usher John Donald Parker off the stage as briskly as possible. They are categorical where they might have been tentative: compare 'Parker was the name of the child's fiddler father' with Clare's own 'and in his stay at this and the neighboring villages *went by the name of* John Donald Parker' (my emphasis), with its hint at the possibility—embellished by Martin—that in other places he might have gone by other names. Conversely, the Tibbles are euphemistic where they might have been explicit: 'He disappeared at the inconvenient rumour of his child' is a lame attempt to replicate the wit of Clare's own 'he left the village and my grandmother soon after the deplorable accident of misplaced love was revealed to him'. Clare's phrase 'The deplorable accident of misplaced love' is at once funny and direct, while 'the inconvenient rumour' is both coy and confusing (village rumours are often false, so the Tibbles' wording inadvertently raises the possibility that Parker was not the father, thus flying in the face of the evidence of the christening).

Brisk dismissiveness caused by moral embarrassment is characteristic of the Tibbles' *Life* in all matters related to drink and extra-marital sex. This was understandable in the original 1932 edition, but hardly necessary in the 1972 revision. In his article 'The Nine *Lives* of John Clare', Greg Crossan asserts that 'a greater degree of frankness is admitted' in the 1972 Tibble, 'except, perhaps, about Clare's drinking' (*JCSJ*, 5 (1986), 41). I would say that sexual activity also remains an exception.

Consider the case of Betty Sell, with whom Clare had a fling whilst Patty was pregnant. Clare writes

> while I [w]as at home in the winter I renewd my acquaintance with a former love and had made a foolish confidence with a young girl at Southorpe and tho it began in a heedless [flirtation] at Stamford fair[,] from accompanying her home it grew up in to an affection that made my heart ach[e] to think it must be broken[,] for patty was then in a situation that marriage could only remedy (*By Himself*, p. 111)

The Tibbles play down the importance of this relationship, despite the fact that Clare was still remembering Betty Sell in lyric poems many years later. They also use the opportunity to deny that Betty was, as Edward Drury claimed, a 'Cyprian' and to suggest that Clare may never have caught a sexually transmitted disease—something they can only do by reading

'Sketches in the Life' very much against the grain ('not only my health but my life has often been on the eve of its sacrafice by an illness too well known, and to[o] disgusting to mention'—*By Himself*, p. 29). Clare wrote in his autobiographical fragment of 'a heedless [blank in manuscript] at Stamford fair'. The Tibbles fill in the blank with the euphemism 'frolic'. Robinson and Powell, in both *John Clare by Himself* and the Oxford edition's note to the poem 'Betty Sell', insert the word 'flirtation' (*Early Poems*, I, p. 580). But if it was an innocent frolic or flirtation, why would Clare have left a blank? I hope I am not betraying my own vulgarity by saying that I can think of another word beginning with 'f' which would fit the context much more aptly.

I mention Betty Sell in the context of John Donald Parker because it seems to me that the 'family origins' section with which biography conventionally begins has the crucial effect of establishing the tone of the later narrative. Think of the way in which biographies of Byron make much of his grandfather, the restless promiscuous sailor known as 'Foulweather Jack' and his father, the dissipated promiscuous soldier known as 'Mad Jack'. The Tibbles' discomfort over the taint of paternal illegitimacy prepares the way for their later awkwardness about Clare's own philandering.

Clare himself was sufficiently interested in his renegade paternal grandfather to talk to old John Cue of Ufford about him. The image he appears to have been given was that of a man of somewhat mysterious identity, an outsider and a wanderer, a rogue and a lady's man, but also a teacher, a bringer of literacy. It does not matter whether the transmission of these attributes to John Clare was genetic or memorial: either way, we can see something of old John Donald Parker in Clare's own life—the unstable identity, the sense of exile, the walk back from Essex, the promiscuity, the commitment to reading and writing. This is why Frederick Martin is not to be dismissed: he intuited a sense of the grandpaternal inheritance and used 'Master Parker' to set up his own themes—tramping, drinking, fiddling, seducing. By making much of the way that Parker came from outside Helpston and disrupted the sleepy village community, he prepares the way for Clare to travel the road—first to London, then to the asylum—away from the cottage of his birth. There is a structural, almost a mythic, truth to Martin's narrative that gives it value despite its factual inventions.

By giving prominence to a tale of seduction early in *The Life of John*

JONATHAN BATE

Clare, Martin opens the way for the reader to reflect on the frequency of such tales in Clare's own poetry. I would say that biographers have been rather too cautious in using the poems as biographical evidence. I see this as the principal deficiency of June Wilson's *Green Shadows* (1950), which I otherwise regard as the best biography of Clare yet written. We have to proceed with caution here. Common sense would suggest that a poem called 'Betty Sell' is about Betty Sell of Southorpe, but knowledge of poetic convention warns us that the hazel eyes and 'ringlets black as gloss rind sloes' in that poem (*Early Poems*, I, p. 487) may be literary attributes more than literal ones. The biographer needs to recognise that the relationship between the life and the work is real but complex. A poem such as 'The Fate of Amy' in *Poems Descriptive of Rural Life and Scenery* is several things at once: a literary tale of seduction in the manner of many a popular ballad (Clare specifically acknowledges the influence of 'The Ballad of Edwin & Emma'), a story from the local folk memory (Robinson and Powell tentatively identify Amy with Amy Levit, laid to rest without Christian burial in Helpston on 15 July 1722), *and* a response to circumstances which struck a chord with Clare because of both his grandfather's and his own acts of seduction— a deleted amendment in one of the manuscripts names Amy's destroyer as 'Johnnie', the name of both Clare and his grandfather (*Early Poems*, I, p. 277).

All subsequent biographies have reiterated Martin's claim that Master Parker was a fiddler as well as a teacher. But that detail is not in Clare's note of John Cue's recollections. Martin seems to have conflated Clare's statement about his grandfather with a more general remark about his ancestors: 'all I can make out is that they were Gardeners Parish Clerks and fiddlers and from these has sprung a large family of the name still increasing' (*By Himself*, p. 34). Martin appears to have assumed that since Alice Clare's father was a parish clerk, it must have been John Donald Parker who was the fiddler. But this is surely wrong: the gardeners, parish clerks and fiddlers must all have been local Helpston Clares. As far as we can tell from the evidence, Parker was a 'fiddler' only in another sense of the word.

The alternative, less likely possibility is that Martin had other evidence, either written or oral, for the existence of Master Parker's violin. I think this is unlikely, but the fact that Martin did frequently embellish and mythologise should not lead us to assume that he is never to be trusted. Eric Robinson and

Geoffrey Summerfield's brief introduction to the 1964 reprint of the 1865 Life reminds us of this, and somewhat redresses the balance in response to the Tibbles' scepticism. In the final section of this essay, I want to suggest that Martin may have been in possession of evidence that has been overlooked by later biographers. I want to look at an absolutely crucial period in Clare's life, late 1823 to early 1824, when he sank for the first time into a deep and prolonged depression.

There are few surviving letters from these months. On 20 April 1824, Clare writes to his publisher Hessey in the following terms:

> I have not written to you a long while ... my insides feels sinking & dead & my memory is worse & worse nearly lost the sensation as if cold water was creeping all about my head is less frequent now tho it comes on now & then in the evening for at that time I am always worse ... my feelings are so unstrung in their company that I can scarcly refrain from shedding tears & when I went church I could scarcly refrain from sleep (*Letters*, p. 294)

All the symptoms, then, suggest the classic torpor and weepiness of depression. The 'company' in question was that of the Ranters or Primitive Methodists, with whom Clare renewed his involvement at this time—recourse to religious enthusiasm as a response to mental illness being not uncommon in the early nineteenth century (one thinks of the case of Prime Minister Spencer Perceval's son, who left a record of his own delusions).[1]

Edward Storey, Clare's most recent biographer, passes over these winter and spring months in a mere three sentences:

> The family continued to grow and, ironically, the winter's one bright ray of happiness was the birth of his first son in January, who was named Frederick. Clare brightened for a while until he realized that it was one more mouth to feed and one more body to find room for in the cottage. His depressions returned and he longed to get away to London where he could receive more expert medical treatment as well as discuss his future with John Taylor. (*A Right to Song*, p. 185)

The second sentence ('Clare brightened for a while...') is mere presumption, while the idea that he was eager to go to London is very dubious. People with depression are not eager to do anything—on 19 May, Clare wrote to Hessey to the effect that 'I have so great an opinion of Dr Darling that I must start *tho I feel very difficult my self to encourage the resolution*' (*Letters*, p. 298, my emphasis).

The twentieth-century biographers are sketchy about the medical treatment Clare received locally, before he went down to London in May 1824 to see Dr Darling. The Tibbles (p. 200) say that 'Lady Milton had sent her own physician, Dr Walker of Peterborough, and he had assured Clare that he would soon recover'—but *Mr* Walker, as Clare calls him, was an apothecary not a physician. The British Library correspondence reveals that he was sent via Henderson, the botanising/lepidopterising head-gardener at Milton who had befriended Clare (Eg. 2246, f. 288). But Clare was unhappy about both Walker's billing procedures and his 'quackery' (*Letters*, pp. 296-7). On 8 May 1824 Clare mentioned to Taylor that Dr Skrimshire had visited four or five times; on one occasion he arrived when apothecary Walker was also present, causing the latter some embarrassment. Later in the year, Skrimshire seems to have discussed Clare's case with Darling in London. Early the following year, Hessey wrote complaining that apothecary Walker had sent Clare's publisher an exorbitant bill for medicines prescribed by Skrimshire. Walker had apparently stated that he had attended Clare at the request of Lady Milton, but didn't see fit to bill her for drugs prescribed by Skrimshire, who was attending at the request of Taylor and Hessey.

Martin gave a much more lengthy and detailed account of Clare's treatment, but it has been ignored by later biographers—perhaps because it begins with what seems to be invention. Martin has Clare walking to Stamford on the day of Octavius Gilchrist's death, 30 June 1823. There is no corroborating evidence for this. He has him falling ill the very next day: there is no evidence for such a precise date, and indeed it does not seem to have been until the autumn that Clare became seriously ill. On 4 November, Mrs Emmerson, his most assiduous correspondent, expressed concern at his two months' silence. Clare's reply is lost, as are nearly all his letters to Mrs Emmerson, but the tenor of it may be reconstructed, for in her next letter she quotes back to him some of his own phrases: 'this "troublesome nothing which haunts you,"' 'this *abiding shadow of misery*,' '"visionary miseries"' (9 November, Eg. 2246, f. 251) .

Again, Martin has Taylor attending Gilchrist's funeral and calling in on Clare on the way back to London. Actually at this time Taylor was ill in London and Clare was writing with the complaint that he had heard nothing from him for so long that he might as well address him as a stranger—Clare himself seems to have been the one to tell Taylor of Gilchrist's death, eliciting a letter of commiseration which apologised for long silence (*Letters*, p. 276).

A hitherto unnoticed pair of letters from Hessey to Clare may explain Martin's error. On 1 November 1823, Hessey writes that Taylor is in the country with his family and that 'He called on Mrs Gilchrist on his way through Stamford' (Eg. 2246, f. 247). Then on 15 November he says that Taylor will be changing coaches in Stamford and suggests that Clare might walk in to meet him. He would be cheered to find you waiting for the arrival of the coach, says Hessey, because he will be in low spirits since 'He is coming up to attend the funeral of a very old friend' (f. 253). I suggest, then, that Martin had access to a version of this information, but that the combination of the visit to the recently widowed Mrs Gilchrist and the attendance at a funeral led him to misplace Taylor's visit to the time of Gilchrist's death. Since the visit was really in November, it coincided with the serious depression revealed in Emmerson's letters of this month. Presumably Clare failed to make the walk to Stamford, and this alerted Taylor to his illness.

The fact that Taylor *did* pass through Stamford *en route* to a funeral shows that this sequence of Martin is no mere tissue of invention. The following passage suggests that he had access to relevant correspondence:

The medical gentleman [engaged by Taylor], while carefully watching all the symptoms of the disease, now began to fear that he would be unable to master it, and wrote to this effect to Mr Taylor, entreating him to use his influence to get Clare removed to some hospital, or other house where he might have the necessary attention. In the letter it was stated without disguise that the illness of the poet was mainly the effect of poverty. His dwelling, the Peterborough physician argued, was altogether unfit for a human habitation, being dark, damp, and ill ventilated, with a space so circumscribed as to be worse than a prison for two families. He insisted, therefore, that to make recovery possible a better home should be found for Clare himself, and, if possible, for his wife and child, pending the removal of his aged and suffering parents. A copy of this note the writer sent to Lord Radstock, knowing that his lordship had taken, from the beginning, a deep interest in Clare's welfare. (Martin, p. 173)

The description here of the content of the physician's letter to Taylor, copied to Radstock, is so specific that Martin must have seen it. A letter from Emmerson to Clare provides corroboration: 'Lord R. has written a second letter to Lord M. in the most feeling manner on your account; soliciting his Lordship's benevolent grant of a cottage & a piece of garden for you' (Eg. 2246, f. 262).

Martin says that this 'medical gentleman' was a 'Peterborough physician'. But Clare's Peterborough doctor was Skrimshire, who had connections with the Fitzwilliam family at Milton, not with Lord Radstock, so he would surely have copied his letter to the former rather than the latter. I think that the true identity of this caring doctor is revealed by another of Taylor's letters:

As you wish to have Dr Arnold's advice I have by this day's post, not to lose a moment's time, written to request he will call upon you, and I feel great hope that as your Disorder seems to be of the same kind as that which he cured you of before, he will be of Service. (8 March 1824, Eg. 2246, f. 308)

Arnold was the Stamford doctor mentioned by Clare in 'Sketches in the Life' as having treated him for the fits from which he suffered earlier in life after seeing a man fall from a haywagon and break his neck (*By Himself*, p. 19). A follow-up letter from Taylor enclosed 'a note for 5£ out of which I wish you would send as soon as you can 2£—(Two Guineas I mean) to Dr Arnold— It is his Fee, he tells me, for going to see you' (Taylor to Clare, 3 April 1824, Eg. 2246, f. 321, *Letters*, p. 290).

This proves that letters passed between Taylor and Arnold. None survive in the Taylor archive in Matlock, but I strongly suspect that Martin had access to some part of the correspondence and used it as the basis for this section of his *Life*.[2] Some of the details of the treatment which he adduces are so specific that they compel attention:

The new doctor ordered absolute rest, plenty of fresh air, and some nourishing food; all which being provided, a visible improvement began to manifest itself. There was some difficulty in getting the second part of the prescription, the fresh air, Clare's narrow bedroom having no ventilation whatever. The energetic doctor, however, got over the obstacle by the simple expedient of knocking a brick out of the top of the wall, which furnished a channel sufficiently large to let in the warm summer air. Perhaps this thrown-out brick, as much as anything else, saved the life of the poet. (Martin, p. 172)

That knocked-out brick seems too strange, too particular a detail to be pure invention.

If I am right that Martin was working here from a documentary record and not just his own lively imagination, then we have to consider the possibility that one of the most romantic, fictionalised-sounding images of Clare which we possess might actually have a basis in fact. It is with this image—the poet seeking therapy in his hollow oak—that I would like to end:

Gradually recovering, he was strong enough when the first blossoms of spring came peeping in at the window, to issue forth once more into the open air. To him the first walk was such boundless enjoyment as to be almost overpowering in its intensity. Never seemed the green fields more glorious, the song of the birds more enchanting, and the whole wide world more full of ecstatic bliss. In vain the good Peterborough [or should we say Stamford?] doctor entreated him not to risk his yet imperfect health in long excursions, but to keep as quiet as possible, and only venture upon short walks during the middle of the day. Clare promised to attend to the injunction, and honestly meant to obey it, yet was lured into forgetfulness whenever the birds sat piping in the trees, and the sun's rays came streaming into his narrow hut. They witched him away almost against his own will, making him creep forth into the fields and woods, heavily leaning on his stick. One day he stayed out longer than usual, and, the doctor arriving, a search was made after him. It was fruitless for some time; at last, however, he was found in his favourite hollow oak, sitting as in a trance, his face illumined by the setting sun. Enraptured joy seemed to pervade his whole being; unutterable bliss to fill his mind. The doctor looked serious, and made an attempt to upbraid his patient, but which was entirely unsuccessful. 'If you loved the sun and flowers as I do,' quietly said Clare, 'you would not blame me.' The words somewhat startled the Peterborough [?] man of science. (Martin, p. 175)

NOTES

1. Referred to by Roy Porter in his essay '"All Madness for Writing": John Clare and the Asylum', in Haughton, *Context*, pp. 259-77. For Clare and 'enthusiastic' religion, see Mark Minor, 'Clare and the Methodists: a Reconsideration', *Studies in Romanticism*, 19, no. 1 (Spring), 31-50.
2. Evidence of the assiduity of Martin's research is preserved in NMS 57 and NMS 58 in the Northampton Clare collection.

2. 'Written By Himself'—Edited by Others: The Autobiographical Writings of John Clare

Valerie Pedlar

Both during his lifetime and since, John Clare has been cast in a variety of roles—peasant poet, countryman, political rebel, social commentator, fugitive, madman—and has been appropriated by various interested parties. Whatever the role, however, he is generally seen as a marginal figure, never fully at home and never fully accepted, even, it could be argued, at the Northampton asylum, a recognized abode of alienated others. Clare himself evinces great interest in the question of personal identity, voicing his concern in both his poetry and his prose. In this essay I shall be concentrating on the prose. In the first part I shall argue that one reason for the perception of Clare as an alienated individual lies in the way he represents himself in his autobiographical writings. I shall discuss, in particular, the emphasis he places on his difference from the others in his life, and on the uniqueness of his experience. But Clare's autobiographical writings pose a problem for readers today, since they were never published in his lifetime, and the fragmentary manuscripts are accessible only to approved readers in (mainly) the Northampton Library and Peterborough Museum. Although, arguably, some of the fragments were silently incorporated into Frederick Martin's biography, and were indubitably incorporated into *John Clare, a Life* (1932) by J.W. and Anne Tibble, the first serious attempt to present the prose on its own terms for the general reader was Edmund Blunden's edition of the *Sketches in the Life of John Clare* in 1931. It was not until 1951 that the Tibbles published the more comprehensive *The Prose of John Clare*. More recently editions have been published by Eric Robinson in 1983 (*Autobiographical Writings*) and by Eric Robinson and David Powell in 1996 (*John Clare By Himself*). The second part of the essay, then, will be devoted to a discussion of the ways in which editorial work can contribute to our perception of Clare. I shall concentrate on comparative readings of the Tibbles' edition of the *Prose* (1951) and the two Robinson-edited editions, looking in particular at

17

the choice and arrangement of the fragments, and at stylistic amendments. I shall illustrate my argument by comparing in some detail the beginnings and endings of their presentations of the fragments.

Clare's construction of identity
Clare's most orderly account of his life is contained in 'Sketches in the Life of John Clare written by himself, addressed to his friend John Taylor Esqr March 1821'. He starts:

> There is a pleasure in recalling ones past years to reccolection: in this I believe every bosom agrees and returns a ready echo of approbation and I think a double gratifycation is witness'd as we turn to a repetition of our early days by writing them down on paper on this head my own approbation must shelter its vanity while thus employ'd, by consieting self-satisfaction a sufficient appology. But I am carless of fame and fearless of censure in the business, my only wish being to give a friend pleasure in its persual for whom and by whose request it is written and as I have little doubt of being able to accomplish that matter those who (strangers to the writer) that it displeases need not be startled at the disappointment   (*Autobiographical Writings*, p. 1; *By Himself*, pp. 1-2)[1]

This rather stately paragraph amplifies the particularity of the title, the sense of relationship between the writer and his past self, the writer and the friend for whom he is writing and—at some remove—the writer and a wider audience, strange to him though he is not strange (in one sense of the word at least) to them.

John Taylor was, of course, the publisher Clare shared with, among others, Keats, and the 'Sketches' are dedicated to explaining the genesis of Clare, the 'peasant' poet. When his first volume of poetry was published in 1820 Taylor wrote a fairly lengthy introduction, describing Clare's background and putting his poetry in the 'peasant' context of agricultural labour, poverty, ill health and a scraped-together education. Clare is represented as exceptional:

> ...no Poet of our country has shewn greater ability, under circumstances so hostile to its developement. And all this is found here without any of

those distressing and revolting alloys, which too often debase the native worth of genius, and make him who was gifted with powers to command admiration, live to be the object of contempt or pity. (*Critical Heritage*, p. 53)

Clearly it is not only for his unexpected poetic talent that Clare is being recommended, but for his lack of corruption, his unspoiled nature.

The 'Sketches' were sent to Taylor in the following year. They read, as Matthew Smith has pointed out,[2] as a response to Taylor's anodyne version of his life, but also more generally as an attempt to put the record straight, to assert his own point of view. Thus in describing his first attempts to get published, Clare details his struggles in writing a prospeċtus, the difficulties of getting it circulated, his inexperience in dealing with these matters and his financial problems. He also tells of his discovery by Taylor's cousin, Edward Drury, a bookseller in Stamford. This is recounted in Taylor's introduction as follows: 'In ... 1818, Mr. Edward Drury ... met by chance with the Sonnet to the Setting Sun, written on a piece of paper in which a letter had been wrapped up and signed' (*Critical Heritage*, p. 53). From this account it would look as though Clare was indeed a flower blushing unseen until chance and Drury's perspicacity rescued him from oblivion. The effort is Drury's: he seeks out Clare in his Helpston cottage and asks him to make a collection of pieces which are then sent to London. Clare's version of events reveals the efforts he had gone to on his own behalf before ever Drury appeared on the scene, and how in fact his poems were in the hands of a local bookseller and printer, J.B. Henson, where the main obstacle to their actually appearing in print was Henson's insistence on an advance from Clare. In this account, Drury is seen as a sharp businessman rather than an altruistic benefactor, and Clare is represented as someone keen to present his poetry to the world, rather than as the passive object of discovery. Clare insists on the veracity of his own version: 'his [Drury's] account of first meeting with the Sonnet to the Setting Sun in MSS is all a hoax and of no other foundation then his own fancy: but wether a mistake or intended falsity I cant justly assert' (p. 21; p. 24). And later he returns to the attack: 'Drury may make what he pleases of his meeting with me at first if I shoud ever become of that consequence in his opinion to require that notice—he may contradict, add, alter, or shuffle it about in what shape he pleases—here is the plain truth without the least

desire to offend or wish to please any of the parties conserned' (p. 22; p. 26).
It is hardly surprising that the 'Sketches' were not published in Clare's lifetime, since the account of his difficulties in getting published is followed by a frank revelation of his dealings with women, his ventures into 'bad houses, those painted pills of poison' where 'not only my health but my life has often been on the eve of its sacrafice by an illness too well known, and to[o] disgusting to mention' (p. 25; p. 29), and his connections with Patty (his wife-to-be) which 'now began to disclose dangers which marriage alone coud remedy' (p. 24; p. 28). The piece ends with his representation of himself as an honest Jack: 'here is as faithful account of myself as I can possibly give I have been as free to disclose my own faults as a meddler is those of his neighbours', but also as one who is constantly under threat: 'and by so doing have doubtless baffled the aims of skulking assasins from throwing weapons in the dark with the force they woud have done had I made myself better then I am. "Tell truth and shame the devil"' (p. 26; pp. 30-1).[3]

A few years later Clare set about writing a more substantial autobiography, as well as keeping a journal (from September 1824 to September 1825 with a few entries for 1828). As I said at the beginning, the autobiography exists only in fragments and there is some disagreement about whether a fair copy ever existed. The Tibbles think not; Robinson agrees with Blunden that 'Clare probably wrote an extended version of his life, for which the "Autobiographical fragments" are the first drafts, but we consider it a possibility that Clare deliberately destroyed the new version' (*By Himself,* p. xix). It would appear that some of the fragments are rough drafts for the 'Sketches', since they encompass the same events, and this second telling has the effect of emphasising certain aspects and incidents of Clare's early life. In other instances, however, the fragments, especially since they cover a longer period, present new material: his experiences with the militia, his descriptions of the gypsies, numerous character sketches both of people he knew and who visited him in Northamptonshire and of people he met during his various visits to London.

In the Introduction to the Penguin edition of J.S. Mill's *Autobiography* John Robson writes that there are two main options open to the autobiographer: 'the assumption that one is typical of the age, seemingly arrogant enough for most; or the even more arrogant presumption that one is unique' (p. 1), and he suggests that in either case there is an implication that reading the life will improve the reader. I think the first option can be re-expressed (and indeed has been, by, for instance, James Olney)[4] as the autobiographer seeing him or herself as representative not necessarily of the age but of a social group. Clearly this is the option that the reviewer for *British Book News* understood Clare to be taking. The quotation on the back cover of Robinson's edition of the *Autobiographical Writings* as published by OUP in paperback in 1986 says the fragments: 'add up to one of the best accounts by any writer of the growth of the creative imagination, and one of the most valuable records we have of the mental, emotional and physical world of the English rural poor of the nineteenth century'. Clare in this assessment is representative of both creative writers and the English rural poor.

These autobiographical writings do indeed give us an insight into the creative impulse, but it is *Clare's* creativity, *his* idiosyncratic approach, which may have affinities with the imagination of other poets; it is not generic, however, and cannot be taken as typical. A long lyrical section in the fragments that does not appear in the 'Sketches' dwells on the particularities of the countryside he knows; it is concerned with conveying his rapturous involvement in the scenes, yet at the same time it is a supremely visual passage which actually demonstrates the verbal skills he has acquired. The passage is written with a self-awareness that precludes the characterization of Clare as naive: 'I observed all this with the same raptures as I have done since but I knew nothing of poetry   it was felt and not utterd' (*Autobiographical Writings*, p. 32; *By Himself*, p. 38). Clare later commented in that well-known distich: 'I found the poems in the fields / And only wrote them down' (*Later Poems*, I, p. 19). It is not just that there is an intrinsic poetry in nature, but that he has discerned it; the inspiration for his poetry is his unique relationship with nature.

Similarly, Clare cannot be seen simply as representative of the rural poor; he takes pains both in the 'Sketches' and in the fragments to emphasise his difference. In the 'Sketches' he marks himself out from his fellows as weak and sickly and therefore unfitted for hard labour; as a secret reader and writer, as a lover of solitude: 'conjectures filld the village about my future destinations on the stage of life, some fanc[y]ing it symtoms of lunacy and that my mothers prophecys would be verified to her sorrow and that my reading of books (they woud jeeringly say) was for no other improvment then quallyfiing an idiot for a workhouse' (pp. 4-5; p. 5).[5] And he relishes his peculiar appreciation of the beauties of nature:

I often wondered that, while I was peeping about and finding such quantitys of pleasing things to stop and pause over, another shoud pass me as carless as if he was blind I thought somtimes that I surely had a taste peculialy by myself and that nobody else thought or saw things as I did (p. 14; p. 17)

But whereas in the 'Sketches' the emphasis is on his early life as forming a poet, in the autobiographical fragments the perspective is different and the writer, disillusioned after several years' experience of the literary scene, looks back to the lost paradise of childhood. Nevertheless, he insists time and again on his difference: 'I know I am foolish enough to have fancys different from others' (p. 57; p. 69); 'tho I was not known as a poet my odd habits did not escape notice' (p. 65; p. 78), and he associates his love of the countryside with solitude. Even when he describes the way he passed his leisure time as a youngster with shepherds and herd boys playing marbles, leapfrog or soldiers, or reading aloud from the Bible, he prefaces the description with the comment that 'it was the leisure of solitude' and refers back to 'this solitary disposition' (p. 33; pp. 39 and 40) His feelings of having been betrayed in later life are apparent throughout the fragments. Although he remarks of his early life that 'I made but few close friendships for I found few with the like tastes inclinations and feelings' (p. 39; p. 49), no bitterness attaches to his recollection of what now seems an idyllic childhood in contrast to the treacherous world of professional writing:

Among all the friendships I have made in life those of school friendship and childish acquaintance are the sweetest to remember there is no deseption among them their is nothing of regret in them but the loss they are the fairest and sunniest pages memory ever doubles down in the checkerd volume of life to refer to there is no blotches upon them—they are not found like bargains or matters of interest nor broken for selfish ends (p. 39; p. 49)[6]

In London Clare is an outsider; it is almost as though he has penetrated fairy-land: 'I had a romantic sort of notion about authors and had an anxious desire to see them fancying they were beings different to other men but the spell was soon broken when I became acquainted with them but I did not see many...' (p. 132; p. 139).[7] Unlike his descriptions of natural phenomena which grow out of a life-long intimacy, his observations of the literati round Taylor's dinner table (Reynolds, Lamb, Hazlitt, Cary) are those of a spectator, as though he is gazing on a cabinet of curiosities. His comments are acute and his prose style astonishingly confident considering his apprehension only a few years previously when he was called on to write that first prospectus for a subscription ('I was very loath and had a worse opinion of my prose abilitys then my poetry for I had never written a letter excepting the silly love epistles aluded [to]' (p. 98; pp. 104-5)).

The Journal gives us yet another perspective on Clare. Unlike an autobiography which is retrospective, typically concerned with making sense of or justifying a life, trying to grasp its overall significance, a journal focuses on the quotidian. Clare announces his aim at the outset: 'I have determined this day of beginning a sort of journal to give my opinion of things I may read or see and set down any thoughts that may arise either in my reading at home or my musings in the Fields' (*By Himself*, p. 171). The striking difference between this document and the other texts mentioned so far is its representation of Clare as a family man, for the fragments are strangely reticent about his domestic life after his marriage to Patty Turner. Touchingly he records the birthdays of his wife, his children, his parents and his sister Sophie, commenting on 13 June 1825, as he mentions his daughter Eliza's birthday: 'I feel anxious to insert these memorandums of my affections as Memory tho a secondary is the soul of time and life the principal but its shadow' (p. 234). Sadly, a recurrent theme for the whole family is ill health: 'Very ill today and very unhappy   my three Childern are all unwell   had a dismal dream of being in hell' (p. 183). Even here, though, Clare gives little detail of his family life. His concern is with his opinions (he reveals himself to be a sharp critic of other writers, watching particularly for truthfulness of expression), his reading and his observations, presenting himself, it would seem, as a man of letters, standing somewhat apart from the world he observes.

It is the *Journey out of Essex*, however, the poignant account of Clare's escape from Allen's madhouse in Epping and his 80-mile, four-day journey home, on foot and penniless, that gives the most powerful representation in prose of Clare as alienated from society. It is the last piece of extended prose that we have, probably the last that he wrote. Clare, the fugitive, is at this point a total outcast, and his sufferings must have been intense, yet he writes about his experiences almost as dispassionately as though it was another task of naturalistic observation. He says little about his feelings and passes lightly over his suffering, focusing on the material details of finding his way, of seeking shelter for the night, of the people he meets, and of how he manages to satisfy his hunger.

The hand of the editor in constructing identity
Even in a piece as short as the *Journey* it is interesting to see how the editor plays a role in constructing the identity of the autobiographical subject. The copy text which Robinson cites in his 1983 edition of the *Autobiographical Writings* (NMS 6) begins:

> July 24 1841 Returned home out of Essex & found no Mary her & her family are nothing to me now—though she herself was once the dearest of all—& how can I forget [my transcription from NMS 6]

The next entry is for 18 July and starts the narrative of his escape. Although this arrangement is preserved in the Tibbles' editions, Robinson chooses to place the 24 July entry, that makes so striking an opening, in its chronological position as the last entry, where it loses much of its dramatic impact and Clare is denied, I feel, the artistry that even in this extreme moment was part of his professional identity. The alternative hypothesis is that Clare made a mistake, but why this one should be silently corrected, when so many others remain, is unclear. Besides, the manuscript at this point is orderly enough and the writing legible. There is also a second manuscript source (NMS 8), which Robinson and Powell cite in their 1996 edition, *By Himself*, which also has the 24 July statement at the beginning. The only editorial note pointing to textual variation notes that this latter manuscript gives 23 July instead of 24 July.

So far I have been focusing on the degree to which Clare's autobiographical prose writings are concerned with his genesis as a poet and his life as a writer, and I have given examples of the way in which his writing is crafted. As I said at the outset, though, these prose writings were not published in Clare's lifetime, and we are dependent on the work of twentieth-century editors for day-to-day access to a chaotic mass of manuscripts. I should like to turn now to a consideration of how our understanding of Clare both as a writer and as a person can be affected by the way in which these pieces are edited. Hugh Haughton, in a review essay in the *John Clare Society Journal* for 1999, discusses the difficulties of editing Clare, which are acute when it comes to the prose writings. In the first place, there are a number of stylistic decisions that have to be taken, since Clare's manuscripts not only use the idioms and vocabulary of his locality (which may or may not be understood by an international readership), but are characterized by variable, idiosyncratic orthography, and above all by the absence of punctuation. His side-stepping of 'that awkward squad of pointings' has caused headaches to editors from John Taylor to the present day; his work has been punctuated and de-punctuated, as well as re-spelled and in any number of ways made more conventional—and less conventional. In the two most recent editions, for instance, 'and' is substituted for the ampersands, punctuation (which may well have been added later, possibly even by someone else) is removed from the 'Sketches' and spaces are inserted in the place of full-stops. Gaps are filled with conjectural words and letters are added to incomplete or apparently misspelled words, whereas the Tibbles (1951) preserve the ampersands and leave the text unpunctuated, even by spaces.

It is a commonplace observation, now, to remark on the function of autobiography in imposing order on, or making order of a life, but what is usually meant is the order imposed by the autobiographical subject himself or herself. In the present instance, the problem is one of the textual order of the material, and the disorder of Clare's autobiographical fragments does pose a great challenge to editors. The Tibbles tackle the problem by creating a continuous narrative, preserving such chapter numbers and titles as Clare provides, but omitting and amalgamating where necessary to reduce confusion when episodes are described in more than one version. Robinson in both the 1983 *Autobiographical Writings* and the 1996 *By Himself* with David Powell, eschews both this strategy and the option of following the order in the manuscripts as catalogued by Powell and Grainger. As the Introduction to the 1996 edition has it: 'we have grouped the "autobiographical fragments" in what appears to us to be the most logical order' (p. xx), though the premise of that logic is left unspecified. This 'logical order' also means, in one or two cases, breaking up what are continuous passages of narrative in the manuscripts, being less respectful of Clare's suggested chapter divisions and headings than the Tibbles and inserting editorial headings (usually, but not consistently, marked by square brackets).

The narrative is further broken up by the insertion of manuscript references at the end of each passage. These are invaluable to scholars and those seriously interested in Clare's work, though I'm not sure how appropriate they are for the 'general reader' the edition is aimed at, but they also emphasise the fragmentary nature of the text, producing what one might call *Verfremdungseffekte*, distancing the reader from the material. Thus, whereas the Tibbles' narrative, entitled incidentally 'The Autobiography', is sustained by chronological continuity, presenting the story of a life as a build-up of incident and experience that contributes to the formation of the writing persona, Robinson and Powell, working in a period in which the credibility of sustained narrative flow has been questioned, create a postmodern text, in which the reader is faced with lack of continuity, different versions of events, a constant awareness of the editing process, and in one instance, a paragraph written by the editors that itself gives yet another version of events. This in turn promotes the sense of a more disordered personality, of someone finding it difficult to put his life in order (and indeed, as his Journal reveals, Clare did find the task more difficult than he had expected), but at the same time the visible presence of the editorial apparatus reminds us that these are working notes, evidence of the efforts of someone who is searching for the right terms of expression.

If I turn now to the beginnings and endings of the two versions, I can elaborate on the difference that the ordering and choice of the fragments can make. The Tibbles start with a fragment of a letter or an address from Clare to his 'childern':

My Dear Childern
Before this meets your knowledge I may be unconsious of your welfare & the laughing schoolboy may be gathering the spring daisey from the sod that covers me with unconsious pleasure yet it matters not good counsil is always in season come when it will (*Prose*, p. 11)

(This does not appear at all in the Robinson version.) Their next fragment is a paragraph that in the manuscript is actually headed 'near conclusion':

Many people will think me a vain fellow perhaps attaching or fancying such importance to these memoirs as to think they will repay my vanity or labour in dwelling on them to this length & in many instances the manner in which they are written may draw on me a juster [condemnation] * for some of my remarks are very weak & some of the anecdotes very trifling & the expressions impertinent but most of the narrative was written in severe illness which may be a sufficient appology for defects in the author though not perhaps for their being thrust on the reader

* omission of perhaps one word—MS. (p. 11)

Thus the Tibbles provide the reader with a sort of preface to the autobiography proper which starts traditionally enough with a reference to his genealogy. Clare is represented as writing with two groups of readers in mind, his own children and a wider public, and as accounting for his writing in two ways. Since the address to his children is an isolated fragment, it is not self-evident that 'this' refers to the autobiography. Nevertheless, it forms a poignant and appropriate way of introducing recollections of a joyous rural childhood, and in the image of himself as under 'the sod' from which a schoolboy is, as he once did, gathering daisies, and in the idea of advice always being 'in season', it constructs an identity for the writer as part of the natural world. His aim in writing, one is given to believe, is didactic, a father giving his children good advice. Although he pictures himself as underground, his stance is elevated. This impression is undermined by the succeeding paragraph in which Clare imagines the likely reception of his autobiography by a wider public. Here from a perception of his own lowly position he apologises, explains and justifies himself in a way that recalls his first prose writing, the Prospectus that he had printed by Henson of Market Deeping in an attempt to gain subscribers to a projected first volume of his poems (1818). In the extract quoted above the aim is expressed as a simple desire to give pleasure, but it means that the reader starts with a warning of 'weak' remarks, 'trifling' anecdotes and 'impertinent' expressions; in a sense Clare seems to be striving for, or even asserting a superior position by pre-empting the reader's possible criticisms.

Robinson on the other hand starts with the genealogical slant, in which

Clare refers to and subverts another convention of autobiographical writing. He speaks out directly: 'I cannot trace my name to any remote period ... I have found no great ancestors to boast in the breed—all I can make out is that they were Gardners Parish Clerks and fiddlers' (*Autobiographical Writings*, p. 29; *By Himself*, p. 34). No apologies here; no explanations as to why he is writing. If, in the Tibbles' version, the link between past and present is made through the prefatory paragraphs I have just quoted, in which the writer addresses his imagined readers, in Robinson's version it is made through the comments on genealogy, which serve, in fact, to show how tenuous a link it is; the family fades into obscurity in the past and loses contact in the future. The next paragraph further distances present from past in the comparison of his life since boyhood with those early days:

[Holidays]

What ups and downs have I met with since I was a boy how barren the world looking about me now years come and go like messengers without errands and are not noticd for the tales which they tell are not worth stopping them to hear nothing but cares and dissa[point]ments when I was a boy a week scarcly came without a promise of some fresh delight Hopes were always awake with expectations the year was crowned with holidays (p. 29; pp. 34-5)[8]

It is worth noting in passing the editorial decision to place the 'now' with the years. In the original there is no gap and where 'now' belongs is therefore ambiguous. Since the writer is concerned to contrast his present situation with his past, the exclamation 'how barren the world looking about me now' confirms the thought of the first sentence. The writer indicates his estrangement from his present circumstances in two ways. In the first place he establishes himself as disillusioned, nourished only by his memories of the glistening joys of childhood; in the second place his rootedness in a society and culture very different from that of the commercial readership he might have been writing for, which has been asserted in the opening paragraph, is further emphasised as he proceeds to detail the popular holidays of the year. The reminiscences which follow are refracted, then, through this lens of despoliation as the jaundiced autobiographer looks back at past innocent glories.

The latter part of the memoirs in both cases covers the three visits that Clare made to London, concluding with Lord Byron's funeral which the young man witnessed. Clare was a great admirer of Byron and during his periods of madness in later life adopted his identity and wrote in free imitation of two of his best-known poems, *Childe Harold* and *Don Juan*. What greatly impresses Clare is the affection in which Byron was regarded by 'the common people', and he concludes:

> I believe that his liberal principles in religion & politics did a great deal towards gaining the notice & affections of the lower orders Be as it will it is better to be beloved by those low & humble for undisguised honesty than flattered by the great for purchased & pensioned hypocrisies (*Prose*, p. 100)

In the Tibbles' edition, a final paragraph (not in Robinson) continues these thoughts:

> Things will fall out in their season wether they are wanted or expected or not Autumn seldom passes away without its tempest & friendship begun upon speculation & self-interest is sure to meet with a shock as chance & changes fall out the man that built his house upon the sand was near drownd by the tide—my friendship is worn out & my memorys are broken (p. 100)

Returning to the image of the seasonal cycle with which it opened, 'The Autobiography' in this edition ends with a dying fall, the words of a man of thirty-one, who has another forty years to live (more than half of them in asylums), but who feels that the best is over. Gone is the balanced, knowing confidence with which Clare wrote to Taylor in 1821:

> my vanity if I have any will end in its proper mortification to know that obscurity is happiness & that John Clare the thresher in the onset & neglected ryhmer in the end are the only two comfortable periods of his life (*Critical Heritage*, p. 141).

Robinson, on the other hand, follows the description of the funeral with a passage—much longer—which takes up some of the ideas that the spectacle of the funeral has aroused, elaborating on the question of human relationships by discussing that between authors and booksellers, where Clare feels that he has been betrayed by false promises. The final sentences of this passage summarize the process of his disillusionment, and also illustrate the lively originality of much of his prose style:

> on my first visit to London I had a glimpse of things as they are and felt doubtful on my second I had more dissapointments and in my last I saw so much mistey shuffling that my fa[i]th of the world shrunk to a skeleton and woud scar[c]e fill a nutt shell or burthen a mouse to bear it—the vastest of wisdoms hath said 'put no confidence in men for they will decieve you' (*Autobiographical Writings*, p. 149; *By Himself*, p. 159)

Following this bleak vision is the fragment that I have already quoted that the Tibbles put at the beginning: 'Many people will think me a vain fellow...' Thus, whereas, in the Tibbles' version Clare is shown as anticipating his readers' possible criticisms, in Robinson's version Clare is situated alongside his audience, evaluating the material he has written and they have read. In *Autobiographical Writings* Robinson then adds six further fragments, which in *By Himself* are augmented by eight more, comprising moral and emotional reflections. These fragments cover a variety of topics, but the overwhelming impression is that this is the voice of a disappointed man, one who has been betrayed and finds himself 'an alien in a strange land' (*By Himself*, p. 161). At the same time he reveals himself as someone who is proud of his achievements and of his free speaking. In this version, then, the concluding section has more weight, which is the result not only of its length, but of its moral assurance and of the apparent finality with which it crystallizes the autobiographer's identity. These then are the last words of the autobiography in Robinson's editions:

> if every any body did or does me a foul barefacd wrong that memory grows with my life and break[s] out with every oppertunity and if there is a resurrection quickning with the dust it is such a vivid spark in my nature that I believe I shall not forget it in my grave (p. 152; p. 165)[9]

Instead of the figure of decline with which the Tibbles' version ended, we have here a vigorous assertion of the man's indestructible fibre. When Clare acknowledges, in the sentence preceding the quotation above, that the faults 'that stick to me were born with me and will dye with me', there is almost pride in the ownership. By describing the wrongs that he will never forget as 'foul' and 'barefacd', he seems to be turning what he claims is a fault into a virtue, and although the final words envisage him in the grave, it seems that he will live on, not so much by virtue of a New Testament resurrection, as by the 'vivid spark' of Old Testament vengefulness.

NOTES

1. Quotations are given throughout as they appear in *Autobiographical Writings*, with a second page reference to *By Himself*. Variations are recorded in these notes. The editors of *By Himself* note that this volume is 'more accurate' than the earlier one. Thus, in this quotation we have 'reccollection' followed by a semi-colon, and 'dissappointment'. Furthermore, in an endnote the editors draw attention to the fact that the final sentence is heavily deleted in manuscript. Blunden, in fact, omits it in his 1931 edition.
2. Matthew Smith, 'The "Peasant Poet" Replies: *Sketches in the Life of John Clare* as a Response to Taylor's Introduction to *Poems Descriptive*', *JCSJ*, 15 (1996), 21-5.
3. *By Himself* has 'Tell the truth...'
4. James Olney, *Metaphors of Self: The Meaning of Autobiography* (Princeton, NJ: Princeton University Press, 1972).
5. *By Himself* changes 'would' to 'woud'.
6. *By Himself* changes 'or' to 'on'.
7. *By Himself* alters the text to: 'I had had a romantic sort of notion...'
8. *By Himself* has an endnote pointing out that instead of 'I was' Clare has written 'I way'.
9. *By Himself* changes 'every' to 'ever'.

3. Writing Clare's Poems: 'The Myth of Solitary Genius'

Bob Heyes

John Clare's autobiographical writings are endlessly fascinating. They were written when he was still a fairly young man, shortly after he had become a published author, and therefore they deal mainly with the events of his childhood and early manhood in the years before his first book, *Poems Descriptive of Rural Life and Scenery*, was published in 1820. Although biographers and critics have treated these writings as a transparent account of Clare's early life, no autobiography is ever that. They are, like all autobiography, a reconstruction, a reinvention, of the past, and at the very least involve a process of selection—what is recalled has a significance for the autobiographer which may or may not be clear to us. What matters in writing an autobiography is to make some sort of pattern out of a life. In reading Clare's autobiographical writings one continually asks: what does that mean, why is he telling us this? Sometimes the significance is obvious, at other times completely obscure. One passage which I find particularly interesting is the following; Clare has been talking about his first experiences of writing poetry, and how he kept his activities secret from his parents:

> at length I begun to shake of[f] this reserve with my parents and half confess what I was doing my father woud sometimes be huming over a song, a wretched composition of those halfpenny ball[a]ds, and my boast was that I thought I coud beat it in a few days afterwards I used to read my composition for his judgment to decide, but their frequent critisisms and laughable remarks drove me to use a process of cunning in the business some time after, for they damp'd me a long time from proceeding. My method on resuming the matter again was to say I had written it out of a borrowd book and that it was not my own the love of rhyming which I was loath to quit, growing fonder of it every day, drove me to the nessesity of a lie to try the value of their critisisms and by this way I got their remarks unadulterated with prejudice—in this case their expressions

woud be, 'Aye, boy, if you coud write so, you woud do.' this got me into the secret at once and without divulging mine I scribbld on unceasing for 2 or 3 years, reciting them every night as I wrote them when my father returnd home from labour and we was all seated by the fire side their remarks was very useful to me at somethings they woud laugh here I distinguishd Affectation and consiet from nature some verses they woud desire me to repeat again as they said they coud not understand them here I discoverd obscurity from common sense and always benefited by making it as much like the latter as I coud, for I thought if they coud not understand me my taste shoud be wrong founded and not agreeable to nature, so I always strove to shun it for the future and wrote my pieces according to their critisisms, little thinking when they heard me read them that I was the author[1]

I find this a significant piece of writing for two reasons. Firstly, it shows how, for Clare, poetry was always closely associated with the spoken word; throughout his life the audience for which he was writing remained real, not something abstract and imagined. Secondly, this piece foreshadows what seems to have been a lifelong habit with Clare, of needing the opinions of others to help him in the correction of his poems, preferably by reading his poems to them or, if that was not possible, by letting them read the manuscript for themselves and pass judgment on it. Clare knew that he wrote too much, and he knew that some of what he wrote was good and some was run-of-the-mill stuff, but he seems to have had real difficulty in distancing himself from his work sufficiently to judge the merits of what he had written, to tell the good from the ordinary. The experience of being laughed at by his parents must have been a particularly painful one for such a sensitive child, and one he was anxious never to repeat. He needed to try his work out on an audience in order to get some reaction, some feedback from them. He was very concerned that his poems should make sense, that they should be comprehensible, to discover 'obscurity from common sense' as he put it.

He was also very concerned that, as he said, he should distinguish 'Affectation and conseit from nature', that his taste should be 'agreeable to nature'. It was vitally important to Clare that he should get things right, that his verse should be accurate. He wanted it to be factually accurate, but also imaginatively and emotionally true. This was crucial for Clare because he saw this as the key to the survival of his poetry. For example, in 'The Eternity of Nature', after fifty lines describing the sights, and particularly the sounds, of nature (he has been describing birdsong), Clare writes:

And so I worship them in bushy spots
And sing with them when all else notice not
And feel the music of their mirth agree
With that sooth quiet that bestirreth me
And if I touch aright that quiet tone
That soothing truth that shadows forth their own
Then many a year shall grow in after days
And still find hearts to love my quiet lays[2]

And again, in 'Shadows of Taste':

A pleasing image to its page conferred
In living character and breathing word
Becomes a landscape heard and felt and seen
Sunshine and shade one harmonizing green
Where meads and brooks and forrests basking lie
Lasting as truth and the eternal sky
Thus truth to nature as the true sublime
Stands a mount atlas overpeering time[3]

'Lasting as truth' is the significant phrase. The survival of his work was a constant preoccupation of Clare's, and it was 'truth to nature' which he saw as the necessary precondition for this, and that in its turn depended on him finding 'pleasing images', which were only pleasing if they were true, if he 'touched aright' whatever he was describing. If he did not get things right his work would be forgotten, and it was on other people that he depended to tell him when he was not getting it right.

I have said nothing so far about who these people were, except for his parents. The truth is that we really don't know, but there are at least some pointers, in Clare's correspondence and elsewhere, as to the sort of help he was able to enlist. The first major influence on Clare, outside his family, was Edward Drury, the Stamford bookseller who discovered Clare. Drury was a younger man than Clare; when they met Clare was in his mid-twenties, whereas Drury had only just turned twenty and was recently arrived in Stamford on his first independent business venture. Drury was clearly a very remarkable young man: he had a wide knowledge of literature, and literature meant a great deal to him—not qualities commonly found in a bookseller then or now. In the first year of their acquaintance Drury, as well as supporting Clare and his family financially, spent a lot of time with Clare, reading through his poems with him, discussing them, sorting out what was good and what was bad, and why, making Clare aware of his strengths and weaknesses, and generally offering him guidance. For example, on 5 May 1819, after copying out some of Clare's poems, Drury wrote to his cousin John Taylor, who became Clare's publisher:

this fresh Copy I have had taken for the purpose of reading it over with Clare, and yesterday we began at 6 o'clock, continued comparing till finished which was in the evening late. There is not a thought or expression altered but what is purely his own; but he begs you, me or anybody capable, will so far be his friend to cut out many puerile passages that weaken the effect of the whole[4]

Later came the reading of the proofs, and here again Drury was closely involved with Clare; it must have been Drury who taught Clare how to read a proof sheet. It would be an exaggeration to say that Drury taught Clare how to write poetry, but theirs was certainly something of a pupil-teacher relationship. Drury had the insight to recognise Clare's genius in its raw state; in one of his letters, written on 9 May 1820, four months after the publication of *Poems Descriptive of Rural Life and Scenery*, he told Clare: 'you have a talent within you of which you are scarcely aware as yet'.[5] Drury also had the sensitivity to realise what it was that Clare was trying to do, to encourage him in his efforts and to suggest suitable models for him to follow.

After Clare's poems were published, his circle of acquaintance widened, and one person he became friendly with was the Stamford grocer and maltster, critic and editor, Octavius Gilchrist. Gilchrist was a well-known figure in literary circles, a man of immense erudition and capacious learning, a friend of John Scott, the editor of the *London Magazine*, of William Gifford, editor of the *Quarterly Review,* and of John Taylor, amongst many others. Gilchrist was another to whom Clare was able to show manuscripts and discuss his poems. Writing to Clare on 17 December 1819, a month after they first became acquainted, Gilchrist said:

It's now "tw'een day and dark", my good friend, and I have only read over the Ballad,—of which I do not think so meanly as you do: but of this, as of some others, it strikes my vanity that we might between us, now and then, suggest a little change which might do them no harm, without altering (as the lawyers say) "matter of substance". But this we can talk over when we meet next Thursday.[6]

A few months later, on 26 May 1820, he told Clare: 'I have got about half way through the Peasant Boy, but have no design to make a single remark upon it in the first reading';[7] 'The Peasant Boy' was the long poem which eventually became the title poem of Clare's second book, *The Village Minstrel.* There are several other instances, preserved in the correspondence, of Clare sending manuscripts for Gilchrist and his wife, Elizabeth, to read through and comment on.

Yet another of Clare's Stamford friends was Frank Simpson, a young man who came from one of the town's leading families. Although he was known for his artistic rather than his literary gifts, Frank Simpson was certainly a well-read man, and on occasion Clare circulated manuscript poetry around the Simpson family, not only showing his work to Frank himself but also to his parents, brothers, sisters and cousins, and no doubt Clare read his poems to them at the literary and musical evenings which the Simpsons held and to which he was invited. One occasion on which Clare sought the advice of both Frank Simpson and his father, Alderman Francis Simpson, is found in 1822; on 13 September Clare received a letter from Frank Simpson which began: 'Dear Clare / I was much disappointed last Week when I heard that Mrs Clare had been here & coud not procure what you wanted & yet it gave me pleasure that such an opportunity occur'd to prove to you that it was sacred—I have now released it from its custody'. Simpson ended the letter by saying: 'your Mother I hear is afraid of being too late for the Cart, & I must conclude. yet if I thought you required the assurance I woud tell you that none *but* my *Father & Myself* have seen the *Mxxxxx*'.[8] I think it is fairly clear that 'Mxxxxx' stands for 'manuscript', and the reason for this secrecy was almost certainly that it was the manuscript of Clare's long satirical poem, 'The Parish', which he was beginning to circulate among his friends at this time. Clare would have realised that this was a sensitive manuscript, and that the contents might upset some highly placed and powerful individuals if they imagined that they were depicted therein. Another friend to whom Clare sent a specimen of 'The Parish', asking for his reaction, was William Sharp, who worked at the Dead Letter Office in London; replying on 31 July 1823 Sharp asked: 'But My Dear Sir do you not fear to provoke these potentates and entail upon yourself a portion of their cruel tyrany?'[9] Perhaps Clare was mindful of this possibility, and the reason for his showing this manuscript to the Simpsons, father and son, was not so much for an opinion on its poetic merits as for a judgment on the wisdom of publishing the poem.

In early 1822 Edward Drury had to leave Stamford to return to his native Lincoln, and at about the same time Octavius Gilchrist's health began to deteriorate—he died the following year. Clare's acquaintance in Stamford therefore was much reduced, but at this time he formed a friendship with someone else who could assist him with his poetry. This was Joseph Henderson, the head gardener at Milton Hall.[10] Henderson came from a family of gardeners in Kinross; the gardening profession in southern England at that time was dominated by Scots, for a variety of reasons, one of which was undoubtedly the superiority of the Scottish educational system.[11] Henderson was certainly well-educated, and a man of high intelligence, but anyone occupying the position of head gardener in a large country house needed to be a very accomplished individual. This was particularly true if you worked for Lord Milton, who was a patron of the sciences—he was the first president of the British Association for the Advancement of Science—and whose particular interests were in botany and horticulture. When it came to gardeners he only employed the best, and in Joseph Cooper at Wentworth Woodhouse and Joseph Henderson at Milton he had two of the best in the business.[12] The scientific papers which Henderson published gained him a considerable reputation in botanical circles, and he was elected an Associate of the Linnaean Society, an honour rarely bestowed on gardeners, on the strength of a paper published in the Society's *Proceedings*;[13] in addition he was an entomologist of note, contributing specimens and information to John Curtis for the latter's *British Entomology* which was published in sixteen volumes between 1824 and 1839. Henderson had a good knowledge of Greek and Latin, so he would have known something about grammar, but he was also a man with a wide knowledge of English and Scottish literature. Moreover he had an acute critical faculty; I suspect that Henderson played a large part in developing Clare's critical abilities, and it is noticeable that from time to time Clare expresses opinions in his letters to his London friends which are largely a repetition of opinions that Henderson had expressed to him.

On one occasion Henderson arrived to visit Clare with *Don Juan* in his pocket; Clare noted in his Journal that:

we talkd about books and flowers and Butterflyes till noon and then he discanted on Don Juan which he admird very much I think a good deal of his opinion and shall read it when I am able[14]

Clare did indeed think a good deal of his opinion, and on 22 April 1822, only a few months after the start of their friendship, we find Henderson writing to Clare about 'The Shadows of Life, Death and Eternity', which John Taylor published two months later in the *London Magazine*.[15] Henderson said:

Yesterday while *groping my way* among "The Shadows of Life, Death, & Eternity", I discovered a mistake which I am afraid may prove fatal to its insertion in the forthcoming Magazine, except Taylor should take upon himself to alter it, but as you will probably have an opportunity of communicating with him yourself before it is too late, I thought it proper to mention it that you may be enabled to correct it yourself.————
The error is in one of the lines which you altered on Saturday.
Wave chasing wave *unceasing never*
This you will at the first glance observe is not grammar, & I am astonished that it should have escaped us both at the time, You will easily perceive that by taking away the negative un from ceasing the line becomes grammar but wants one syllable to fill up the measure.[16]

It is obvious from this that Clare and Henderson had gone through the poem together with some care and in great detail, discussing it and making corrections to it, and Clare seems to have made considerable use of Henderson in this way over the years. They also sometimes went over the proofs of

Clare's work together, because of course everything which Taylor printed, either in book form or in the *London Magazine*, was submitted to Clare in proof for his approval or alteration.

If Clare was unable to visit Henderson then he would send manuscripts to him for his comments and suggestions. For example, on 12 May 1823 Henderson told Clare:

I have been so busy that I have hardly been able to look at the "Parish" & to tell you the truth there is a good deal of it that I cannot make out, I shall be unengaged this evening & shall have another try at it. I will return it in a day or two with any remarks that I may be able to make.[17]

Just over a week later, on 21 May, Henderson fulfilled his promise:

My Dear Clare

I have been hard at work on the Parish every night since I wrote you last & I hope I have not transgressed by keeping it so long.—I have no doubt that you must feel anxious about it as every one would about an unpublished manuscript, but I can solemnly assure you that it has been as sacred in my hands as if it had been locked up in your own possession I have read it only in the evenings when no one was near to interrupt me, & no person knows that it has been in my posession except ourselves.[18]

There is a strong similarity here with the language Frank Simpson used when he apparently had the manuscript of 'The Parish' in his possession, even down to the use of the same word, 'sacred'. This may be coincidence, of course, although I doubt it; even if it is, it shows how strongly Clare had impressed upon both men the importance of discretion and secrecy. Henderson continued his letter:

From the hasty manner in which you have written it down, I found a good deal of difficulty in making it out, but I believe I have succeeded in all except about half a doz. words. ————
I do not know whether I have not taken too great a liberty in marking with a pencil those parts which I thought would want ammendment, I did it however to save time it would have taken so much more to have

transcribed them, in some of the parts marked it is possible that I have misconstrued some of the words & consequently may have mistaken the sense, however it may have the effect, (when you rub out the pencil marks,) of making you reconsider the poem, which I think you should do, the subject is one which in your hands is capable of being turned to considerable advantage.—No one posesses in a greater degree the natural simplicity of language fited for such a subject & few are better acquainted with the general details of the subject. Your general plan, & the characters you have marked out, are in my opinion just what should be, & you have already succeeded in making the poem sufficiantly interesting to deserve your attention in removing its triffling <objections> deffects,. I will now tell you what in my humble opinion is objectionable in it, & you must treat it as an humble opinion only.[19]

Henderson included in his letter comments about the general structure and plan of the poem; in addition to writing comments in pencil on the manuscript he had also inserted slips of paper at various points with yet more comments on them.

There are a number of other pieces of evidence of Henderson's assistance with the revision of manuscripts, and I will just give one more example, of a poem not published in Clare's lifetime:

My Dear Clare
    After a long interval I have at last returned your poem of "Edmund & Helen" & I am quite ashamed of myself for having kept it so long, I wished to read it over once more & at the time you wrote to me I was so busy with my accounts, that I had not time to do it,—& since then it has quite slipt my recollection, till now. I have now travelled all through it & in the course have erased several of the marks where I on first reading, thought the parts wanted ammendment.—I still think that by picking out the best parts of it & condensing the matter you will make it one of the most interesting of your poems.[20]

Again Henderson offered a general observation, regarding the excessive use of the words 'hope' and 'hopes' in the poem, before continuing:

I have marked those parts which I thought wanted ammendment thus }
& my other observations are written on slips of paper I have as you
desired me made my remarks freely & without reserve, because I know
that you would not have sent me the poem if you had not intended me to
do so.—there are many parts of it which I very much admire & I do
assure you that I think it will well repay you for a little amendment &
revision.[21]

In this instance the manuscript which Henderson saw, with his underlinings,
markings and a few comments, has survived, although the slips of paper on
which he wrote most of his remarks, sadly but unsurprisingly, have not.[22]

Of course there must have been many more people, besides those I have
mentioned, to whom Clare read or showed his work. Clare tells us nothing
about his writing and revising practices; we know a little about the people I
have discussed because they wrote letters to Clare, and the evidence, however
slight, is there in their letters, but those who were closest to Clare, his friends
and neighbours in Helpston, had no need to write to him and therefore we
know nothing about the part they played in the revision of Clare's work. Just
occasionally we are given a hint of what went on; for example, in a letter
which Clare wrote to John Taylor on 19 March 1820, he mentioned 'The
Lodge House', saying: 'it is undergone the Critiscism of my father & mother
& several rustic Neighbours of the town & all aprove it'.[23]

There were many people in and around Helpston, as well as further
afield at Milton Hall and in Peterborough and Stamford, to whom Clare lent
books, from whom he borrowed books, and with whom he shared newspapers
and periodicals—a whole circle or network of readers. The names of a few
of these people are known, but they are only a fraction of the men and women
with whom Clare shared his passion for the written word, and any of them
might, on occasion, have been asked to help him out with his poems.

Although the evidence is very fragmentary, we can see, therefore, that
Clare's poems were subject to a process of revision in collaboration with
others before they were submitted to Clare's publishers (and far fewer poems
than is commonly supposed were ever sent to London to be read by Taylor
and Hessey). Even those poems which were not published in Clare's lifetime
may have been to some extent the result of a collaborative process, and
provide a good illustration of the argument put forward by Jack Stillinger, in

his *Multiple Authorship and the Myth of Solitary Genius*, that the solitary author may be a necessary myth, but is a myth nonetheless. In his chapter on 'Keats and his Helpers: The Multiple Authorship of *Isabella*', Stillinger writes: 'The abundant documentary evidence concerning the revising, editing, and printing of Keats's nonposthumous poems gives us a rather attractive overall picture of Keats, Woodhouse, Taylor, and other friends (Reynolds and Charles Brown in particular) all pulling together to make the poems presentable to the public and to the reviewers'.[24] In the case of Clare the documentary evidence is far from abundant, and the Clare Circle was very different from the Keats Circle, although the splendid Taylor is a common factor, but we have a similarly attractive picture of Clare's friends helping to see his poems into publishable form.

Stillinger argues that critical, textual, and interpretive theories, even those that posit the death of the author, presuppose that there is *an* author,[25] but with Clare, as with so many others, we find that if we examine in detail the actual circumstances of composition and publication, the situation is much more complicated than that; any simple ideas of authorial intention fall down when confronted by the actual complexity of the process of writing. This idea, of the text as a social product, also has much in common with the ideas put forward by Jerome McGann, who has argued that '[t]he textual histories of poems ... are paradigm instances of the historically specific character of all poetry', and advocated the elucidation of 'the larger social act which is the poem in its specific (and quite various) human history'.[26] Each text, whether published or not, has to be seen in the light of the social, material and intellectual circumstances in which it was conceived and written, as an artifact belonging to a specific time and place, taking into account the known biographical facts and the historical context in which the work was composed. As Arthur Marotti has argued: 'What modern idealistic textual criticism, from an author-centered point of view, regards as "corruptions" we can view as interesting evidence of the social history of particular texts'.[27]

I have discussed Clare's reading aloud or circulation of his manuscripts, and in some senses Clare remained, throughout his life, a manuscript poet. I don't want to present him as a historical throwback, but in many respects Clare worked in the manuscript tradition which had been commonplace in earlier centuries, but which was still alive and well in the Romantic era. The absence of punctuation in Clare's manuscripts is one example. Clare's commentators often seem to think there was something unusual, or even unique, in this, but it was common enough in earlier times for people not to punctuate manuscript poetry and in the early nineteenth century it was still far from unusual—we need look no further than Keats's manuscripts to see that, and Byron and Wordsworth provide further examples. Many writers of that period had not internalised the conventions of print culture, and therefore did not punctuate at all, or only lightly.

In other respects too Clare operated in the manuscript tradition. As we have seen he circulated manuscript poems among his friends, as well as manuscript books. He sewed together the letters he received to make books from them, and these too he would sometimes lend to his friends. He filled manuscript books *for* his friends; Eliza Emmerson had one, as well as many individual poems he had sent to her. Clare also filled a manuscript book for Octavius Gilchrist's widow, Elizabeth, which contained, amongst much else, 'The Parish'. In such ways, Clare had the assistance of his friends in judging, in correcting, and in contributing to, his poetry. Purists and idealists in textual matters, who look upon any intervention by an editor, or any other collaborator, as a corruption of the text, miss the point and miss much of the interest. All texts have a social history attached to them, and are not simply an expression of an individual consciousness; they owe something to the wider milieu in which the writer moved, and are an expression of communal rather than purely personal values. For those who seek textual purity, the works of John Clare are no place to look.

NOTES

I am grateful to Northamptonshire Libraries and Information Service and to the Department of Manuscripts, British Library, for permission to quote from manuscripts in their keeping.

1. *By Himself*, pp. 13-14; a similar passage is to be found on p. 98.
2. *Middle Period*, III, p. 529.
3. *Middle Period*, III, p. 306.
4. NMS 43 (3).
5. Eg. 2245, f. 116r.
6. Eg. 2245, f. 15r.

7. Eg. 2245, f. 134r.
8. Eg. 2246, f. 109r.
9. Eg. 2246, f. 226r.
10. It is commonly stated, in the biographies of Clare and elsewhere, that his friendships with Joseph Henderson and Edmund Artis began early in 1820, when he first visited Milton Hall; however, the evidence indicates that these friendships date from late 1821.
11. The preponderance of Scots in the gardening profession is discussed by Alice M. Coats, 'When Scottish Gardeners Came South', *Country Life*, 12 March 1964, pp. 572-3.
12. For details of Lord Milton's interest in horticulture generally, and the cultivation of orchids in particular, see Ray Desmond, *Dictionary of British and Irish Botanists and Horticulturists including Plant Collectors, Flower Painters and Garden Designers* (London: Taylor & Francis and The Natural History Museum, 1994), p. 249, and G.G. Yearsley, 'Earl Fitzwilliam and His Gardener, J. Cooper: 18th-19th Century Orchid Growers', *American Orchid Society Bulletin*, 45 (1976), 484-5.
13. For some details of Joseph Henderson see Desmond, *Dictionary*, p. 334. Henderson himself is sadly absent from the *Dictionary of National Biography*, but one of his brothers, Andrew, can be found therein.
14. *By Himself*, p. 174.
15. *Middle Period*, I, pp. 338-9.
16. Eg. 2246, ff. 52r-v.
17. Eg. 2246, f. 196v.
18. Eg. 2246, f. 198r.
19. Eg. 2246, ff. 198r-v.
20. Eg. 2246, f. 467r.
21. Eg. 2246, ff. 467v-468r.
22. PMS A31, pp. 86-112. For all textual variants of the poem see *Early Poems*, II, pp. 549-76; the editors mistakenly attribute the pencil emendations in A31 to Taylor rather than Henderson.
23. *Letters*, p. 38.
24. Jack Stillinger, *Multiple Authorship and the Myth of Solitary Genius* (New York: Oxford University Press, 1991), pp. 25-49 (p. 45).
25. Stillinger, *Multiple Authorship*, p. 193.
26. Jerome J. McGann, *The Beauty of Inflections: Literary Investigations in Historical Method and Theory* (Oxford: Clarendon Press, 1985), pp. 131, 24.
27. Arthur F. Marotti, *Manuscript, Print, and the English Renaissance Lyric* (Ithaca and London: Cornell University Press, 1995), p. 135.

4. Clare and Community: The 'Old Poets' and the *London Magazine*

Mina Gorji

> Inclosure came & every path was stopt
> Each tyrant fixt his sign where pads was found
> To hint a trespass now who crossd the ground
> ('The Village Minstrel' (1821), 107, ll. 1086-8)

In *The Idea of Landscape and the Sense of Place*,[1] John Barrell relates the success of 'The Lament of Swordy Well' (1821-4) to its freedom from 'the sort of dependence on eighteenth-century models which was so apparent in the earlier poems.'[2] It serves as an example of a wider pattern Barrell discerns in Clare's verse during the 1820s, a shift away from derivative and imitative poetry, towards a more individual tone and style, a digging in of local heels.[3] Barrell praises Clare for his ability to 'emancipate himself' from the influence of eighteenth-century poets, and to 'discover a language of his own.'[4] 'Emancipate' suggests that Barrell's notion of poetic influence is Bloomian and antagonistic. Such a model does not allow for the possibility that influence might be positive and friendly. This may be partly because such a model of influence seems to rest on a notion of poetic language or voice as enclosed and singular, what we might term monoglossic, so that influence is seen in terms of ventriloquism or imitation. Clare's 'own' language could be seen as composite, or heteroglossic, its particularity consisting in his way of crafting combinations of words from various registers and sources, weaving in various influences, rather than being entirely possessed or overwhelmed by them.

Barrell suggests that Clare's poetry is best when most 'original', 'individual', 'local' and 'direct'. These aesthetic terms correspond with a vocabulary he uses to describe the ideology of enclosure which, he argues, 'sought to de-localise, to take away the individuality of a place'.[5] Barrell insists that he is not trying to argue 'in a simple fashion'[6] for a causal connection between Clare's response to enclosure and what he perceives as Clare's increasingly 'local' style. Nonetheless, linking the 'idea of the local' in terms of place and style, he implies that Clare's localisation of language was a counter movement to enclosure. The speaking piece of land, Swordy Well, whose voice is colloquial and seemingly unliterary, serves as a symbolic example of this linkage of land and language in terms of the concept of the local. However, such coincidence is not characteristic of all Clare's poetry, nor is a pattern of localisation of language as evident as Barrell suggests. Barrell's seminal study was written before the publication of *The Midsummer Cushion* (1979), a volume which reveals perhaps more than any other the rich variety of Clare's poetic output. Although the volume's title refers to a local custom, the poems which it contains do not all reveal a preoccupation with local subjects, nor are they all couched in a localised poetic language, but written in a wide range of styles, tones and languages. *The Midsummer Cushion* contains several of the forgeries of 'old' poems which Clare published in periodicals during the 1820s. This essay will pay particular attention to the ways in which these forgery poems unsettle Barrell's claims for the importance of the local and original in Clare's verse.

Barrell considers the effects of enclosure in terms of landscape, focusing on the process of de-localisation. As Clare perceived it, enclosure also had wider social implications: it seemed to be destroying the cohesion and sociability of his village community. Rather than considering enclosure, and its linguistic correspondences, in terms of landscape, and, as a result, focusing on the concepts of the 'local' and 'individual', I will consider enclosure from the perspective of sociological effect, and suggest that its stylistic correspondences can be seen in terms of literary sociability and community. I propose that Clare's intertextuality rather than his originality was a response to enclosure. Clare responded poetically to the disintegration of local communities, which he associated with enclosure, by involving himself in poetic communities, intertextually, rather than through evolving a 'language of his own', independently. I suggest that Clare associated originality—a discourse shot through with ideas of property and individualism—with enclosure, and that he opted for a more communitarian, open poetic model. For Clare, this friendly poetic model seems to have been represented by two distinct, but (as I hope to show) *interrelated* literary groups: the *London Magazine* circle, and a group of sixteenth- and seventeenth-century poets whom Clare referred to as the 'old poets'.[7]

Barrell argues that despite Clare's increasing exposure to the London literary world in the 1820s, he became 'more tenacious in his desire to write exclusively about Helpston, to "describe the feelings of a rhyming peasant locally".[8] However, although Clare may have been intimidated by the urbane world of polite letters, he nonetheless profited personally and poetically from his involvement in this literary community. During the mid-1820s, Clare was composing a series of poems which he later hoped would form a collection bearing the name of 'Visits of the Early Muses'.[9] The idea for the collection had been proposed by Clare's publisher, John Taylor, as a way of presenting the body of work Clare had been producing in the 'old' style. In a letter of 15 July 1826, Clare thanks Taylor:

> I am very pleased with your idea of 'Visits of the early Muses' as a Title for my *old* Poems & shall keep adding to the number as I feel inclined & I shall not publish any more of them in pereodicals now you have past your opinion of them so favourably[10]

These 'old' poems'[11] were not originally published under Clare's name, but had appeared in print as forgeries, ascribed to various 'old poets' in periodicals and journals such as Hone's *Everyday Book,* the *European Magazine*, and the *Sheffield Iris.* Taylor encouraged Clare to acknowledge these poems as his own, and publish them as a collection. Although 'Visits of the Early Muses' was never published, Clare eventually placed most of the 'forgery' poems in *The Midsummer Cushion.*[12]

Clare shared his interest in the 'old poets' with the circle to whom he was introduced by Taylor in the early 1820s, a group of literary men, linked in their involvement with the *London Magazine* (which Taylor edited between 1821 and 1825). Clare's poetic career had been launched in the first number of the *London* in January 1820, in an essay by Octavius Gilchrist, 'Some Account of John Clare, an Agricultural Labourer and Poet,' and Clare's poems regularly appeared on the *London*'s pages in the early 1820s. Lamb, Hazlitt, Darley, Cary, Cunningham, Reynolds, Gilchrist, and Keats (whom Clare never actually met), *London Magazine* men, shared Clare's fondness for the 'old poets'. Darley wrote verses in the antique style, indeed his most famous lyric, 'It is not Beautie I Demande', was printed as a genuine anonymous Caroline lyric by F.T. Palgrave in his *Golden Treasury* (it was eventually banished from the selection when assigned to Darley). Uncannily, Clare had played a similar literary trick in 1825, also pretending to have found forgotten poems on the 'fly-leaves' of old books. Rather than appearing anonymously, these forgeries were attributed to 'old poets' in the journals in which they appeared.

Clare discussed his penchant for the 'old poets' in letters to Darley, Cary and Taylor. In *John Keats and the Culture of Dissent*,[13] Nicholas Roe has discussed the radical significance of a taste for the 'old poets' which Keats, Hazlitt and Hunt shared. He points out that these literary figures perceived a connection between Robin Hood and the 'old poets', linking them in terms of a radical and levelling sense of conviviality and sociability. Keats's 'Lines Written at the Mermaid Tavern' and Hazlitt's 'Lectures on the Literature of the Age of Elizabeth' are examples of this sociable understanding of the 'old poets'. Roe also draws our attention to the stylistic implications of the generous amplitude associated with the 'old poets' (particularly the Elizabethans for Keats) who seemed to afford a sociable poetic model which resists the Wordsworthian and egotistical. The *London Magazine* itself acted as a focus for this sociable interest in the 'old poets': its motto, printed on the title page, was taken from Jonson's *Discoveries*, and a review of *The Memoirs of the Life of Sir John Suckling,* which appeared in the April 1820 number of the *London*, spelled out this enthusiasm, declaring, 'we have a great passion for our early poets, lyric, epic and dramatic', and promised to 'intersperse our pages with observations, selections, or criticisms, arising from a prevailing attachment.'[14] On his London visits, Clare was likely to have been involved in and influenced by this shared enthusiasm. Clare visited London three times between 1820 and 1824, and during these visits became acquainted with the *London*'s luminaries at dinners held by Taylor.[15] The exchanges between Clare and this circle were also material, in the form of letters and books. The catalogue of Clare's library at Northampton[16] reveals that he owned books by Lamb, Hazlitt, Cary, Reynolds, Darley and Keats, often presented to him by the authors themselves, or by Taylor.

Clare describes the London literary community in his autobiographical writings:

I had not means of meeting the constellations of Genius in one mass they were mingld partys some few were fixd stars in the worlds hemisphere others glimmerd every month in the [London] Magazine[17]

His starry metaphor echoes Hazlitt's description of Shakespeare's contemporaries in his introductory 'Lecture on The Age of Elizabeth':

Mr. Wordsworth says of Milton, 'that his soul was like a star, and dwelt apart.' This cannot be said with any propriety of Shakspear, who certainly moved in a constellation of bright luminaries, and 'drew after him a third part of the heavens.' ... The sweetness of Decker, the thought of Marston, the gravity of Chapman, the grace of Fletcher and his young-eyed wit, Jonson's learned sock, the flowing vein of Middleton, Heywood's ease, the pathos of Webster, and Marlow's deep designs, add a double lustre to the sweetness, thought, gravity, grace, wit, artless nature, copiousness, ease, pathos, and sublime conceptions of Shakspear's Muse. They are indeed the scale by which we can best ascend to the true knowledge and love of him.[18]

For Clare, the 'constellation' of London literary men were linked with the 'constellation' of lesser-known sixteenth- and seventeenth-century poets. Both offered appealing and interrelated models of poetic community. Hazlitt, one of the *London Magazine* circle, makes the sociability of the 'old poets' explicit when he describes reading the 'old authors':

They sit with me at breakfast; they walk with me before dinner ... Ben Jonson, learned Chapman, Master Webster, and Master Heywood, are there; and seated round, discourse the silent hours away.19

This sociable link is also made apparent in Clare's sonnet 'To Charles Lamb', which Clare placed in *The Midsummer Cushion*.[20] The poem applauds Lamb for championing the 'old bygone bards' in the teeth of popular neglect. Clare's praise is couched in terms borrowed from Lamb's essay 'Detatched Thoughts on Books and Reading':[21]

Friend Lamb thou chusest well to love the lore
Of our old by gone bards whose racey page
Rich mellowing Time made sweeter then before
The blossom left for the long garnered store
Of fruitage now right luscious in its age (ll. 1-5)

Here the blossom's sweetness and the delicious consumability of 'fruitage' recall Lamb's sensuous terms:

> Shall I be thought fantastical, if I confess that the names of some of our poets sound sweeter, and have a finer relish to the ear—to mine, at least— than that of Milton or Shakspeare? It may be, that the latter are more staled and rung up in common discourse. The sweetest names, and which carry a perfume in the mention, are, Kit Marlowe, Drayton, Drummond of Hawthornden, and Cowley.[22]

Although it was not Lamb who introduced Clare to such poets, reading *Elia*, Clare felt less alone in his enthusiasm for the 'warm homely phrase' of these half-forgotten poets. The phrase itself suggests comfort and conviviality:

> Me much it grieved as I did erst presage
> Vain fashions foils had every heart deterred
> From the warm homely phrase of other days
> Until thy muses auncient voice I heard
> & now right fain yet fearing honest bard
> I pause to greet thee with so poor a praise (ll. 9-14)

The sonnet is couched in archaic language and cadences. Archaic language bonds in two directions, Clare to the 'old poets', and Clare to Lamb. Lamb's fondness for 'old' poetry releases Clare from his melancholy isolated appreciation of these neglected poets. The 'warm homely phrase of other days' affords Clare the opportunity of conviviality, offering him a sociable connection to the contemporary literary world.

Clare's reception of these 'old poets' probably contributed further to his sense of their sociability. He came into contact with Herrick, Herbert, Suckling, Raleigh, Cotton, Wotton and Marvell, in collections such as Ellis's *Specimens of the Early English Poets*, Percy's *Reliques of Ancient English Poetry*, Ritson's *Songs*, and Walton's *Compleat Angler*. He also found 'old' poems in almanac magazines such as *Time's Telescope* and Hone's *Everyday Book*, which place poems in broader contexts, using them to exemplify and illustrate country customs, folklore, and natural history. Percy's *Reliques* mingled Elizabethan lyrics with (anonymous) ballads, so that not only were Elizabethan poets grouped together, they were also associated with a characteristic 'low culture' form—the ballad. Such familiar company may have heightened Clare's sense of the homeliness of the 'old poets'. Associated in Percy's *Reliques* with ballads, the 'old poets' probably appeared to Clare as a vital link between the 'low' and 'high' cultures which he tries to mingle in his poetry. The contemporary association of the ballad form with sociability and community may have contributed to Clare's sense of the conviviality of the 'old poets'. Mingled with ballads in the *Reliques*, and associated with country customs and folklore in Hone's *Everyday Book* and *Time's Telescope*, the 'old poets' mediate between worlds Clare often felt torn between—the realm of verse and the rural village community.

In his essay 'Detatched Thoughts', Lamb situates his fondness for the 'old poets' in comparison with Shakespeare and Milton. For Lamb, the two stand apart. For Coleridge, Shakespeare and Milton stood on 'the two glory-smitten summits of the poetic mountain.'[23] In Lamb's estimation they stand less gloriously apart from the other poets 'Marlowe, Drayton ... &c', and are 'staled' by the comparison rather than elevated. Lamb is opening up spaces in the emerging canon, whose fixed poles were Milton and Shakespeare. The poets he praises here provide a more community-based model of poetry: they do not stand aloof like Milton and Shakespeare, but cluster together sweetly. Their names are 'perfumed', not awe-inspiring. The sociability associated with these poets is expressed in Clare's sonnet 'To Charles Lamb', in which he uses a pastiche of their 'old' language to communicate a shared enthusiasm with Lamb. Clare associates this 'old' language with sociability, and uses it in allusion, to counteract the isolating treatment he received from publishers and critics alike. Clare's isolation was not so sublime and glorious as Milton and Shakespeare's. Originality carried with it, as it does in Lamb's essay, notions of singularity.[24] Where Hazlitt's description of Milton's solitude is glorious, for Clare solitude carried the taint of his critics—not so much sublime as inglorious.

Clare's imitative style in his sonnet to Lamb presents in writing what Lamb suggests about his reading—an indifference to originality, if it involves separating oneself from others. Lamb begins his essay 'Detached Thoughts on Books and Reading' with a quotation:

To mind the inside of a book is to entertain one's self with the forced product of another man's brain. Now I think a man of quality and breeding may be much amused with the natural sprouts of his own.[25]

Beginning his essay with the words of another, Lamb immediately engages in the 'product of another man's brain': merely using the quotation as an epigraph to his essay reveals his disagreements with its sentiments, so that Lamb ironically distances himself from the quotation before uttering a single word of his own. He goes on to relate how a friend of his, struck by the passage he quoted, 'left off reading altogether, to the great improvement of his originality.'[26] It is clear at this point that Lamb does not value 'originality' as much as his friend did. Lamb has not so far made much of a personal appearance in the essay, moving from the words of another to describing the effect of those words on a friend of his. He goes on to confess that he is not very much interested in 'originality', but rather 'I love to lose myself in other men's minds'.[27] In his sonnet to Lamb, Clare loses himself in other men's words, and words which he knew that Lamb also liked to lose himself in. Lamb's tone disguises the significance of his claims: his hostility to originality is bold, given the high premium set on originality when he wrote. Coleridge's defensive Preface to *Christabel* reveals his sensitivity to the conflation of poetic value with originality. The need for such an intricate defensive strategy is indicative of the dominance of the discourse of originality.

The discourse of originality was intrinsically involved with ideas of ownership, as Mark Rose has pointed out at useful length in *Authors and Owners*.[28] In *Conjectures Upon Original Composition* (1759), Edward Young, arguably the most influential advocate of originality, uses a metaphor of land and property to describe originality. Whereas 'an *Imitator* ... builds on another's foundation'.[29] 'Originals', he claims, 'extend the Republic of Letters, and add a new province to its dominion.'[30] Private property and poetry are interrelated: Young places great value on ownership, claiming that an original genius has 'sole property' of his works, and that, such 'Property alone can confer the noble title of an *Author.*'[31] Rose summarises the implications succinctly: 'The production of poetry becomes the production of property'.[32] More recently, John Goodridge has pointed out the implications of this relationship for 'dispossessed poets from humble backgrounds, like Clare and Chatterton,' who, he suggests, 'were especially vulnerable'[33] to a discourse of genius grounded in ownership.

Clare no doubt took a pattern from the example of Chatterton's famous forgeries. Both Chatterton and Clare's poetical responses to the discourse of originality, and the privileging of individual property which it encoded, were to some extent shaped by their dispossession. However, for Clare, this sense of dispossession was heightened by enclosure. In 1809, when Clare was sixteen years old, his local parish, Helpston, began to be enclosed. Clare perceived the enclosure of hitherto open common fields and parklands as a vicious assertion of ownership, and of the rights of individual property, as fierce lines from 'The Village Minstrel', published in 1821, reveal:

> Inclosure came & every path was stopt
> Each tyrant fixt his sign where pads was found
> To hint a trespass now who crossd the ground...
> —Inclosure thourt a curse upon the land
> & tastless was the wretch who thy existance pland (107, ll. 1086-8, 1091-2)[34]

Clare's use of dialect—here 'pads' are paths—is one sign of his resistance to attempts to enclose his verse in standard English. If attempts to confine Clare's language were one source of frustration, the image of Clare as an original genius which Taylor had sold to the public was equally restrictive:

> CLARE has a great delight in trying to run races with other men, and unluckily this cannot always be attempted without subjecting him to the charge of imitating; but he will be found free from that imputation in all the best parts of his poetry.[35]

Taylor seems blind to the ironies of conflating 'peasant poet' with 'original genius', where the discourse of original genius, as I have shown, was so bound up with the language of ownership and property. Clare was alive to the restrictions his 'peasant-ness' imposed on his 'genius', and to the freedoms from those restrictions which imitation afforded him.

Packaged as a peasant poet, Clare was expected to write accordingly: as a poet inspired by nature, writing his responses in original, underivative verse. Clare, sensitive to the centrality of individual property in the discourse of originality, which linked it to the ideology of enclosure, resisted the constraints of originality. The discourses of both originality and enclosure value individual ownership. Both made trespass a crime. Coleridge, figuring influence as the perforation of a tank, in the Preface to *Christabel*,[36] shows his awareness of the relationship of originality and ownership, which Young propounds in *Conjectures Upon Original Composition*: both figure influence as theft. The discourse of originality and the practice of enclosure both stressed the boundaries of individual property. Clare's poetry is full of transgressions of these bounds—full of the echoes of poetic voices and intertextual words. He imitated and mimicked poets such as Burns, Pope and Cowper frequently, and drew on their vocabularies intertextually. His verse is also enriched by the phrases and rhythms of popular songs and ballads. More boldly, he wrote under pseudonyms, ranging from 'Percy Green', to 'Giles Scroggins' in the asylum, abandoning the proprietorial claims implied in naming himself as the author. Eventually, in the madhouse, he was actually to claim to be Byron and Shakespeare, an extreme example of a resistance to originality and its firm location of the bounds of individuality. Such confusion of personalities registers a resistance to the dominant discourse of individual ownership and originality, and should not be brushed aside as a symptom of mere 'madness'.

Clare's forgeries of the 'old poets' offer another striking example of his hostility to the discourse of originality. Unlike Coleridge, anxiously trying to prove ownership in the Preface to *Christabel*, Clare abandons his own name and claims to property altogether. That Clare chose to produce forgeries of a specific group of real poets renders his forgeries distinct from the more famous productions of Chatterton and Macpherson, who each invented one specific bard (though Chatterton's 'Rowley' is socialised within a wider, largely invented, literary group). I have suggested that Clare was drawn toward the 'old poets' in part because of the sociability with which he associated both them and their nineteenth-century admirers. I'd like to consider in more detail why it might be that Clare was drawn to the 'old poets'.

The publication of *Paradise Lost*, as Lucy Newlyn has argued,[37] had a democratising effect on the franchise of poetry, making literature more accessible to a wider range of readers. The major literary events Stuart Curran describes as the recovery of Britain's national literature perhaps had an even greater effect on Britain's writers, since the cluster of authors who were 'recovered' were not seen as intimidating or inhibiting to succeeding poets as

Milton tended to be perceived. They offered an alternative model for vernacular poetry. Curran describes this momentous 'event' as taking place 'between 1765, when Percy first put to press his *Reliques of Ancient Poetry*, and 1819 [the date of the publication of Chalmers's twenty-one volume *Works of the British Poets*]'.[38] Curran points to the importance of historiography in the eighteenth century for the new generation of poets emerging after 1780. Due to the endeavours of men like Warton and Percy, poets of the period we term Romantic inherited a literary past hitherto largely unknown. The process was not suddenly complete in 1819, but its implications were immense. One of the epigraphs Curran chooses for his chapter 'The Second Renaissance' reveals how dramatic the change was; it is an extract from an 1818 essay 'On the Revival of a Taste for our Ancient Literature' in *Blackwood's Magazine* :

...we have raised up, as it were, from the tomb, a spirit that was only lying asleep, and that now, from the dust and darkness, walks abroad among us, in the renovation of all its strength and beauty.[39]

That the order of things could be seen to have shifted so dramatically, that poets once buried deep in 'dust and darkness' could suddenly emerge and come to life in the public consciousness, must surely have changed notions of poetic obscurity in some way, making the 'dust and darkness', seem more permeable than before. If the dead were now walking, then perhaps there was hope for those living unknown, and hope also for Clare. Gray was sensitive to the pressures exerted by those yet-undiscovered, mute inglorious Miltons, from under the dust and darkness in his 'Elegy Written in a Country Churchyard' (a seminal text for Clare). But Gray's conservatism registers a sense of threat from the graveyard.[40] Most of Clare's forgeries reveal a preoccupation with the themes of neglect and death.

The recovery of forgotten 'old poets' was very important to Clare. It presents an opening up of the realms of verse which can be viewed as a countermovement to the enclosure encoded in the Romantic discourse of originality, and on another level, the enclosure of Helpston. Clare associated the 'old poets' with an ideal, pre-enclosure landscape, where people were free to wander at will, unhampered by fences. He says as much in a letter to George Darley of 3 September 1827:

I intend for my own part to strike out on a new road if I can & my greatest ambition is to write something in the spirit of the old Poets not those of Dr. Johnson but those half unknowns who as yet have no settled residence in the <city> Land of Fame but wander about it like so many Pilgrims who are happy to meet a stranger by the way to make themselves known or heard once in a century & I think from these you have made your own model for there is a 'sweet savour' stirs my imagination when I read your Poems ... the same as when I read those above mentioned[41]

These 'half unknowns', these 'old poets', were not the landed gentry of Parnassus; they had 'no settled residence'. This must have appealed to the unenfranchised Clare, antagonistic to the idea of individual property after enclosure had changed his world. These 'sweet songsters' offer a 'new road' for Clare to take—an alternative model.

In 1825, Clare composed 'To John Milton, From his Honoured Friend William Davenant'. The poem was first published as a forgery in the *Sheffield Iris*.[42] In this poem, 'Davenant' addresses Milton and asks:

Poet of mighty power I fain
Would court the muse that honoured thee
& like Elishas spirit gain
A part of thy intensity
& share the mantle which she flung
Around thee when thy lyre was strung. (ll. 1-6)

Through one of the 'old poets', Clare attempts to open out Milton's grand solitude. Whereas Marvell (in 'On Mr Milton's Paradise Lost') and Collins (in 'Ode on the Poetical Character') despair that Milton has closed off a particular poetic space, leaving succeeding writers 'no room' for expression, Clare seems less pessimistic about the effects of Milton's fame. Clare, through Davenant, addresses Milton as a friend, and asks, touchingly, to share his mantle. Where Collins saw Milton as *curtaining close* poetic space, Clare seems to have associated the 'old poets' with opening up such space, expressively and canonically. Gradually, as Stuart Curran has pointed out, these 'old poets' were emerging into an English canon, through anthologies and in newspapers and magazines. Hazlitt, for example, gives space to the starry poets and dramatists whom Shakespeare dragged down from the skies with him in his 'Lectures on the Age of Elizabeth'.[43] Clare attempts to convert this opening up of canonical space to his own poetic ambitions, in the forgeries and through allusion.[44]

'To John Milton, From his Honoured friend William Davenant', describes Milton's rise to fame as brightness shining through the darkness of initial unpopularity:

> Though factions scorn at first did shun
> With coldness thy inspired song
> Though clouds of malice passed thy sun
> They could not hide it long
> Its brightness soon exaled away
> Dank night & gained eternal day (ll. 7-12)

Clare seems to have perceived the trajectory of Milton's career, from obscurity to fame, as a hopeful sign. Clare's 'forgery' poem reveals his sensitivity both to the complex mechanism of reception, and to the importance of sociability in that process. Clare's interest in and witnessing of the recovery of a literary past, marks his hope that he too, in time, may be acknowledged and noticed as a great poet, showing an awareness of the slow processes of reception. Establishing relationships with poets who have been neglected and later remembered by fame, Clare perhaps hoped that his reception would follow a similar pattern.

The years between 1820, when Clare's first volume was published, and 1832, when he completed his manuscript of *The Midsummer Cushion,* had witnessed the rise and fall of Clare's literary career. His fame peaked in the early 1820s, buoyed up by the enthusiastic reception of *Poems Descriptive of Rural Life and Scenery,* and from then began the decline, and Clare's increasing detachment from the literary world. His growing loneliness in these years perhaps made his desire for a sociable poetic community stronger than ever. His friendly address to Lamb in pastiche archaic language was written during this time. Not only was Clare's sense of solitude coloured by his growing isolation, but the range of implication of solitude was widened by less individual concerns: Clare associated detachment with enclosure.

As well as fencing up the face of the countryside, enclosure profoundly changed village social life. Common land had been used for village games and local customs, so its ploughing up and fencing off not only curtailed individual freedoms (the right to roam), but also affected the village community as a whole. George Deacon gives numerous examples of Clare's descriptions of country customs, and his insistence that they had been destroyed by enclosure.[45] In one example, Clare describes enclosure's role in the demise of the custom of stone-gathering in the fields and the games which accompanied it:

inclosure came & destroyed it with hundreds of others—leaving in its place nothing but a love for doing neighbours mischief & public house oratory that dwells upon mob law as absolute justice[46]

Clare sees enclosure as destructive of the cohesive traditions which held the village community together. He describes a community broken apart by enclosure, a society collapsed into crime, mischief and mob law. For Clare, poetry was one means of preserving these customs being lost. *The Shepherd's Calendar* records Clare's regret at the passing of these old customs, and registers his attempt to record and preserve them in verse.

I mentioned earlier that Clare found 'old' poems in almanacs such as Hone's *Everyday Book* and *Time's Telescope,* where they were used to exemplify old customs and folklore, and I suggested that Clare was alive to this connection between the 'old poets' and the rural community. Marvell's poetry, unlike Herrick's for example, was not shot through with country lore. However, he was part of a group of older poets Clare believed needed rescuing from neglect, one of the 'half unknowns' whom he and the *London Magazine* circle shared a fondness for. Indeed Marvell's separation from a group of poets interested in country customs, as well as the solitary themes of his poems, may have induced Clare to try and assimilate him into a poetic community. Clare's fear of the loss of his village community heightened his sense of the need for a poetic community, and made him sensitive to those excluded from such a community, marginalised and half-forgotten writers such as Marvell. Placing Marvell's lines from 'The Garden' as an epigraph to *The Midsummer Cushion,* Clare places this 'old poet' in the context of a particular village ritual, the custom of making cushions of flowers to celebrate midsummer, thus enacting a twofold weaving in of a marginalised and isolated figure.

I have tried to show how Clare's growing personal isolation, and his fear of the break-up of his village community, which he ascribed to the disappearance of customs caused by enclosure, are important factors in his interest in 'old' poetry. Clare uses poetic sociability as a means of establishing himself canonically, linking himself and his fate to poets who were neglected, and had since risen to fame, or were beginning to be noticed during Clare's lifetime. Clare seems to have been sensitive to the association between the Romantic discourse of originality and enclosure and isolation. I have suggested that his intertextuality was a means of writing himself out of the 'inclosure' which the model of originality imposed on him, as well as providing him with a strategy of opening up space for himself in the canon. I have tried to unsettle John Barrell's association of the emergence of Clare's 'individual' voice with the de-localising effects of enclosure, suggesting instead how Clare's efforts to involve himself in poetic communities—to open out his solitude into company—was perhaps a response to the disintegration of the local community he attributed to the enclosure of Helpston: that his intertextuality, rather than his originality, was a response to enclosure.

NOTES

1. Barrell, pp. 98-188, 'The Sense of Place in the Poetry of John Clare'.
2. Barrell, p. 116.
3. The phrase is Seamus Heaney's, 'John Clare: a bi-centenary lecture', in Haughton, *Context*, pp. 130-47 (p. 131). Heaney, like Barrell, privileges the local in Clare's verse, describing him as a 'monoglot genius' (p. 131), distinguished from the heteroglossic geniuses Joyce and Shakespeare.
4. Barrell, p. 120.
5. Barrell, p. 120.
6. Barrell, p. 119.
7. *Clare-George Darley*, 3 September 1827, *Letters*, pp. 396-8 (p. 398).
8. Barrell, p. 122.
9. NMS 32, Letter 94; George Deacon, *John Clare and the Folk Tradition* (London: Sinclair Browne, 1983), p. 23.
10. *Letters*, pp. 381-4 (p. 383).

11. These poems are grouped together by J.W. Tibble in a section of his edition entitled 'Poems Written in the Manner of the Older Poets', *The Poems of John Clare*, 2 vols. (London: Dent, 1935), II, pp. 181-212. I have cited the texts from *The Midsummer Cushion* as printed in *Middle Period*, III-IV.

12. 'Vanitys of Life', first published as an anonymous seventeenth-century poem in the *Sheffield Iris*; 'Thoughts in a Churchyard', first fathered on Sir Henry Wotton; 'To John Milton, From his Honoured friend William Davenant' fathered on Davenant, and published in the *Sheffield Iris*, renamed 'To a Poet' in the *Midsummer Cushion* version; 'Farewell and Defiance to Love', fathered on Sir John Harington, published in the *European Magazine*, renamed 'Farewell to Love' in *The Midsummer Cushion*; 'Death', attributed to Andrew Marvell, published in Hone's *Everyday Book*; 'The Gipsey Song', attributed to Tom Davies, published in the *European Magazine*.

13. Oxford: Clarendon Press, 1997, pp. 111-59.

14. [Octavius Gilchrist], *London Magazine*, iv (April 1820), I, 369-79 (369).

15. See 'My Visit to London', in *Prose*, pp. 79-93.

16. [David Powell], *Catalogue of the John Clare Collection in the Northampton Public Library* (Northampton: Northampton Public Library, 1964).

17. *Prose*, pp. 86-99 (86).

18. The quotation is reproduced in an anonymous review of *Hazlitt's Lectures on the Literature of the Age of Elizabeth; delivered at the Surrey Institution. By William Hazlitt*, *London Magazine*, ii (February 1820), I, 189, where Clare would have most probably read it.

19. See previous note.

20. *Middle Period*, IV, pp. 205-6.

21. Elia (Charles Lamb), 'Detached Thoughts on Books and Reading', *London Magazine*, xxxi (July 1822), VI, 33-6.

22. Lamb, 'Detached Thoughts', 35.

23. Samuel Taylor Coleridge, *Biographia Literaria*, ed. by James Engell and W. Jackson Bate (Princeton, New Jersey, 1983), II, p. 27.

24. Francis Jeffrey states as much in his (unsigned) review of Southey's *Thalaba*, in the October 1802 issue of the *Edinburgh Review*. He links the 'originality' which the Lakers 'boast of', their 'having broken loose from the bondage of antient authority, and reasserted the individuality of genius', with 'the antisocial principles ... of Rousseau' (my italics). *Robert Southey, The Critical Heritage*, ed. by Richard Madden (London and Boston: Routledge & Kegan Paul, 1972), pp. 68-90 (p. 69).

25. *London Magazine*, xxxi (July 1822), VI, p. 33.

26. *London Magazine*, xxxi (July 1822), VI, p. 33

27. *London Magazine*, xxxi (July 1822), VI, p. 33

28. Mark Rose, *Authors and Owners. The Invention of Copyright* (Cambridge, Massachusetts and London: Harvard University Press, 1993), hereafter *Authors and Owners*.
29. Edward Young, *Conjectures on Original Composition*, 1759 (Leeds: Scolar Press, 1966), p. 11.
30. Young, *Conjectures*, p. 10.
31. Young, *Conjectures*, p. 54.
32. *Authors and Owners*, p. 8.
33. John Goodridge, 'Identity, Authenticity, Class: John Clare and the Mask of Chatterton', *Angelaki*, 1 (2) (Winter 1993-4), 131-48 (131).
34. *Early Poems*, II, p. 169.
35. John Taylor, 'Introduction' to *Poems Descriptive of Rural Life and Scenery* (London: Taylor and Hessey, Stamford: E. Drury, 1820), in *Critical Heritage*, pp. 43-54 (p. 52). See also Gilchrist's 'Some Account of John Clare, an Agricultural Labourer and Poet', *London Magazine*, i (January 1820), 7-11, *Critical Heritage*, pp. 35-42 (p. 38).
36. *The Oxford Authors. Samuel Taylor Coleridge*, ed. by H.J. Jackson (Oxford and New York: Oxford University Press, 1985), p. 66.
37. Lucy Newlyn, *Paradise Lost and the Romantic Reader* (Oxford: Clarendon Press, 1993), p. 43.
38. Stuart Curran, *Poetic Form and British Romanticism* (New York and Oxford: Oxford University Press, 1986), p. 19.
39. *Blackwood's Magazine*, 4 (1818), 266.
40. As William Empson has pointed out in 'Proletarian Literature', *Some Versions of Pastoral* (Harmondsworth: Penguin Books, 1935), pp. 11-25.
41. *Letters*, pp. 396-8 (p. 398).
42. *Middle Period*, III, pp. 253-4.
43. Hazlitt discusses Marston, Chapman, Decker, Lyly, Marlowe, Heywood, Middleton, Webster, Jonson, Drummond of Hawthornden, Herrick and Marvell, among others.
44. Clare also attempted to write Jacobean style tragedy, as exemplified in the dramatic fragments printed in *Middle Period*, II, pp. 77-90.
45. Deacon, pp. 67-69.
46. Deacon, p. 68.

5. Boys, Marvellous Boys: John Clare's 'Natural Genius'

Bridget Keegan

In a recent essay on the patronage of eighteenth-century self-taught poets, Betty Rizzo describes how the theory of natural genius was manipulated by Samuel Richardson, Elizabeth Montagu, and Hannah More in their promotional efforts on behalf of Mary Leapor, James Woodhouse and Ann Yearsley respectively.[1] While Rizzo's reading provides several fine insights into the patrons' motives, her analysis neglects the fact that natural genius was not just a marketing tool for insecure patrons. It was also an important category of self-presentation for the labourer poets themselves. In ignoring this fact, Rizzo participates in a persistent critical pattern of disallowing self-taught poets active creative agency. Such an assumption is untenable insofar as it is easy to demonstrate that plebeian artists from Stephen Duck and Robert Dodsley in the 1730s to John Clare in the 1820s were well aware of the opportunities and limits which the aesthetic category of natural or original genius provided for them. Because one of the primary characteristics of the concept of genius was that it could not (nor should not) be tainted by learning, it was a category that was easy, if ultimately dangerous, for the poets to appropriate to themselves. I say dangerous because the cult of original, untaught genius developed in opposition to the rapid 'professionalization' of authorship in the eighteenth century.[2] The danger of self-identifying as a 'natural genius' was further compounded once Romanticism had succeeded in recasting the image of the poet from an empty vessel for the Muse to the 'legislator of the World.' As such, asserting that the definitive lack of agency of the genius was the special condition of autodidact authors, made them worthy of polite attention only to the extent that they deviated from prevailing norms of poetic creativity. While their 'genius' might be a sign of their 'purity' and their originality, it was also a continued excuse to dismiss their creation as a happy accident. By accounting for their poetry as one might account for the formation of a diamond or the blooming of a rose, critics could and did belittle the poet and intellectually dismiss the content and craft of his or her poetry.

In focussing on how John Clare represented 'youthful genius,' my essay has two objectives. The first is to underscore that Clare was entirely self-aware in his self-fashioning as a boy genius, and, more importantly, that his representations of genial poetic youthfulness both transform and extend a tradition of thinking about the category of genius in poetry and philosophy. Clare's work conscientiously participates in a broader history of theorizing aesthetic ability. In making this argument, I want to suggest further that we need to continue to resist the critical trend that was established by all the eighteenth- and nineteenth-century theories of genius and (if Rizzo's essay is any indication) is still occurring in contemporary criticism. This trend is one in which labelling the poet an 'original genius' denies him or her self-conscious creative control. We do Clare and his self-educated precursors a serious injustice if we do not correct those readings that persist in viewing their poems not as the works of artists but as symptoms of some mysterious, irrational force, where the poet is merely a passive puppet. Not to do so would be to continue to deny Clare's work the serious and sustained analytic and stylistic attention it merits. In short, I want to argue that we do Clare greater service as a poet once we refuse to continue calling him a genius.

Before sketching how Clare worked within and against prevailing notions of natural genius, I should review briefly those theories and their role in the cultivation of a tradition of plebeian poetry prior to Clare. It is generally agreed that the modern notion of 'genius' had its genesis in the eighteenth century. Although Penelope Murray has traced similar concepts in ancient Greece and Rome, Jonathan Bate, among others, has isolated the origin of the contemporary sense of the idea to the early eighteenth century. In his important essay 'Shakespeare and Original Genius' Bate attributes the rise of the cult of the uneducated genius in part to a resistance to neo-classical rules governing literary production.[3] As Bate notes, the first significant eighteenth-century discussion of genius comes in Addison's *Spectator*, no. 160 (1711). Addison establishes the fundamental premise reiterated in all subsequent poetical and philosophical investigations: namely, that genius cannot be the product of education. In fact, genius and learning are largely antithetical. Geniuses create 'by the meer strength of natural parts, and without any assistance of art or learning'.[4] Addison's formulation was reiterated by all the subsequent texts devoted to the subject. In the 1740s, Akenside's popular poem *The Pleasures of Imagination* further promoted the idea of natural or uneducated genius. Akenside asserts: 'Nature's kindling breath / Must fire the chosen genius; Nature's hand / Must string his nerves, and imp his eagle-wings / Impatient of the painful steep, to soar / High as the summit'.[5] What Addison and Akenside further agreed upon, was that genius was more likely during the 'childhood' of civilization. As Glenn Most has argued, a great deal of eighteenth-century thinking about genius derived from the 'rediscovery' of Homer and the glorification of Homeric (and later Ossianic) primitivism. Addison writes: 'Many of these great natural geniuses that were never disciplined and broken by rules of art, are to be found among the ancients.' Although neither Addison nor Akenside explicitly associates genius with actual childhood, they do provide a metaphoric connection by linking it with the period of *civilization*'s youth.

The third important British contribution to theories of natural genius, Young's *Conjectures on Original Composition* of 1759, once again stresses the opposition between genius and learning: 'As Riches are most wanted where there is least Virtue; so Learning where there is least Genius. As Virtue without much Riches can give Happiness, so Genius without much Learning can give Renown'.[6] Young furthermore takes the notion of genial passivity to an extreme only hinted at in Addison. As M.H. Abrams has noted in *The Mirror and the Lamp*, though Addison had used landscape metaphors to distinguish between natural or passive and artful or purposeful creativity, Young goes a step further in the famous passage: 'An *Original* may be said to be of a *vegetable* nature; it rises spontaneously from the vital root of genius; it *grows*, it is not *made*'.[7] While one might, at first, be flattered to be declared a genius, it would be the most backhanded of compliments if this also meant that one was simultaneously being identified as the mental equivalent of a potted plant.

The potential harm of being labelled a genius can be seen also in that not only did most theorists, even while seeming to celebrate it, claim its unconsciousness and lack of active animation, they also elaborated upon its necessary immaturity. Being a genius meant being not only plant-like but also puerile. By rendering genius the domain of gifted boys (and as Christine Battersby has proven in no uncertain terms, geniuses have always been gendered masculine),[8] the potential threat that a genius could pose to the artistic establishment was sufficiently diminished. The connection between genius and boyishness or childlikeness is unambiguously established by 1767 in William Duff's *Essay on Original Genius*. Indeed, it would seem that youth is as much a necessary precondition for genius as the lack of education. As Duff writes, imagination, which is the foundation of genius, is 'peculiarly adapted to the gay, delightful, vacant season of childhood [and] appears in those early periods in all its puerile brilliance and simplicity, long before the reasoning faculty discovers itself in any considerable degree' (p. 29). Duff continues: 'one who is born with a Genius for Poetry will discover a peculiar relish and love for it in his earliest years' (p. 37). He then proceeds to cite as examples Tasso, who wrote poetry at the tender age of five, Pope who began at twelve and Milton at thirteen or fourteen. Although original genius is in its purest state in antiquity, it could be recaptured in the early stages of the individual (male) human life. Duff states even more vehemently than earlier critics that not only is original genius youthful, it is also entirely self-taught:

> The truth is, a Poet of Original Genius has very little occasion for the weak aid of Literature: he is self-taught. He comes into the world as it were completely accomplished. Nature supplies the materials of his compositions; his senses are the underworkmen while Imagination, like a Masterly Architect superintends the whole. (p. 281)[9]

Given such unequivocal statements as this, it is not difficult to see how the full-scale development of theories of natural genius in the eighteenth century was in part responsible for increased interest in poets who were *literally* young and self-taught. The archetypal relationship between Oxford Professor of Poetry, Joseph Spence, and thresher-poet Stephen Duck is one of the many cases throughout the century where, as Rizzo has noted, aesthetic theory was applied, in procrustean fashion, to poetic practice and to actual poets, more often than not with personally and professionally damaging results for the poets involved. Spence's paternalistic biographical introduction of Duck is exemplary of the ways in which both youth and ignorance were marshalled to muster interest in Duck's work. Spence writes that 'Stephen is all Simplicity,' and that, moreover, as with Tasso, Pope and Milton, he was assuredly a *born* poet, with the appropriate symptoms appearing in boyhood: 'I find by him, that from his Infancy, he had a cast in his Mind toward Poetry. He has delighted, as far back as he can remember, in Verses and in singing'.[10]

The association of genius with youth and ignorance, however, was not just a product of the theorists and bourgeois patrons, but was given one of its most significant poetic articulations in James Beattie's influential poem *The Minstrel* (1771-4)—a poem which was intertextually crucial for Clare's major vocational poem 'The Village Minstrel'. It is, in fact, perhaps, more because of Beattie than Young or Duff that the self-taught poets themselves, like Robert Bloomfield in his debut volume, *The Farmer's Boy*, announced themselves as simple, untutored, rural, and young. Soon after Beattie's poem, the figure of the juvenile, socially underprivileged genius was given its most popular and certainly most powerful embodiment in the person of that marvellous boy *par excellence,* Thomas Chatterton. And although it was doubtless inspired by Bloomfield more than Chatterton, the first decade of the nineteenth century saw a marked increase of a genre which one might label 'Gifted Boy' poems: David Service penned first 'The Caledonian Herd Boy' (1802) and 'Crispin, the Apprentice Boy' (1804);[11] W.H. Ireland was responsible for 'The Fisher Boy' (1808) and 'The Sailor Boy' (1809).[12] These were only a few of the more popular manifestations of this veritable 'movement' in minor poetry.

From the beginning of his poetic career, Clare self-consciously placed himself squarely in this lineage of adolescent, unlettered, critically-acclaimed genii. In his autobiographical writings, he not only invokes them by name, but works to show how he too demonstrates the same pattern of development. Clare notes that his awareness of his poetic gift dawned upon him, as it did upon Milton and Pope, at the tender age of twelve or thirteen, the time of his famous first encounter with *The Seasons*. Moreoever, as Clare tells it, one of his very first attempts at poetic composition was made in imitation of Chatterton's poem 'The Resignation' which came to him by way of a souvenir handkerchief his mother had purchased at a country fair (*By Himself*, p. 99). Finally, Clare's connections with his most immediate boy-genius predecessor were the strongest of all: he corresponded with Bloomfield, whose poetic works he tells us were among the first books he collected and 'great Favourites.' By 1824, Clare was planning to writing a critical biography of Bloomfield to improve upon the one produced by Capel Lofft.

That Clare explicitly capitalized upon the audience for charming, artless boys is evident in the more public self-representations attached to his first volume. In the Prospectus he prepared for Henson, Clare announces in the first sentence that his poems are '*Juvenile* productions' (duly italicizing the word 'juvenile') and calling attention to the 'humble situation which distinguishes their author'. While these formulations were self-protective, one can imagine that they were also inserted to arouse curiosity. That John Taylor would repeat the same information in the very first paragraph of his introduction to *Poems Descriptive*, reveals the importance of these terms as a marketing device. Taylor writes: 'The following Poems will probably attract some notice by their intrinsic merit; but they are also entitled to attention from the circumstances under which they were written. They are the genuine productions of a *young* Peasant, a day-labourer in husbandry, who has had *no advantages of education* beyond others of his class' (my emphasis).[13] Taylor knew that part of what would lure readers to Clare's volume was the same curiosity that rendered Chatterton and Bloomfield popular (and even to a certain degree, Keats). Taylor, and, I do not doubt, Clare as well, knew that there was a market for marvellous boys.

It is unfortunate, however, that although we can speculate that Clare may have initially been complicit in Taylor's marketing scheme, indeed moulding himself to fit it, we all know very well how soon he came to resist and resent it. This resentment is apparent in any number of selections from Clare's correspondence. However, what I would like to focus on here is the way in which Clare both wrote within and against this formulation in three important *poems*. By looking at 'Dawning of Genius', 'The Fate of Genius: A Tale,' and 'The Village Minstrel', I hope to indicate how Clare revises and resists the nostalgic topos of the unlearned child genius as undeniably detrimental and debilitating to his continued poetic production. Boys grow up (unless, like Chatterton and Keats, they have the good fortune to die in early adulthood) and the primary goal of most untutored poets, Clare not excepted, was to further their education.

In the three poems, Clare critiques the very factors which supposed define original genius in the first place. For example, in 'Dawning of Genius', it is the requisite lack of education which precludes the rustic genius from ever being able to express himself. As Clare writes in line 13, a line which, I think importantly, was expunged from the version printed in *Poems Descriptive*, 'The sparks of genius Ignorance conceals' (*Early Poems*, I, p. 451). Clare thus reveals disagreement with the simplistic celebration of ignorance as a valuable poetic attribute. Clare's definition of genius in this poem is original in other ways. Although he initially defines it, in the opening lines, in familiar terms as 'a pleasing rapture of the mind / A kindling warmth to Learning unconfin'd' (ll. 1-2), Clare's concept of genius is more radically democratic than that of any of his poetic or philosophical forbears. Genius is not manifested only in a select few, but present in all, regardless of their relationship to culture—it 'Glows in each breast & flutters in every vein / From arts Refinements to th'unculter'd swain' (ll. 3-4).

Although genius makes no distinctions in rank, the central message of the poem is clear. In order to speak, in order to reveal or share his genius, the nascent swain-poet must have some kind of knowledge, or he will be forever silenced. The poem's final lines reveal the true tragedy of untutored genius. It does not produce great works of art. Rather, as Clare tells us:

Vain burns the soul & throbs the fluttering heart
Their painfull pleasing feelings to impart
Till by successles sallies wearied quite
The memory fails & fancy takes her flight
The wickett nipt within its socket dies
Born down & smother'd in a thousand sighs (ll. 47-52)

The poem articulates what Clare knew all too well from his own experience and from his familiarity with the fate of other self-taught poets: ignorance is never bliss. It is a kind of death.

The doomed state of the uneducated juvenile swain, and the fact that this doom is directly related not to the boy's genius but to his lack of education, is made even more explicit in 'The Village Minstrel' and 'The Fate of Genius.' The fact that the protagonists of both poems are ill-fated from the first lines presents a strong criticism of the glorification of poetic primitivism. The opening verses of 'The Village Minstrel' set up the crucial distinction between learning and what is implied by a lack of it:

While learned genius rush to bold extreemes
& sun beams snatch to light the muses fires
A humble rustic hums his lowly dreams
Far in the swail where poverty retires (ll. 1-4; *Early Poems*, II, p. 123).

Learning allows the educated genius the power to 'light the muses fire'. Unlike his precursor, Beattie's Edwin, who from the third stanza of *The Minstrel* is destined for 'The rolls of fame', young Lubin is destined, already by stanza two, to remain 'Where black neglect spreads one continual frown' (l. 14). Although Lubin, Clare's poetic alter-ego, is well-read in 'The Book of Nature' and has quite an astonishing mastery of what we would today call the 'texts of popular culture', by the poem's conclusion, in stanza 129, as he wishes to attain poetic maturity and 'to manhoods cares aspire', his unlettered state contributes to crushing such hopes as

...malice mocks him wi a rude disdain
Proving pretensions to the muse as vain
They deem her talents far beyond his skill
& hiss his efforts as some forged strain' (ll. 1294-7)

As with Chatterton, critical readers insinuate that only plagiarism (not native talent) can explain Lubin's poetry. Although this poem ends somewhat less gloomily than the other two, with the remote hope that 'the low muse his sleepless night may cheer' (l. 1324), the message remains the same. Aesthetic theories to the contrary, genius untrained, even if it can be articulated, risked mockery—a fact of which Clare was all too well aware as he wrote this, the title piece to his second collection.

Clare knew by this time as well that despite vogues of primitivism, cults of Shakespeare and Ossian, and aesthetic philosophies, the absence of appropriate cultural credentials would subject the poet to the condescending critical reception. The following excerpt from an 1820 review in *The Guardian* is exemplary. Its author writes: 'The lower orders are singularly apt to place an idle estimate upon their own powers, to be of course easily inflated, and in their inflation too easy to desert the path of wisdom. It *requires an educated mind* to make a true estimate of itself, and feel the deference due to the talents and the common sense of society'.[14] A trawl through Mark Storey's *Critical Heritage* collection reveals similar assessments of Clare's poetry even into the twentieth century.

Written, no doubt, as a response to these harsh and condescending reviews, 'The Fate of Genius' (*Early Poems*, II, pp. 666-70) provides the most depressing and most striking analysis of the problems that claims for untutored genius presented to the poets themselves. In this poem, we begin not with the poet silenced or criticized, but literally dead due (albeit indirectly) to his lack of education. Considering its potentially radical message, this poem was understandably not published during Clare's lifetime. It begins by telling the now familiar story of 'A rustic genius from the darkness sprung' who 'sought the muses mid his toils & sung' (ll. 9-10). Due to the critical confusion produced by the genius's learned friends, 'The damps of disappointment provd too much / & warm hopes witherd at the chilly touch' (ll. 25-6). Not only does hope wither, but so does the poet, and the majority of the poem is transferred to the voice of the old sexton 'Who knew the bard & dug his early grave' (l. 34). The story the sexton tells us of the young poet's short life is quite familiar. His poetic proclivities were evident almost from infancy and his affinity with nature and the natural world nurtured his innate gifts. But once again, Clare explicitly identifies the poet's lack of learning as the cause of his untimely demise. The sexton relates how, though some enjoyed his poetry, there were others

> ...like serpents in the grass
> That skulk in ways which learning has to pass
> To slander worth which they would feign posses
> & dissappointment urges to suppress
> Snarling at faults too bright for common minds
> & hiding beautys wisdom warmly finds
> Such marr'd his powers & slanderd in disguise
> & tryd to black his merits with their lyes (ll. 89-96).

Reading these lines, one cannot help but (and I believe one is meant to) think about another young poet with whom Clare shared a publisher and whose death was also attributed to a vicious critical reception, namely John Keats, who died the year before this poem was composed. While Keats was not rural and uneducated, his status was socially and educationally marginal enough to have earned him jibes for being one of the 'Cockney School of Poetry'. Clare's concern for Keats's fate is further evidenced in a letter written to Taylor on 5 May 1821. Clare argued that Taylor would do well to promptly bring out another volume of Keats:

...while the ashes of genius is warm the public look with a tender anxiety for what it leaves behind—to let this get cold woud in my opinion do him an injury—the ill treatment he has met will now be productive of more advantages—tho the warm heart that once felt it—is cold and carless to praise or to censure now—still he left those hopes behind him— which his friends cherish in remembrance that justice woud be done him (*Letters,* p. 188)

Like the wise old sexton in the poem, wishing to keep alive the memory of the victimized bard, Clare comes to Keats's defence. In the next sentence of his letter, Clare asks, at this point clearly rhetorically, 'is polotics to rule genius'? Clare knew better than any that it did and his shrewd analysis of the term and its implications differentiates him from the boy geniuses he writes about. For it is important to note that in all three poems, Clare is clearly writing *about* others and not explicitly about *himself.* Though there is much autobiography in Clare's poetry about boy geniuses, formally the poems' speakers are an external or framing voice—a voice that is clearly older, wiser, and we assume, better educated than the simple singers whose sad stories they narrate.

It is precisely because they were uneducated that these geniuses were doomed. Clare is quick to reveal the cheat and the critical hypocrisy that he himself felt. He was praised for his natural genius which was by definition the result of his 'artlessness', but his poetry was frequently condemned because it lacked artfulness. As a 'Child of Nature', Clare attracted patrons and an audience. As a grown-up poet with a hunger for knowledge and a passion for books, Clare met more often with scorn. In his attention to the figure of the boy genius, Clare responded to and attempted to reshape the eighteenth-century aesthetic concept of natural genius which was imposed upon him and his self-taught precursors, and which conditions readerly expectations of their work even to this day. Clare reacted to and revised—for himself, at least—and for us, if we would but choose to see it—the potentially detrimental nostalgising of male adolescence surrounding the reception of the work of Chatterton, Bloomfield, Keats, and most importantly Clare himself.

NOTES

1. Betty Rizzo, 'The Patron as Poet Maker: The Politics of Benefaction,' *Studies in Eighteenth-Century Culture*, 20 (1990), 241-66.
2. For an excellent recent discussion of the development of literature as profession, see Clifford Siskin's study *The Work of Literature: Literature and Social Change in Britain, 1730-1830* (Baltimore: The Johns Hopkins University Press, 1998).
3. Penelope Murray, 'Poetic Genius and Its Classical Origins'; Jonathan Bate, 'Shakespeare and Original Genius', both in *Genius: The History of an Idea*, ed. by Penelope Murray (Oxford: Blackwell, 1989), pp. 9-31 and 76-97. See also Glenn Most, 'The Second Homeric Renaissance: Allegoresis and Genius in Early Modern Poetics', in Murray, *Genius*, pp. 54-75.
4. *The Works of Joseph Addison* (Philadelphia: J.B. Lippincott, 1883), VI, p. 383.
5. *The Poetical Works of Mark Akenside* (New York: AMS Press, 1969), p. 87.
6. Edward Young, *Conjectures on Original Composition* (London: R. & J. Dodsley, 1759), p. 29.
7. M.H. Abrams, *The Mirror and the Lamp: Romantic Theory and the Critical Tradition* (New York: Oxford University Press, 1953).
8. Christine Battersby, *Gender and Genius: Towards a Feminist Aesthetics* (Bloomington: Indiana UP, 1989). Approaching the boyishness of genius from a feminist perspective, Battersby reminds us of the importance of gender in formulations of genius, namely that throughout the classical, neoclassical, Romantic and even contemporary eras, geniuses are male. Battersby underscores the paradox, however, that what differentiates the genius from ordinary men are characteristics that are traditionally gendered feminine: 'instinct, emotion, sensibility, intuition ... even madness'. As she notes, in many formulations, 'The great artist is feminine male.' This state of feminized male would seem to fit well with the adolescent status of the genius. Adolescents are not fully masculine or feminine, but in a liminal and more androgynous state. Recall Coleridge's celebrated assertion, reiterated by Virginia Woolf, that the true artist is androgynous.
9. William Duff, *An Essay on Original Genius* (London: Edward and Charles Dilly, 1767).
10. Joseph Spence, in *The Beautiful Works of Stephen Duck* (London: Printed and Sold for the Booksellers, 1753), p. xiii.
11. Dwight Durling, *Georgic Tradition in English Poetry* (Port Washington, NY: Kennikat Press, 1963), p. 97.
12. Durling, p. 102.

13. *Critical Heritage*, p. 43.
14. *Critical Heritage*, pp. 100-101.

6. 'Labour and Luxury': Clare's Lost Pastoral and the Importance of the Voice of Labour in the Early Poems

Stephen Colclough

This essay is divided into three sections. Section one aims to establish the link between the prose description of the lost pastoral poem 'labour and luxury' and the fragment of text which begins 'Thy eye can witness more then others', first published in the Clarendon edition of the *Early Poems* in 1989. Section two provides an introduction to the various voices of labour found amongst the unpublished, often unfinished or fragmentary, texts of the *Early Poems*, and suggests that these voices constitute an important area of study for Clare scholars. The third section re-examines a canonical text, 'Helpstone', in order to assess the impact of one of these voices of labour upon Clare's first audience. It investigates the controversy surrounding the ten lines excluded from the fourth edition of *Poems Descriptive of Rural Life and Scenery* and argues that the voice of labour acts as a disruptive, politicising force within the poem.

1. 'Labour and Luxury'

Clare's reference to 'labour and luxury' as a 'lost' poem occurs in a passage written in the mid-1820s as part of the 'life' that was intended to be a much fuller account of his development as a poet than the 'Sketches' written for Taylor to promote *The Village Minstrel* in 1821. It follows a description of his earliest attempts at verse and the transcription of some poems of a 'satirical nature' that had remained unpublished:

> I only regret the loss of one of my early poems a sort of Pastoral the title was 'labour and luxury' the plan was a labourers going to his work one morning overheard a lean figure [accosted] in a taunting manner by a bloated stranger the phantom of luxury whence the dialogue ensues labour makes its complaints and the other taunts and jeers him till the lean figure turns away in dispair[.]¹

As this statement makes clear, Clare considered 'labour and luxury' to be an important poem both in the history of his development as a poet and in terms of the subject matter dealt with in the text, which he describes here in some detail. The manuscript NMS 7 contains an untitled fragment which begins 'Thy eye can witness more then others...', the concluding lines of which connect it directly to the lost poem:

> Im Labour friend & thats what I am
> & that fat podgy knave
> Is Luxury ye know 'nough on him
> & I am Luxurys slave[2]

These lines declare that the speaker of the text is the personified Labour and they identify the poem as a version of the lost pastoral. In describing the poem as 'a sort of pastoral' in the autobiography Clare is employing the term in a very specific sense. Many of Clare's poems can be described as pastoral in the sense that they are concerned with descriptions of the rural world, but in this instance he is using it in the traditional sense as a description of a poem in which two or more voices are heard in dialogue. I want to suggest that the fragment is the voice of labour from a text which, when complete, would have presented a dialogue between labour and luxury, witnessed by the labourer referred to in Clare's recollection of the poem. This is the fragment in full:

> Thy eye can witness more then others
>   Thy feelings are thy own
> & labours anguish & her sorrows
>   To thee has long been known
> Luxurys wealth & pride uphold my <   >
>   Poor labours slav'd to dead
> While they die gorg'd like beast in clover
>   We die for wants of bread
>
> & what is worse—our little earnings
>   For which we toil & sweat
> To uphold em [a]nd urge their coaches

They tax back half we get
We wear no rags but they ha part ont
They tax yer sho & shoetye
Yer barly bannock—theyle ha share
    Like robber oer a booty

They run so eager arter wealth
    Such upstarts & contrivers
Im made a very slave among em
    Curst witling negroe drivers
Our p——s talk of hardships bless em
    Well hells doom they unravel
But labour here in luxury proves
    The devils very devil

& thou thought right their ansrs matey
    Tho plain to all thy kind
Thy feelings only coud disern it
    Poor ignorance is blind Im
Labour friend & thats what I am
    & that fat podgy knave Is Luxury
ye know 'nough on him
    & I am Luxurys slave (*Early Poems*, I, p. 505)

The internal evidence suggests that this voice was supposed to be heard by two listening figures. The first, referred to in lines 1-4, is a figure who shares the speaker's experience of labour, 'labours anguish & her sorrows / To thee hast long been known' (ll. 3-4), and this is perhaps the labourer 'going to his work' described in the autobiography. This figure is referred to again in lines 25-8:

& thou thought right their ans[we]rs matey
    Tho plain to all thy kind
Thy feelings only coud disern it
    Poor ignorance is blind

The second figure is identified as 'Luxury' (l. 31) and the description of him as a 'fat podgy knave' echoes the reference in the prose passage to 'a bloated stranger the phantom of luxury'. That the figure of Luxury was designed to have already spoken in the full version of the text is suggested by the reference to ignorance's acceptance of 'their ans[we]rs'.

Robinson and Powell date NMS 7 to the period 1818-20 which would make the composition of this poem somewhat later than the other 'early poems' with which it is placed in the autobiography, but it is also possible that the NMS 7 text is a transcription of an earlier draft. Clare is, however, writing at some distance from the time of composition and may be more concerned with the loss of the poem than the time of its creation. Its completion before the publication of *Poems Descriptive* in 1820 may also have led to his recollection of the poem as 'early'. Clare's inclusion of two alternative endings to the poem in the autobiography perhaps indicates that the poem was never completed and that he was still planning its conclusion at the time of writing the autobiography. The NMS 7 fragment may be either a work in progress, a transcript of an earlier draft, or a later re-creation of a text that he considered particularly important. Its position in the manuscript, where it is surrounded by other fragments and texts that appear in different versions elsewhere, suggests that Clare was using this book to sound out versions of texts that he would later work up for publication or abandon.

In the 'life', the voice of Labour is described as making its 'complaints' and then being challenged by the voice of Luxury. The existence of the voice of labour alone in 'Thy eye can witness...' suggests that Clare's major interest in this poem was the achievement of this voice of complaint, and that he was less concerned with the voice of Luxury. Clare regrets the loss of this poem, I want to suggest, because it allowed him to experiment with a voice that could express the anger and frustration that he felt as a wage labourer.

We therefore need to understand the characteristics of this voice if we are to explain its importance to Clare and if we are to recognise its presence in other texts. The voice of labour in 'Thy eye can witness...' is characterised by the use of the collective terms 'we' and 'our':

While they die gorg'd like beast in clover
We die for wants of bread

& what is worse—our little earnings
For which we toil & sweat
To uphold em [a]nd urge their coaches
They tax back half we get (ll. 7-12).

This strategy of writing from a collective position—of privileging the 'we' over the 'I'—produces a very different voice from the one that we often associate with the author of 'I Am'. The function of this voice is rhetorical. It aims to convince the listener that the labourer's poverty is the direct result of Luxury's greed. Labour, the poem argues, is exploited both at the site of labour ('we' 'urge their coaches') and through the systems of taxation ('They tax back half we get'). The phrase 'wealth & pride' (l. 5) is found in many of Clare's poems from this period in conjunction with an image of exploitation.[3] The voice of labour is the voice of insult and condemnation and one of the poem's rhetorical strategies involves turning the status of 'wealth & pride' upside-down. The poem argues that luxury 'acts like robber oer a booty', and that as a class it is made up of 'upstarts and contrivers' and 'curst witling negroe drivers'. The image of master and slave recurs throughout the poem and is the basis of Clare's radical critique of the exploitation of labour. In choosing 'Luxury' as a figure to attack, Clare is following the precedent of Goldsmith's *The Deserted Village*, a text with which we know he was familiar, and of other late-eighteenth-century texts which emphasise the dangers of excessive 'wealth' and 'luxury'.[4] As James Raven has noted, the concept of luxury has a complex history from the early eighteenth century onwards, and is inveighed against and praised as a symptom of economic growth in equal measure.[5] The poem imagines the figure of luxury through images of trade and new wealth ('upstarts and contrivers'), but it is remarkable in that it does not posit an ideology of gentlemanly morality, of the responsible use of wealth, as an alternative to Luxury's abuse of his position.

This fact may be a matter of Clare's historical and cultural context. His contemporaries would have recognised the similarities between this text and the form of the 'Pindaric satire' written and published by 'Peter Pindar' and William Hone. These texts, frequently published as pamphlets in the post-war years, often attacked George IV (both as Prince Regent and King) as a figure of excessive 'luxury', as the engravings that accompanied Rosco's *Horrida Bella. Pains and Penalties Versus Truth and Justice* (1820) demonstrate (see Fig. 1).[6] Clare's poem echoes the distinctive method of partially deleting names used in these pamphlets:

Our p——s talk of hardship bless em
　　Well hells doom they unravel
But labour here in luxury proves
　　The devils very devil (ll. 21-4)

Like the original readers of these texts we are left to fill in the blanks. Clare's editors have joined in this game and their suggestion, 'princes', fits the context of the radical pamphleteers' attacks against the Prince Regent and 'Old Corruption'. This form, with its use of grotesque caricature, was important to Clare because it allowed a critique of authority figures to be expressed in a context that appealed to the trans-historical concepts of 'truth and justice'.[7] The voice of Labour is therefore a political voice in the sense that it is taking on issues such as corruption and taxation that contemporaries would have read as political. In this poem Clare articulates his grievances through the existing language of radicalism, and in its connection of economic exploitation to political repression—'they tax yr sho & shoetye'—the poem displays the same mix of traditional and class-specific grievances that Gareth Stedman Jones suggests characterises working-class movements before 1832.[8] The re-articulation and re-voicing of existing modes of expression is a characteristic of many of Clare's early poems.

　　Clare may be paying homage to a form that he was familiar with because it was relatively cheap and accessible, but he also re-invigorates the tradition of attacking luxury by allowing the normally silenced labourer to voice this critique. As in the enclosure elegies, Clare uses the contrast as his mode of attack. In the elegies the beauty of the pre-enclosure world contrasts with the ugliness of the enclosed fields. In this instance the poverty of the starving labourer is made to contrast with the bloated figure of luxury. Clare's lack of punctuation in this passage produces a punning ambiguity that is also typical of this form of satire. We can read 'hells doom' as a possessive singular (Hell's doom), which perhaps suggests that the blank should be filled by 'parsons' or 'priests', but the contemporary reader would also have been aware of the use of 'Hells' as a slang term for the London gaming houses, which Clare plays with to produce the image of the devil.[9]

This brings us to the second major characteristic of the voice of Labour in the poem: its use of slang and dialect:

We wear no rags but they ha part ont
They tax yer sho & shoetye
Yer barly bannock—theyle ha share
Like robber oer a booty (ll. 13-16)

In using dialect Clare is experimenting with the accepted ways of presenting a working-class voice, but this strategy is also part of the poem's attempt to subvert the qualities usually associated with 'wealth & pride'. The voice of the labourer normally excluded from authority because of its lack of refinement is here given the authority to 'prove' that Luxury, described in the prose as 'taunting' Labour, is a witler ('curst witling negroe drivers'), a contemporary term for one who talks aimlessly.

This poem is important because it suggests that Clare wanted to articulate a voice that could speak both for his own concerns about the condition of the agricultural labourer and for labour as a class. By creating a dialogue between voices which are given distinctive class characteristics the poem explicitly reveals the forms of class tension that often remain implicit in many of the other early poems.

2. Voices of Labour

I now want to draw attention to the voices of labour found in three other early poems in order to demonstrate their variety and suggest that they constitute an important area for further study.[10] Lobin Clouts Satirical Sollilouquy on the Times' (*Early Poems,* I, pp. 137-8) has a similar setting to 'labour and luxury' and is introduced by the couplet:

A lab'rour journeying to his work betimes
Thus reak'd his vengance on the awkard times (ll. 1-2)

This couplet distances the author from the voice of labour that is presented in the remainder of the text. This voice, like the voice of 'Labour' in 'Thy eye can witness...', speaks in dialect:

Poor men hod now be batter nokt o' t' head
Thon ha' to wok fo' nothin' else but bred (ll. 5-6)

It is used to focus the violent feelings of dissent felt by many labourers towards their employers, and 'Lobin' delivers a list of violent acts he would like to see performed on his master: 'How I shud like a bruzzer at his joul' (l. 10). However, Clare distances himself from this voice through the opening couplet and the framing device of the title, which foregrounds the poem's relationship to pastoral dialogue by echoing Gay's 'Lobbin Clout' from *The Shepherd's Week*, itself an echo of Spenser's 'Colin Clout'.[11] By describing the poem as a 'soliloquy' Clare is suggesting that he is using the dramatist's art to create a character through speech. Given the inflammatory rhetoric of Lobin this is perhaps understandable, but the poem nevertheless expresses Clare's concern for the material conditions of the labourer. Lobin speaks out against new modes of exploitation, 'Ney ar old ma'stur nosty fleerin' to'k / Say's I've no time for 'atins wen I wok' (ll. 7-8), but the poem's conclusion, 'beggin' prayin' nothink's a' no use' (l. 42), is despairing. The poem does not offer the reader a solution to the exploitation of the labourer and Lobin's presentation is never less than ambiguous.

Despite this distancing Clare could also express a voice of labour through an autobiographical 'I':

One monday morning sour & loath
     To labour like a turk
A tween the hour o' five & six
     I took my corpse to work
Deuce take a labourers life thought I
     They talk o slaves els where
I sees much choice in foreighn parts
     As I do in Slavery here (*Early Poems*, I, p. 352)

This text, with its redeployment of the theme of labour and slavery, is marginal, its unfinished status indicative of Clare's uncertainty about the way in which the production of such voices of protest could help him to escape the very dependence upon wage labour described in the poem and to gain 'reward ... with my pen' as a professional author.[12] Without access to a culture of protest such texts were more likely to inhibit rather than increase his chances of publication. This fragmentary autobiographical record of the alienation of the labourer was too radical to complete, as a comparison with the description of labour in the 'Sketches' makes clear. In this text, which was intended for publication, Clare describes 'labouring' as a 'perpetual curse from god' experienced by all humankind, but in the poem this mythic interpretation of the harshness of labour is exchanged for a social explanation that compares the labourer's existence to that of the slave.[13] This image, repeated many times in the early poems, famously in 'The Village Minstrel', and twice in 'Thy eye can witness...', comes so naturally to Clare that we are apt to overlook its true significance.[14] Clare takes the discourse of opposition to slavery—'they talk o slaves els where'—and subverts it by including the freeborn English labourer within its terms: 'Deuce take a labourers life thought I'. Similarly, in 'Thy eye can witness...' the economic drive behind colonial slavery, the exploitation of labour, is revealed as connected to the exploitation of 'Labour' at home who is made to complain: 'Im made a very slave among em / Curst witling negroe drivers' (ll. 19-20).

In 'Chubs Reply' (*Early Poems*, I, pp. 111-12) the voice of the labourer again comes into conflict with a voice of authority. In this ostensibly humorous poem a comic figure on horseback, described as a 'Tom Thumb', verbally attacks the labourer 'Chub' for staring at him. The labourer's 'reply' to this insult is both unexpected and witty and the poem concludes with the reassuring couplet: 'For Madam Wit no chuser of her place / Is often cloath'd in rags as well as lace' (ll. 43-4). However, the central section of the text registers the radical effect of the creation of this voice. The voice of the labourer, as in the 'Thy eye can witness...' fragment, is able to outwit a voice that is, in class terms, its superior, and the horseman is depicted as leaving the marketplace:

For fear the crowd that gaping round 'em stood
Should catch the sharp reply and run him down
By joining chorus with the gauling clown (ll. 38-40)

In this instance Clare's voice of 'labour', a collective term for a class, opens up the possibility of collective action, of 'joining chorus'. Thumb's authority comes from his class position on horseback above the crowd of the marketplace, and his insulting language is itself hierarchical. He describes

Chub, in an echo of Burke's famous reference to the 'swinish multitude', as a 'two leg'd bastard of the swinish breed'.[15] The poem thus imagines the defeat of the insulting attitude towards the labourer that is also displayed in 'Lobin Clout's' satire. However, by providing a comic context for this defeat, Clare signals something of his own nervousness about creating a voice of dissent that could encourage the collective action feared by Thumb in the poem.

Each of these poems contains a voice that is recognisably a voice of labour, but Clare's modes of presentation and content vary greatly between the individual texts. They do not articulate a politics, an ideological position, but constantly return to the site of conflict outlined in the recollection of 'labour and luxury' in the autobiography.

3. The 'Helpstone' Controversy, or the Voice of Labour in Print
Clare's most infamous voice of labour occurs in 'Helpstone', the poem that opened his first published volume, *Poems Descriptive of Rural Life and Scenery* (1820). Its presence in the following lines caused immediate controversy:

Accursed Wealth! o'er-bounding human laws,
Of every evil thou remain'st the cause:
Victims of want, those wretches such as me,
Too truly lay their wretchedness to thee:
Thou art the bar that keeps from being fed,
And thine our loss of labour & of bread;
Thou art the cause that levels every tree,
And woods bow down to clear a way for thee. (second edition, p. 9)

Captain Sherwill, one of the volume's earliest readers, suggested that Clare should 'expunge' these lines from the poem because 'they have in fact very little to do with the subject'.[16] In a sense this criticism is justified: the voice of labour that emerges in this section of the poem is a disruptive force shifting the text's focus from personal nostalgia to collectively focused anger. The personal pronoun appears five times in quick succession in the section of the text which begins 'Hail scenes obscure so near & dear to me' (ll. 47-94) and allows the poem to focus on the destroyed 'native' landscape:

These joys all known in happy infancy
& all I ever knew where spent on thee
& who but loves to view where these where past
& who that views but loves em to the last
Feels his heart warm to view his native place
A fondness still those past delights to trace
The vanish'd green to mourn the spot to see (ll. 67-73)

This nostalgia, which appears both personal ('all I ever knew') and at the same time universal ('& who but loves'), is disrupted by the voice of labour which begins to speak from a collective position ('thine our loss of labour & of bread'). Clare gives a 'cause' (l. 133) for his nostalgia that is historically specific rather than universal and links the poverty of the labourer to the changes in the landscape. Sherwill's comments were part of a concerted effort by Clare's post-publication patrons to alter the way in which the poet was presented to the public. Clare recognised that the deletion of these lines would almost certainly lead to the excision of the later passage:

When peace & plenty known but now to few
Were known to all & labour had his [its] due
When mirth & toil companions thro' the day
Made labour light & pass'd the hours away (ll. 137-40)

(The word 'peace' is 'ease' in *Poems Descriptive*.) Clare's correspondence seems to suggest that Radstock did indeed question these lines and that Taylor attempted to please both patrons and poet by removing the 'accursed wealth' passage but allowing these lines to remain.[17] The significant word in this passage is 'labour' which is used to refer both to an abstraction, a class, as in 'labour and luxury', and to the act of work ('made labour light'). Clare recognised that the 'Accursed wealth' passage was being accused of radicalism not only because it attacked the aristocracy, who now made up a significant proportion of his patrons, but because it spoke from the perspective of the labourer, and made significant demands about his material existence, about the provision of 'labour & bread'. This nascent materialism is further explored in the later passage which argues that before the alteration of the landscape the material needs of the labourer were met—'labour had his due'—and met to the extent that he knew 'peace [ease] & plenty'. Clare develops this argument about the ability of the pre-desolation, open-field, landscape to support the labourer in the mature enclosure elegies. The shift in the text from the individual to labour as a class also signifies a shift from the 'native scene' of the village to the national context:

Now all laid waste by desolations hand
Whose cursed weapons levels half the land (ll. 123-4)

The 'land' here is not the speaker's native fields but England, and a similar shift occurs in the enclosure stanzas of 'The Village Minstrel' when Clare begins to talk of the nation's lost liberties.[18] In other words, Clare uses the voice of labour to give the poem a materialist politics that, although disruptive of the nostalgic elements of the early stanzas, also takes strength from the images of 'plenty' found in these stanzas. Both 'Helpstone' and 'The Village Minstrel' suggest the possibility of collective action, of labour's resistance to change, by moving from the personal to the political via the use of a voice tensed towards collective resistance. 'Helpstone' recreates the site of conflict produced in 'Thy eye can witness...' by addressing 'wealth' as though it is a figure present in the poem. The repetition of lines 131-5, 'Thou art ... & thine ... Thou art', emphasises the accusatory, dialogic nature of this passage. That the voice of labour was a subversive force within the early poems was recognised both by his early readers, as the intervention of Clare's patrons attests, and by Taylor who chose not to publish complete texts such as 'Lobin Clout'.

The various voices of labour contained in these early manuscripts conflict and contradict. They do not create an ideological centre or produce a coherent argument for the rights of labour but constantly return to the site of dialogic conflict depicted in 'labour & luxury'. The Clarendon edition of the *Early Poems* has revealed a poet who is able to produce many voices and, as a consequence, the search for an essentially Clarean voice that has preoccupied many critics in the past must be exchanged for an investigation of the poet's many voices. The poems explored in this essay suggest that this investigation will discover new voices and help to ground Clare's texts in his personal and cultural context.

NOTES

1. *By Himself*, p. 64. This edition of the autobiographical writings notes that Clare described two alternative endings to this poem which follow 'in dispair' in PMS A25: 'when the phantom of liberty in[s]tantly appears to cheer the lean figure with prophetic' and 'when the bloated pha[n]tom shrinks from its presence and fades away', p. 297.
2. *Early Poems*, I, p. 505. The poem is taken from NMS 7, p. 41. Further references to this volume are given after quotations in the text.
3. The phrase occurs in both 'Dawning Of Genius' (*Early Poems*, I, pp. 451-2, ll. 17- 18) and 'On Labour' (p. 141).
4. Clare recognised the similarities between 'Helpstone' and Goldsmith's poem and defended himself against accusations of plagiarism: see *Early Poems*, I, p. 169.
5. James Raven, *Judging New Wealth. Popular Publishing and Responses to Commerce in England 1750-1800* (Oxford: Clarendon Press, 1992), pp. 157-82.
6. The phrase 'Pindaric Satires' comes from a collection of pamphlets bound *c.* 1820 and now in the British Library (C.131.d.11). Examples of these texts include [William Hone], *The Midnight Intruder or Old Nick at C—lt–n H—se, a Poem by W.R.H* (William Hone, 1816), and *The R—l Marriage, Or Miss Lump and the Grenadier. A Poem by Peter Pindar* (Johnson, n.d.). These pamphlets, particularly popular during the Queen Caroline affair, ranged in price from 1/2d to 1s 12d.
7. Clare refused to side with the Queen in the Caroline affair. See *Letters*, pp. 109-10. His later poems 'The Hue & Cry' and 'The Summons' contain similar echoes of the pamphlets and his attempt to get Cruikshank to illustrate these texts suggests a continuing familiarity with the genre (*Letters*, pp. 524-5).
8. Gareth Stedman Jones, *Languages of Class: Studies in English Working Class History 1832-1982* (Cambridge: Cambridge University Press, 1983), pp. 102-10. Stedman Jones's suggestion that working-class movements often conceived of oppression as 'legal and political' in the early century indicates that there are similarities between Clare's position in the enclosure elegies, which emphasise the role of the law, and the working-class movements to which he was in many other ways opposed.
9. For a contemporary use of the term 'hells' see Byron, *Don Juan*, Canto XI (1823), xxix:
   Don Juan, our young diplomatic sinner,
   Pursued his path, and drove past some Hotels,
   St James's Palace, and St James's 'Hells'. (ll. 230-2)
   Jerome J. McGann, *The New Oxford Book of Romantic Period Verse* (Oxford:

Oxford University Press, 1994), p. 647.

10. For a discussion of the voice of alienated labour in the early poems see, Stephen M. Colclough, 'Voicing Loss: Versions of Pastoral in the Poetry of John Clare, 1817-1832' (unpublished doctoral thesis, University of Keele, 1996), pp. 5-23.

11. *John Gay: Poetry and Prose*, ed. by Vinton A. Dearing and Charles E. Beckwith (Oxford: Oxford University Press, 1974), I, pp. 90-126; *The Yale Edition of the Shorter Poems of Edmund Spenser*, ed. by William A. Oram, Einar Bjorvand, Ronald Bond, Thomas H. Cain, Alexander Dunlop and Richard Schell (New Haven and London: Yale, 1989), pp. 1-213. Both of these poems contain dialogues between two representative characters. Gay's poem contains a burlesque of the pastoral singing match that may have influenced Clare when writing both this poem and 'labour and luxury'.

12. *By Himself*, p. 5

13. *By Himself*, p. 3.

14. 'The Village Minstrel', *Early Poems*, II, p. 169:
> O england boasted land of liberty
> Wi strangers still thou mayst thy title own
> But thy poor slaves the alteration see (ll. 1093-5)

15. Edmund Burke, *Reflections on the Revolution in France* (London: Dodsley, 1790), p. 117.

16. Margaret Powell, 'Clare and His Patrons in 1820: Some Unpublished Papers', *JCSJ*, 6 (1987), 4-9 (p. 7). Sherwill's letter was written on 11 May 1820, less than four months after the publication of *Poems Descriptive*.

17. *Letters*, pp. 68-70.

18. 'The Village Minstrel', *Early Poems*, II, p. 169 (ll. 1093-1101).

ILLUSTRATION OPPOSITE

The words beneath the image read:

> W, for the wine and liqueurs he swallow'd
> While writhing he lay on the sofa and hallow'd.

ROSCO (pseud.), *Horrida Bella, Pains and Penalties Versus Truth and Justice* (London: Humphrey, 1820), p. 23. A contemporary depiction of 'Luxury', issued during the Queen Caroline affair. The 'bloated figure' is George IV, and his 'lean' companion, Lord Hutchinson. Other contemporary caricaturists frequently depicted Hutchinson offering the Queen a bag containing £50,000. (Reproduced by permission of the British Library.)

91

7. 'Like Clover Through Lime': Rural Ruins and the Language of the Past

Paul Chirico

I would like to discuss some issues of labour, leisure and community in the light of Clare's writings on antiquity. Before turning to two poems about the discovery and contemplation of ruins, it is worth considering three conflicting descriptions of Clare's own labour. The first is by John Wilson, whose review of *The Rural Muse* in *Blackwood's Edinburgh Magazine* is a sustained evocation of a nation at ease with itself. This one-nation complacency, so representative of contemporary reviews of Clare's publications, is predicated on a reading of the rural poet as naive beneficiary of a generous Nature. In his eagerness to celebrate an authentic, national culture as natural and uncultivated, he denies the labour involved in breaking up earth or making up poetry:

The soil in which the native virtues of the English character grow, is unexhausted and inexhaustible; let him break it up on any spot he chooses, and poetry will spring to light like clover through lime.[1]

Wilson was either unaware or negligent of Clare's occupation during the three years immediately preceding his first publication. In Clare's own account of one period of this work, the soil harbours not simply a blueprint for native virtue, but the fragmented remnants of an earlier civilisation:

Pickworth is a place of other days   it appears to be the ruins of a large town or city   the place were we dug the kiln was full of foundations and human bones.[2]

John Taylor had in fact drawn attention to Clare's recent employment in his 'Introduction' to *Poems Descriptive of Rural Life and Scenery*, back in 1820, quoting Clare's account of the composition of one particular poem:

The Elegy on the Ruins of Pickworth was written one Sunday morning,

PAUL CHIRICO

after I had been helping to dig the hole for a lime-kiln, where the many fragments of mortality and perished ruins inspired me with thoughts of other times, and warmed me into song.[3]

Clare is anxious, as always, to trace the borders between labour, leisure and poetic production. Taylor prefixes to Clare's comment his own assessment of those complex relationships, which begins to escape Wilson's complacency:

To describe the occupations of Clare, we must not say that Labour and the Muse went hand in hand: they rather kept alternate watch, and when Labour was exhausted with fatigue, she "cheer'd his needy toilings with a song."[4]

If this seems a curious blend of cheerfulness and realism, it is noteworthy that Taylor takes his quotation from the opening poem of the volume, 'Helpstone', where it follows very closely after the infamous lines—excised in subsequent editions—condemning 'Accursed wealth'.[5] In fact Taylor's account bears a certain relation to Clare's own. In 1817 Clare 'left Helpstone in company with an out of town labourer who followed the employment of burning lime, named Stephen Gordon'.[6] Moving between the villages of Casterton, Pickworth and Ryhall, to the north of Stamford, this work lasted until late 1819. By this stage his first collection of poems was imminent and Martha Turner ('Patty') was pregnant with his child. Writing of his motivation during this period of poetic creativity, Clare describes himself 'getting a many more poems written as ex[c]ited by change of Scenery, and from being for the first time over head and ears in love, above all the most urgent propensity to scribbling'.[7] It is, unsurprisingly perhaps, Clare's leisure activities that he cites as his primary inspiration. More explicitly, he recalls that at the beginning of 1819 frost rendered his employment at Casterton impossible; his account—'I then returnd home and had a good winters work of Scribbling etc for the forthcoming book'—provides a realistic corrective to Wilson's sentimental assertion of the implicit connection of labour and poetry.[8]

In his 'Introduction' Taylor repeats Clare's claim that, late in 1819, his employer had broken an agreement and cut his wages. His account is strikingly detailed:

94

He had an engagement during the greater part of the year with Mr. Wilders, of Bridge-Casterton, two miles north of Stamford; where the river Gwash, which crosses the road, gave him a subject for one of his Sonnets. (p. 203.) His wages were nine shillings a week, and his food; out of which he had to pay one shilling and sixpence a week for a bed, it being impossible that he could return every night to Helpstone, a distance of nine miles: but at the beginning of November, his employer proposed to allow him only seven shillings a week, on which, he quitted his service and returned home.[9]

Taylor's writing here demonstrates exactly the characteristics grudgingly acknowledged by Clare in a short, unusually critical sketch of the publisher.[10] He is detailed but dry, judiciously summarising the material facts but refraining from offering a leading interpretation. If this sort of understatement eschews the radical claims which now appear more tempting and less problematic, it also avoids the complacency expressed by some of Clare's reviewers. In part Taylor is acting as literary promoter, for example connecting the biography to the actual content of the new volume by giving the page reference for the sonnet 'The River Gwash'. Meanwhile that final, brief description of Clare's withdrawal of his labour adds a moral energy and a temporal urgency to Taylor's comments about Clare's future financial security, without implying any threat to the social order. The poet 'is again residing with his parents, working for any one who will employ him, but without any regular occupation'.[11]

The wage dispute had already been reported in the *London Magazine* by Octavius Gilchrist. In contrast to Taylor's painstaking account, Gilchrist had merely recorded that 'when the writer of this narrative first saw the poet, he had just quitted an engagement in the vicinity of Stamford, because his employer had reduced his stipend from eighteen to fourteen pence *per diem*!'[12] That rendering of Clare's wage by the day is striking, when set alongside Clare's declaration—published by Taylor, and cited above—of his composition of the Pickworth elegy on Sunday. Certainly the timing—'after I had been helping to dig'—does not necessarily imply that the work had taken place on the Sabbath. Yet the poem was printed in *Poems Descriptive* as 'Elegy on the Ruins of Pickworth, / Rutlandshire. / Hastily composed, and written with a Pencil on / the Spot.'[13] The title goes to some length to emphasise the conditions of composition, which match Clare's habit—stressed in his autobiographical prose and, more prominently, in Taylor's 'Introduction'—of writing his poems hastily and surreptitiously, in pencil, at dinner-time or in a stolen break from work.[14] This context of labour deliberately undermines another tradition to which he alludes and which could be characterised very roughly as the leisured ruin poem, where the emphasis is on spontaneous first-hand moralistic reflections, arising from the triumphant yet humbling contemplation of a picturesque prospect of decay.

In addition to the labouring context, the title suggests an anxious awareness that the subsequent account shares with its subject matter the qualities of provisionality and impermanence. And in fact, as might be expected, the original manuscript seems not to have survived, while the pencil version of the first half of the poem in PMS A3 has been erased and overwritten in ink with the hunting song 'To day the fox must dye'. Yet despite the apparently incidental uncovering of the 'buried Ruins' (l. 1) as a result of considerable labour carried out for a quite unconnected reason, the opening stanza makes it clear that the history of those ruins has never been forgotten locally, signalled as it is by the heaped stones and by the place names:

> The 'Old Foundations' still they call the spot
> Which plainly tells Enqu[i]rey what has been (ll. 3-4)

For the inquisitive reader of this poem, as for the interested local, access to historical information is straightforward. The realm of mystery—which, in the sonnet 'To Mystery' (discussed below), exerts a fundamental organizing force—is here limited to the uneven distribution of wealth:

> Mysterious cause! Still more mysterious pland
> (—Altho undoubtedly the will of heaven)
> To think what carless & unequal hand
> Met[e]s out each portion that to man is given (ll. 13-16)

In the context of the surrounding lines it is hard to resist an ironic reading of the conservative moral drawn here. In fact the whole of the first half of the poem is driven by a vehement political engagement; a further irony is the overwriting of these sentiments with that hunting song, cheerful verse in the service of a class pretty unambiguously described here as the enemy.

In the preceding and following stanzas the economic protest is no mere subtext, yet it seems not to have provoked the sort of discomfort and irritation prompted by (for example) Clare's attack on 'Accursed wealth' in 'Helpstone'. This is partly because, rather than being directed against the acute and (in local terms) personal issue of enclosure, the poem was to a degree assimilable to a perceived tradition of rural nostalgia.[15] Having been selected and printed in Clare's first volume it apparently provoked no criticism. On the contrary: in the *Gentleman's Magazine*, for example, it is singled out for particular praise, and compared to Gray's 'Elegy': 'there is ... much that forcibly reminds us of the sublime and impassioned moral painting which characterizes the "Church-yard."'[16] This can be taken as an indication of the quality of Clare's imposture, the skill with which he deploys various poetic voices and inhabits various literary conventions in the very act of undermining them. Some recent critics, also, have felt that the identification outweighs the irony. Timothy Brownlow, for example, ignores Clare's complaints about wealth distribution in favour of his echoes of Gray's 'Elegy'. He clearly regards Clare's use of the devices of eighteenth-century visual organisation as exhausting all his linguistic and narrative resources (at this stage in his writing career):

> Clare is never at home with this verse-form; if the quatrain suits Gray's 'divine truisms', it is quite inappropriate to the mature Clare's purpose, which is to catch the animation and detail of nature without imprisoning it in the frame of conventional form or manner. Clare is also uneasy with the visual demands of the perspective, with space used pictorially (the assumption of foreground, middle-distance and background), the time-projections (the retrospective use of a prospect), and the moral vision controlled by the optical vision.[17]

Brownlow contrasts this poem with Clare's more complex later style, and while the certainty of his identification of 'the mature Clare's purpose' is surprising, so too is his repeated suggestion that Clare is here unsettled by a verse-form beyond his control. Brownlow's assessment of Clare in 1818 as prisoner rather than master of form and convention also informs his implication that Clare masks his own labouring presence in Pickworth and adopts the role of itinerant picturesque tourist. Yet it is true that the brief reference within the poem itself to the manual labour which has revealed the ruins is obscured by personification, and thus fails to match the clarity of Clare's note on the composition of the poem:

How contemplation mourns your lost decay
To view thy pride laid level with the ground
To see where labour clears the soil away
What fragments of mortality abound (ll. 37-40)

Contemplation is apparently prioritised over labour; the poem, Brownlow suggests, implies that the ruin is 'sought out ... by a picturesque tourist'.[18] Perhaps the point is precisely that this is an *implication*, and that this implication means that the poem—again in Brownlow's analysis—'*seems* all the more in the topographical mode'(my italics).[19] The talent which Clare is beginning to perfect in this poem is the convincing adoption of the various conventional postures of melancholy and grandeur. Brownlow's complaint that Clare 'repeats in a *laboured* way the eighteenth-century device of pointing out landmarks within an ordered design' (my italics) replicates in its unintentional, almost unnoticeable pun the subtlety with which Clare in fact supplements, rather than subverts, initially unsympathetic poetic traditions, by simply refusing to choose between identification with contemplation or with labour.[20]

After the early attention to the distribution of wealth, the terminology of prosperity comes to be more widely applied as the elegy continues. In fact the pressing sense of present economic destitution is overtaken by a metaphor of the present as impoverished in relation to the past. This is put to moralistic use: 'what was once is lost / Who would be proud of what this world bestows?' (ll. 35-6). Finally human history is seen as shrouded in mystery; but what might have been framed as a consolatory moral levelling, is described instead as a threatening isolation:

Ye busy bustling mortals known before
Of what you've done—where went—or what you see
Of what your hopes attain to (now no more)
For everlasting lyes a mystery

Like yours awaits for me that 'common lot'
Tis mine to be of every hope bereft
—A few more years & I shall be forgot
& not a Vestige of my memory left (ll. 53-60)

This final stanza asserts the obliteration of human history in the wake of the passage of time. Earlier in the poem the victory of natural process over architecture is described in more specific terms:

A time was once—tho now the nettle grows
In triumph oer each heap that swells the ground
When they in buildings pil'd a village rose (ll. 5-7)

The presentation of nature as partaking in the decay of the ruins carries the moral implication of the vanity of mortal endeavour against the eternal natural (dis)order. But a complementary or even contradictory inference can be drawn from the way in which the continuity of nature is enacted in the detail of individual locations or plants. The nettle is the agent of nature's triumph, yet the ground from which it grows is swollen by the ruins. This idea of the land as physically constituted by the past is later confidently expressed in terms which are at once more explicit and more general:

Theres not a Rood of Land demands our toil
Theres not a foot of ground we daily tread
But gains increase from times devouring spoil
& holds some fragment of the human dead (ll. 41-4)[21]

Here the adjective 'human', logically redundant, emphasises Clare's notion of an eternal, organic community. Clare's poems on the theme of antiquity explore the connection between the concealment of these artefacts of the past within the earth and the metaphorical revelation of information about the past. At the end of this poem the human remains refuse to give up their story, but the capacity of the narrator to give his present account remains unchallenged. This is a highly political poem, driven by a powerful anger and anxiety about economic standing and emphasising the narrator's identification with the labour of digging. But the anxiety also looks forward, into uncertain career prospects. The means by which the narrator hopes to avoid the 'common lot' (l. 57) and establish a claim to a continued public 'memory' (l. 60) are unstated; his identity with the labour of narration itself remains implicit.

* * *

In a longer essay I would have liked to discuss the connections between Clare's poetic ambitions and his local attachments. The tensions are played out, more or less explicitly, in his various accounts of the rural poet, such as 'Helpstone' and 'The Fate of Genius'.[22] In many other poems nature escapes from its position as backdrop to a biographical narrative and becomes a metaphorical battleground, where to control the language of natural description is to seize control of the tools of commercial success. There is a parallel movement in Clare's treatment of antiquity, as the very question of the applicability of metaphor and narrative begins to take centre stage. This is evident in the sonnet 'To Mystery', printed in *The Rural Muse* as 'Antiquity'. The following version is that of the Oxford English Texts edition, taken from Clare's *Midsummer Cushion* manuscript (PMS A54); beneath it I print a rejected version of lines 5-6, which appear as an alternative to that couplet in another manuscript (PMS A37):

Mystery thou subtle essence—ages gain
New light from darkness—still thy blanks remain
& reason trys [to] chase old night from thee
When chaos fled thy parent took the key
Blank darkness—& the things age left behind *
Are lockt for aye in thy unspeaking mind *
Towers temples ruins on & under ground
So old—so dark—so mystic—so profound
Old time himself so old is like a child
& cant remember when their blocks were piled
Or caverns scooped & with a wondering eye
He seems to pause like other standers bye
Half thinking that the wonders left unknown

Was born in ages older then his own

* Look at the wonders man hath left behind
* That wake reflections in a thinking mind[23]

It is worth first looking at the lines which are *not* in the final version, and considering the light which their exclusion sheds on the central themes of time, subjectivity and social process. The rejection of the first version of the fifth and sixth lines in PMS A37 suggests a dissatisfaction with what is in truth a hackneyed sentiment. The eighteenth-century ruin poem is by no means politically homogenous, given the varying emphases placed by writers of the genre on implications of continuity, decay, civilisation and inevitability in their treatment of the physical remnants of the past. But there is an undeniable familiarity about the situation sketched in the rejected couplet: a leisured observer, possessed of unusual faculties—'a thinking mind'—invited to consider a specific ruin and to exercise a sort of moral responsibility to construct that ruin as symptomatic of a grander historical process.

The rejected lines, then, provide a brief model of one conceptual response to ruins, based on the subordination of observed detail to a moralistic structure. Clare often uses such phraseology as the 'thinking mind' to distinguish a few members of the rural community from the average labourer, and to emphasize the quality of the mental processes which those few bring to bear on their sense information.[24] The invocation of representative figures—the poet, the unthinking swain—is a tool for potential irony, as has been noted by Margaret Grainger in relation to the prose piece 'The Woodman or the Beauties of a Winter Forest'.[25] But, as Grainger implies, any such irony tends to remain speculative and inconsistent, and such passages often end up illustrating principally Clare's own intellectual anxiety and cultural ambition. These implicit autobiographical reservations themselves act as an ironic subtext to Clare's every intimation of a shared, reflective response to natural observation.

While asserting an intellectual community the cancelled lines also suggest a social responsibility and responsiveness. The wonders 'wake reflections'— in other words the reflections are both morally and temporally prompted. This introduction of a timescale of present response contrasts markedly with the grand but vague historical scheme which begins the poem. A parallel innovation in the cancelled lines is the introduction of a new (implied) addressee. Each of the first four lines is addressed to the obscurely personified figure of 'Mystery'. The rejected couplet, in contrast, seems to be directed to an implied companion or companions possessed of the kind of 'thinking mind' which has prompted this narrator's 'reflections'. So, while they stood, these lines formed an uncomfortable bridge between the second-person address to Mystery and the third-person account of 'old time'.

The cancelled fifth line invokes social achievement while simultaneously implying social decay. The responsibility of 'man' for the creation of 'wonders' upsets the dense, mythological account of history packed into the opening four lines. There the terms describing social process remain indirect: ages, reason, darkness. These terms lend themselves to homiletic use, and the disjointed syntax also encourages a reading of those opening lines as a series of proverbial attempts to summarise an abstract. This sense of colliding, even overlapping assessments reaches its height in the opening words of the retained fifth line—'Blank darkness'—with the conjunction of two terms from separate earlier clauses.

Lines seven and eight revert to a cataloguing style, though one in which the earlier tautological tendencies survive. The seventh line is concentrated from its original form in PMS A37—'Temples & caves above & underground'—encouraging a sense of cluttered proliferation which stretches descriptive language to its limits, or rather reduces it to its bare bones. Adjectives replace nouns in the following line as the tempo is carefully lowered before the turn of the sonnet from octave to sestet. It is tempting to regard this eighth line as tautological, but to do so is to underestimate the important function of its echoes. First of all each adjective seems to pair off with a noun from the final version of the preceding line—old towers, dark (perhaps pagan) temples, mystic ruins, profound buried ruins. But the first three adjectives also recall their own nominal forms which have shaped the opening lines: age, darkness, mystery. Although, as I have suggested, the opening statements seem to relate to each other only tangentially, if there is a cumulative sense it is of age and darkness retreating beyond the illuminating beam of human inquiry. The (already abstract) terms used to define Mystery retreat behind their initial definition—leaving 'Blank darkness', where blank seems to propel the darkness back beyond the possibility of discovery. It is this idea of incommunicability which is described in the final version of lines five and six, where the 'thinking mind' of the moralistic observer from the rejected version is replaced by the 'unspeaking mind' of Mystery itself. A centre of knowledge is located as eternally isolated in the abstract spirit of the ruins which constitute the following catalogue.

I have noted that, despite its composition in couplets, this sonnet is divided into octave and sestet, and before going on to discuss the striking change of style in the last six lines, it is worth paying some attention to the final, transitional word of the eighth line. While the first three adjectives of line eight recall important concepts from earlier in the poem, the only apparent echo in the fourth, 'profound', is a bad pun with the 'under ground' with which it rhymes.[26] The appearance of the word here is bathetic; his particular adjective is notable for its relative lack of profundity. There is more than a hint of irony in this unconvincing use of a commonplace but fairly meaningless expression just two lines after the assertion that true understanding resides in the 'unspeaking mind' of mystery. This recalls Clare's record of a similarly hackneyed response in the sonnet 'Pleasant Places'—'Where wonder pauses to exclaim "divine"'.[27] Despite the difficulties mentioned above in any identification of irony in Clare, that sonnet would be vital in any fuller discussion of his deliberate and playful subversion of landscape techniques through a concentration on the constitutive function of both spoken and written language. Here, though, there is a stronger echo of the terms in which Clare proposes, in his Journal for Sunday 24 October 1824, to write his own guide to wild flowers, illustrated—like Elizabeth Kent's *Flora Domestica* (1824) which he greatly admired —with quotations from poetry:

an English Botany on this plan woud be very interesting & serve to make Botany popular while the hard nicknaming sy<s>tem of unuterable words now in vogue only overloads it in mystery till it makes darkness visable[28]

These references to the incommunicable and the mysterious demonstrate Clare's attention both to the intricate politics of language and to the forms of cultural production; and the coincidence of the terms used in the Journal and the sonnet illustrates the sonnet's deliberate and concentrated allusions to similar themes.

After the mythologising, the cataloguing and the recognition of the failure of description, the poem shifts into narrative mode in the final six lines, escaping syntactic density in a single flowing sentence. Important earlier elements are subsumed within the new mode: the alternative forms of ruin—piles and caverns—and the epistemological isolation. Above all a timeframe of observation is introduced. But whereas in the cancelled lines from PMS A37 this observation was exclamatory and moralistic, here it is habitual and deferential. The figure of 'Old time'—clarified within PMS A37, where 'Old' is written over the first word of the original 'That time, himself...'—is both a mythological trope and an emblematic rural figure, a kind of aged everyman representing the old shepherds who preserved local knowledge of customs, events and narratives, and whose passing Clare frequently lamented as fatal to his community. This character, in his dual role, embodies the investment of rural history in individuals. His inability to remember the historical origin of the ruins introduces an implied interlocutor, another level of ignorance. But with the reference in the final line to 'ages older then his own' the deliberate ambiguity is shattered, exposing the hubris of the claim made for the character, of the implication of his immortality. The illusion of a preserved and knowable rural culture is undermined.

There are significant implications here for the viability of poetry as a means of cultural transmission. Two central themes emerge: the autobiographical anxiety of the rural poet attempting to establish a cultural community, and the desire to reaffirm an ongoing oral tradition capable of knowing and preserving both the past and the present of nature. Elsewhere Clare introduces non-human life, such as a pair of birds, a solitary insect or an old tree, as alternative and arguably more permanent repositories of knowledge. In the sonnet 'To Mystery' all hints at community are heavily compromised by the emphasis on the absolute unknowability of the past. 'Mystery' is invoked, in the first line, as a 'subtle essence'. Johnson's sixth and final definition for the word 'subtile' is 'Refined; acute beyond exactness'; it is this mysterious capacity of ancient artefacts to evade exact description that haunts the poem.[29]

NOTES

1. [John Wilson], [Review of *The Rural Muse*], *Blackwood's Edinburgh Magazine*, 38 (August 1835), 231-47 (239), reprinted in *Critical Heritage*, pp. 225-38 (p. 233).
2. *By Himself*, p. 92.

3. John Taylor, 'Introduction' to John Clare, *Poems Descriptive of Rural Life and Scenery* (London: Taylor and Hessey, Stamford: E. Drury, 1820), first edition, pp. vii-xxviii (p. xxii).

4. Taylor, 'Introduction', p. xxii.

5. See 'Helpstone', ll. 144, 127-34, in *Early Poems*, I, pp. 156-63.

6. *By Himself*, p. 21.

7. *By Himself*, p. 21.

8. *By Himself*, p. 28.

9. Taylor, 'Introduction', p. xxv.

10. *By Himself*, pp. 131-2.

11. Taylor, 'Introduction', pp. xxiv-xxv.

12. Octavius Gilchrist, 'Some Account of John Clare, an Agricultural Labourer and Poet', *London Magazine*, i (January 1820), 7-11 (9), reprinted in *Critical Heritage*, pp. 35-42 (p. 38).

13. See *Early Poems,* I, pp. 402-4. Subsequent line numbers refer to this edition.

14. See, for example, Taylor, 'Introduction', p. xx; *By Himself*, pp. 77-8.

15. Although a great deal more space would be required to argue the point forcefully, I mean to suggest that in such a perceived tradition the egalitarian implications of a poem such as Gray's 'Elegy' have been effectively (and lastingly) disarmed.

16. 'E.P.', 'Remarks on the spontaneous display of Native Genius', *Gentleman's Magazine*, xci (April 1821), 308-12 (309), reprinted in *Critical Heritage*, pp. 111-17 (pp. 116-17).

17. Timothy Brownlow, *John Clare and Picturesque Landscape* (Oxford: Clarendon Press, 1983), p. 29.

18. Brownlow, p. 28.

19. Brownlow, p. 28.

20. Brownlow, p. 29.

21. Cf. Thomas Gray, 'Elegy Written in a Country Church-Yard', l. 14: 'Where heaves the turf in many a mould'ring heap'.

22. *Early Poems*, I, pp. 156-63; II, pp. 666-70.

23. *Middle Period*, IV, pp. 245-6. This edition contains a fuller account of manuscript variations.

24. See, for example, 'Obscurity', l. 6, *Middle Period*, IV, p. 256; 'Taste', *Natural History*, pp. 283-5.

25. *Natural History*, p. 3.

26. Johnson's dictionary records usage similar to today's, with connotations of both physical and intellectual depth.

27. 'Pleasant Places', l. 8, in *Middle Period*, IV, pp. 224-5.

28. *Natural History*, p. 195. Clare is quoting *Paradise Lost*, I, l. 63.

29. Samuel Johnson, *A Dictionary of the English Language* (London: W. Strachan for J. and P. Knapton [et al], 1755). The citation given for this definition is from Milton: 'Things remote from use, obscure and *subtle.*' Clare uses the word in a similar sense to describe the protective timidity of the nightingale: see 'The Nightingale's Nest', l. 57, *Middle Period*, III, pp. 456-61.

8. Viewing and Reviewing Clare

Alan Vardy

When John Clare's first volume of poetry, *Poems Descriptive of Rural Life and Scenery*, appeared in 1820, it was reviewed in aesthetic terms familiar to contemporary readers of magazines and reviews, those of the georgic tradition of the unspoiled rustic poet. During this period Wordsworth's adaptation and revision of pastoral traditions in his Preface to *Lyrical Ballads*, and Coleridge's re-interrogation of them in *Biographia Literaria*, were gaining currency. Those formulations founded one of the most influential varieties of what we now call Romanticism,[1] and much of present-day criticism of Clare's poetry relies more on Wordsworth and Coleridge's refinements than on the older georgic tradition itself. The initial reviews of Clare's poems occurred before such adaptations of the georgic had become ubiquitous, and they clearly demonstrated a powerful gentlemanly taste for new poetic 'discoveries' among the labouring classes. Reviewers sought after images of a pastoral world where peasant poets could represent a rural landscape lost to them in their hectic urban milieus—'represent' both in the sense of composing the images of nature that constituted that landscape and in the sense of standing for that lost pastoral world. John Taylor, Clare's publisher, was keenly aware of this immediate aesthetic context as he attempted to situate Clare's poetry in his Introduction to the volume, and his intellectual lead shaped much of the critical response. Taylor's own tastes were highly refined. He had incorporated the Wordsworth/Coleridge debates into his aesthetic views, and those complex considerations colour his advice to prospective readers of Clare. Echoes of Wordsworth's Preface to *Lyrical Ballads* occur throughout Taylor's introduction, and define Clare in several Wordsworthian ways.

Clare was, wrote Taylor, 'the Poet as well as the Child of Nature'.[2] In other words, Clare, like Wordsworth, drew poetic inspiration directly from the objects of nature. As we will see, while this reliance on the natural world was shared in Wordsworthian and georgic poetics, the distinctly Wordsworthian idea that philosophical reflection was necessary in order to give form to the finished poem, produced anxiety in Taylor's account of Clare's poetic practice. Clare also conformed to a Wordsworthian type, the rustic, who provided not only the model of the natural unaffected artist, but also a source of inspiration. Clare was himself an object of poetic contemplation for a Wordsworthian poet, and, more conventionally, a prize for the discriminating patron.[3] Discovered as a detail in a picturesque natural landscape, he was a kind of living leech-gatherer. Taylor's Introduction moved between these two views, the declaration of Clare's poetic genius, and an insistence on his exceptional status as an object of nature: 'a young Peasant, a day-labourer in husbandry, who has had no advantages of education beyond others of his class' (p. [i]).

This essay addresses and explores several related questions concerning the reception of Clare's first two books: how were reviewers reliant on established versions of pastoral poetry and on Taylor's intellectual lead in defining Clare's genius, how did the issue of class penetrate aesthetic discourse and critical judgements about Clare, and how did Clare attempt to resist such judgements?

Viewing

Hugh Blair's 'Lecture Thirty-nine, Pastoral Poetry' from his *Lectures on Rhetoric and Belles Lettres* (1785)[4] provides the most concise statement of the aesthetic and cultural values of eighteenth-century pastoral poetry. Blair's history of the classical invention of pastoral poetry made it clear that pastoral was not rural poetry produced by rustics, Clare's idiom, but a pleasing mode of urban nostalgia:

> It was not till men had begun to be assembled in great cities, after the distinctions of rank and station were formed, and the bustle of Courts and large Societies was known, that Pastoral Poetry assumed its present form. Men then began to look back upon the more simple and innocent life, which their forefathers led, or which, at least, they fancied them to have led: they looked back upon it with pleasure; and in those rural scenes, and pastoral occupations, imagining a degree of felicity to take place, superior to what they now enjoyed, conceived the idea of celebrating it in poetry. (pp. 115-16)

Pastoral poetry was an urban affectation, quite unlike Clare's faithful record of a rural landscape meticulously viewed and represented. In order to satisfy this particular taste, a peasant poet had to become a part of their own pastoral world, and thus a living evocation of the nostalgia the reader sought. Blair wrote that the purpose of pastoral poetry was to 'banish from our thoughts the cares of the world, and to transport us into calm Elysian regions' (p. 116). Clare's poetry could hardly fulfil this need while the 'Elysian regions' that he represented in his poems were being torn up and enclosed. The stark realism of many of Clare's descriptions of rural hardship and privation challenged readers, and potentially produced the opposite effect to the one Blair described. Blair made it clear that neither actual peasants nor over-idealised ones made good poetic subjects:

> Pastoral life may be considered in three different views; either as it now actually is; when the state of Shepherds is reduced to be a mean, servile and laborious state; when their employments are become disagreeable, and their ideas gross and low: or such as we may suppose it once to have been, in the more early and simple ages, when it was a life of ease and abundance; when the wealth of men consisted chiefly in flocks and herds, and the Shepherd, though unrefined in his manners, was respectable in his state: or, lastly, such as it never was, and never in reality can be, when, to the ease, innocence, and simplicity of the early ages, we attempt to add the polished taste, and cultivated manners, of modern times. Of these three states, the first is too gross and mean, the last too refined and unnatural, to be the groundwork of Pastoral Poetry. Either of these extremes is a rock upon which the Poet will split, if he approach too near it. We shall be disgusted if he give us too much of the servile employments and low ideas of actual peasants ... and, if ... he makes his Shepherds discourse as if they were courtiers and scholars, he then retains the name only, but wants the spirit of Pastoral Poetry. (pp. 117-18)[5]

As we shall see, the anxiety that Clare's status as an 'actual peasant' might be a source of 'disgust' to his potential audience permeated Taylor's Introduction to *Poems Descriptive of Rural Life and Scenery*, and he constantly responded to fears that Clare's ideas were 'gross and low'. Clare's vulgarity became an important subject for reviewers, and the most bawdy of his early poems met with calls for censorship. In short, the critical terrain that Taylor had to negotiate, and the gentlemanly taste it represented, was full of pitfalls seemingly designed to ensnare Clare, and, more importantly, critical taste was directly at odds with many of Clare's own poetic principles. Clare could not always be persuaded to walk this impossibly fine line. He was asked on the one hand to be exceptional, not an 'actual peasant', so he would not be contaminated by 'gross and low' ideas, and on the other hand he had to guard against affecting philosophical airs beyond his station. When readers objected to the 'low and gross' subjects of some of the early poems, Clare bitterly resented being asked to conform to genteel, and in his view false, taste. His exchanges with Taylor and Hessey over 'Dolly's Mistake' and other bawdy poems illustrate both Clare's frustration at having to submit to polite society, and the expectations that society placed on peasant poets.[6] These expectations were clearly in Taylor's mind as he introduced Clare to the reading public.

Clare's class identity as 'the peasant poet' was integral to Taylor's construction of poetic genius in the Introduction, and informed his discussions of Clare's poetic practices. Aesthetic judgements were inseparable from class judgements in the Introduction, and that conflation produced a double bind that continues to constrain our understanding of Clare. Taylor's argument that Clare was a natural genius whose work was of intrinsic interest was undermined by a special pleading based on class origins. Taylor's rhetorical strategy, while successful in shaping public opinion and securing sales, guaranteed that Clare be viewed and reviewed with condescension. His genius was limited by his background, making it impossible for him to aspire to true poetic genius because, as a peasant, he lacked the philosophical education necessary for Wordsworthian reflection. And furthermore, in the view of the dominant critics of the day, such reflection represented fatal over-reaching. For a critic like Francis Jeffrey,[7] for example, following Blair's lead, the peasant poet could only be admitted as an object of condescension, and pretence to philosophical reflection was seen as a threat to the poet's 'natural' simplicity. As a result, in his contemporary milieu, Clare would be considered a failure if he aspired to a version of poetic genius beyond his class. The antithesis is true in present-day criticism. For Harold Bloom, Clare becomes a failed Wordsworthian poet precisely because of his lack of a suitable reflective mode, the same poetic mode that would have been decried as over-reaching by Jeffrey.[8] Taylor was left with the unenviable task in his Introduction of attempting to please both the conservative georgic tradition of the unaffected natural genius, and the emerging, and contradictory, Wordsworthian emphasis on philosophical reflection. This essay quarrels with the cultural assumptions of these views by analysing Taylor's Introduction, and by evaluating its impact on public reception in the magazines and reviews, tracing the influence of both the conventional taste for georgic pastorals and the emerging Wordsworthian aesthetic of reflection. These aesthetic formulations, as echoed by the reviewers, betray a clear, and for Clare debilitating, set of cultural assumptions in relation to questions of class. Class-bound aesthetics dominate critical judgments of Clare's career and poetry from the beginning. Yet despite his almost total lack of cultural power, Clare developed a poetics that both confounded the conservative aesthetics that authorised his career, and challenged the assumptions reviewers claimed were integral to an appreciation of his work.

Clare's peasant background inevitably played a part in Taylor's account of the typical composition of a poem: 'Most of his poems were composed under the immediate impression of this feeling [the love of nature], in the fields, or on the road-sides' (p. xv). The emphasis on 'immediate impression' echoed Wordsworth's most famous formulation; according to Taylor the poems were the natural result of 'the spontaneous overflow of powerful feelings', but they were recorded as immediate impressions of those feelings, rather than conforming to the second half of Wordsworth's dictum: 'Poems to which any value can be attached, were never produced on any variety of subjects but by a man who being possessed of more than usual organic sensibility had also thought long and deeply'.[9] Taylor argued that special allowances should be made for Clare. Circumstances did not allow for the full expression of the Wordsworthian ideal, but Clare's poems should be valued anyway because of the special 'circumstances under which they were written' (p. i). A critical paternalism was therefore deemed necessary in order to extract the aesthetic value from the work; the critic could complete the poetic equation and provide the products of Clare's 'organic sensibility' with the philosophical reflection that they lacked. The critic or reader could reflect on the meaning of the landscape that Clare artistically supplied. This was a well-established strategy in marketing peasant poets; patronage was integral to the creation of poetic meaning. Taylor's rhetorical strategy was largely successful, but the cost was an abundance of self-congratulatory condescension on the part of reviewers, and ultimately the foundation of the false view of Clare as a 'failed Wordsworthian'. The persistence of this view is ironic given that Clare was suspicious of the self-dramatisations of Wordsworth's poetics, and attempted to resist their focus on poetic recuperation through reflection—the self-reflexive quality he was judged by many critics to lack. In his references to Wordsworth in letters from this period Clare clearly values spontaneity in Wordsworth's poetry over reflection: 'wordsworth defies all art & in all the lunatic Enthuseism of nature he sets down his thoughts from the tongue of the inspirer'. In his discussions of Wordsworth with Taylor, he commented in December 1821 that Wordsworth's recent efforts at philosophical poetry were 'ridiculous' and gave him an 'itch after parody'.[10] Clare's were not a naive poetics of place, incapable of philosophical reflection, but rather an insistence on the ethical representation of objects for their own sake. In other words, Clare's poetic defence of the objects of nature was not an incomplete Wordsworthian gesture, apprehension without reflection, but a deliberate choice that implicitly, and often explicitly, contained ethical and political commitments. Taylor's sanitised version of Clare's origins and the origins of the poems was careful to disclaim any knowledge of such poetic principles.

Taylor's Introduction also drew on Wordsworth's poetics in establishing the poetic value of rustic or idiomatic language, and this was subsequently reflected in reviews. Wordsworth valorised rustic speech as authentically representing human experience, free from the taint of decadent urban acculturation manifested as faddish 'social vanity' (Preface, p. 744). This argument was a clear source of aesthetic value that Taylor could exploit in constructing Clare's poetic pedigree. Wordsworth had claimed that rural life created 'a plainer and more emphatic language', integrated as it was into a natural scene where 'the passions of men are incorporated with the beautiful and permanent forms of nature' (pp. 743-7). He further claimed that the rural idiom best served the contemplation of these natural forms:

The language too of these men [rustics] is adopted (purified indeed from what appear to be its real defects, from all lasting and rational causes of dislike or disgust) because such men hourly communicate with the best objects from which the best part of language is originally derived. (p.

744)

Clare was the most authentic of poets in these terms, yet Wordsworth's parenthesis suggested that Clare, as a rustic, required purification lest his language inspire 'dislike or disgust'. In his Introduction to *Poems Descriptive of Rural Life and Scenery*, Taylor attempted to serve, in his role as editor, as the purifier of Clare's work, removing its 'real defects' of grammar and spelling. More importantly, he attempted to answer potential criticism of Clare's vulgarity.

Taylor ingeniously argued that Clare, naturally enough given his background, lacked the language to communicate the poetic conceptions that arose during his intense observations of nature. His poverty of language was explicitly connected to his physical poverty: 'his vocabulary would have been too scanty to express even what his imagination had strength enough to conceive' (p. vii). Had John Turnill not taught Clare to write, presumably, such inchoate conceptions would have remained pre-linguistic—a powerful sensibility without expression. Taylor's argument made two important claims: first, that Clare was the true 'Child of Nature' endowed with the 'simplicity' that georgic taste craved and the extraordinary 'organic sensibility' that Wordsworthian aesthetics demanded (Preface, p. 745), and second, that Clare was a special case whose impoverished circumstances had to be taken into account before he was dismissed as vulgar and lacking in the philosophical depth to be gained by reflection. Taylor's solution was to turn on its head the argument that Clare was restricted by his linguistic poverty. After concluding that the poet 'seems to labour under great disadvantages' (p. viii), he exploded the idea as a mere 'seeming'. Clare, Taylor argued, turned his disadvantages into a new source of poetic value:

> On the other hand, his want forces him to an extraordinary exertion of his native powers, in order to supply the deficiency. He employs the language under his command with great effect, in those unusual and unprecedented combinations of words which must be made, even by the learned, when they attempt to describe perfectly something which they have never seen or heard expressed before. And in this respect Clare's deficiencies are the cause of many beauties... (pp. viii-ix)

This was an ingenious argument in that it took advantage of Wordsworth's claim that rural folk expressed themselves in a 'more emphatic language', while it claimed that Clare's search was for new knowledge and that his language, which at first may have appeared crude, was actually the only language capable of representing what had hitherto been unrepresented and thus unknown (this claim appealed both to the conventional taste for the primitive and to Wordsworth's formulations). Clare's native speech was the only possible source of aesthetic value in that landscape. Indeed, Clare himself argued the point more forcefully in a manuscript note to Taylor concerning the use of the invented word 'twitatwit' in the poem 'Helpstone':

> The word 'twitatwit' (if a word it may be calld) you will undoubtedly smile at but I wish you to print it as it is for it is the Language of Nature & that can never be disgusting.[11]

Clare's resistance to having his language 'purified from what indeed appear to be its real defects', and his forceful denial of the potential 'dislike or disgust' inherent in such language challenged the Wordsworthian conception of a natural rural poetics, and insisted on the inherent beauty of 'deficient'[12] idiomatic speech.

As we will see, reviewers followed Taylor's lead in noting the special circumstances of the poet's life; his class position became a key to a proper reading strategy, and an extraordinary ambivalence about the value of Clare's presumably vulgar language coloured most reviews. Provincialisms were alternately decried as coarse or vulgar, and celebrated as the source of startling poetic beauty. But, before turning to the reviews, it is important to remember that Wordsworth's ideas, on which Taylor drew, were still being contested, by Coleridge, and, more importantly for reviewers of the time, by Jeffrey. Coleridge was unwilling to accept claims of a greater authenticity for rustic speech, and, in chapter twenty-two of *Biographia Literaria*, characterised Wordsworth's use of colloquial speech in *Lyrical Ballads* as a weak 'ventriloquism',[13] and a failed poetic experiment. Even with philosophic reflection as part of the poetic process, Coleridge remained sceptical of the value of such works. Worse, he argued, was the predominance of Wordsworth's imitators, both poetic and theoretical. In chapter four, Coleridge bitterly complained:

But that a downright simpleness, under the affectation of simplicity, prosaic words in feeble metre, silly thoughts in childish phrases, and a preference of mean, degrading, or at best trivial associations and characters, should succeed in forming a school of imitators, a company of almost *religious* admirers, ... and that this bare and bald *counterfeit* of poetry, which is characterised as *below* criticism, should for nearly twenty years have well-nigh *engrossed* criticism, as the main, if not the only, *butt* of review, magazine, poem, and pamphlet;— this is indeed a matter of wonder. (p. 75)

This passage provides abundant evidence of the perceived influence of Wordsworth's poetics at the time of Clare's first publication, and the heated nature of the ensuing debate. Jeffrey was, of course, even more harsh in his estimations. Taylor went to some pains to rationalise Clare's idiosyncratic grammar and diction in response to the possibility of such attacks; he was especially sensitive to Jeffrey's antipathy towards affected 'lowliness', and wary of his cultural power as a critic. The aesthetic value of Clare's poetic vocabulary was at stake in these attacks, and therefore a careful counter-argument about the aptness of rural diction in Clare's poetry was required. The claim that such language was inherently 'deficient' could not go unanswered. Taylor's response certainly could be accused of arguing that the verse was '*below* criticism', in Coleridge's phrase, exempt owing to the author's class status. Taylor's constructed view of Clare as a 'natural' and necessarily naive poetic genius risked identifying him as one of Wordsworth's many 'simple' imitators, and, despite Taylor's apparent awareness of this risk, that view became widespread once the reviews appeared. According to Taylor's Introduction Clare was a genius, but one severely limited by the deprivations of his class. As a result, he was believed to be incapable of philosophic reflection, and that lack of reflection was partly converted into a poetic virtue both by Taylor, for strategic reasons, and by conservative critics suspicious of philosophical affectations. Taylor related that Clare had to record the poems immediately because 'He could not trust his memory, and therefore he wrote them down with a pencil on the spot, his hat serving him for a desk; and if it happened that he had no opportunity soon after of transcribing these imperfect memorials, he could seldom decypher them, or recover his first thoughts' (p. xv). In describing Clare as completely dependent on the moment of sensation, the power of his sensibility excited by nature, Taylor painted a portrait of a brilliant child for whom even the act of memory was a puzzle beyond his grasp, let alone the careful meditation required by a more philosophical poetics. Such then were the hazards of the critical terrain that Taylor negotiated in his Introduction, and the real effects of his efforts, for good and ill, were soon revealed by the reviewers of *Poems Descriptive of Rural Life and Scenery*.

Reviewing

As I have indicated, Taylor's preparation of the public conformed to pre-existing critical notions, and made Clare's class identity, his exceptional status as the 'peasant poet', integral to public consumption of his poems. The responses of reviews and magazines of different political stripes revealed how the meaning of Clare's peasant-ness shifted to meet specific pre-conceived political and cultural assumptions and expectations. Clare's unusual strength of sensibility, for example, was taken as evidence of dramatically different ideas about rural life and labour depending on the political orientation of the reviewer. While the reviews recapitulated most of Taylor's aesthetic leads, they drew varying cultural meanings from that material. Was Clare's genius evidence of the inherent rightness of rural relationships of power and patronage, or a challenge to class-bound social assumptions about the source of genius?

One of the most curious events surrounding the initial reception of *Poems Descriptive of Rural Life and Scenery* was the delayed reaction of one of Clare's patrons to radical elements in the poetry. This delay tells us much about the motivated reading strategies of various segments of Clare's audience. Lord Radstock, a conservative Evangelical landowner and naval hero, reacted angrily to what he called 'radical and ungrateful' sentiments in the very first poem in the collection, 'Helpstone'. The offending lines offered a succinct analysis of the effects of enclosure on Clare and those like him:

Accursed Wealth! o'er-bounding human laws,
Of every evil thou remain'st the cause:
Victims of want, those wretches such as me,
Too truly lay their wretchedness to thee:

Thou art the bar that keeps from being fed,
And thine our loss of labour and of bread;
Thou art the cause that levels every tree,
And woods bow down to clear a way for thee.[14]

Radstock became aware of these lines and demanded their removal from the third edition.[15] How could such sentiments have escaped notice? The answer may lie in the power patronage bestowed on the reader. Radstock had taken the decision to patronise Clare after *Poems Descriptive* had appeared, and apparently without reading the poems. He was, in fact, patronising an idea of what Clare might represent, and was shocked to discover his error after the fact. Various versions of this kind of self-confirming patronage, prepared for by Taylor, and obligatory to gentlemanly taste, permeated the reviews. The critics' power created blind spots as they attempted to reconfirm their own tastes and cultural values through the vehicle of Clare's poems.

The 'radical and ungrateful' lines from 'Helpstone' had a similar, spectral existence in many of the reviews. Perhaps simply because it was the first poem in the volume, it was almost always quoted, but Clare's dangerous piece of political analysis was never commented on. The conservative *British Critic* provides a good example. Their June 1820 review quoted three stanzas from 'Helpstone' in support of the view that 'the tendency of his [Clare's] book [was] moral'.[16] This abridged version of the poem contributed to this view. The radical passage on enclosure was as we have seen omitted. Coupled with the fact that Taylor had already edited out the final lines describing:

… when the Traveller uncertain roams
On lost roads leading every where but home,

before publication, the result was a poem that began with a conventional evocation of place,—'Hail, humble Helpstone' (p. 3)—moved through a catalogue of the natural beauty found in the place:

Where golden kingcups open'd into view;
Where silver daisies in profusion grew; (p. 7)

and concluded with a nostalgic hope that the speaker could return to this 'happy Eden' to end his days:

> And as reward for all my troubles past,
> Find one hope true—to die at home at last! (p. 11)

In short, the edited version of the poem that appeared in the review became a sentimental encomium on the natural 'delights' of the countryside, and of the peasant speaker's contentment in that scene. The fact that the poem was an elegy on the irrevocable loss of that landscape, a 'paradise lost' at the hands of the local 'improving' gentry, was replaced by moralising about rural pleasures. It is impossible to know whether the review was a deliberate attempt to constrain Clare's subversive potential through careful omission, or whether, like Lord Radstock, the reviewer's paternalistic assumptions about Clare's peasant identity blinded him to the 'radical and ungrateful' sentiments of the poem's political analysis. On the one hand, the reviewer's condescension towards Clare, prompted by Taylor's special pleading concerning the poet's circumstances, made it possible to read both for evidence of Wordsworthian natural genius and for confirmation of the critic's social superiority. The review deferred judgement because the poet's 'peculiar situation effectually disarm(ed) ... criticism', yet went on to claim that if any vulgar coinages, 'which cannot fail to offend every reader', managed 'to creep in', they could be set aside as the inevitable result of the poet's simplicity. The 'principal merit of the poems' *was* 'the circumstances of the writer'. Confirmed in his social power, and reading to locate a humble Arcadia, the reviewer, conceivably, could have missed the radicalism of the poem.

On the other hand, the brief note introducing a lengthy quotation from 'The Village Funeral' suggests that political anxieties were provoked in the writer of the *British Critic* review. Overall, he viewed the poem as 'commonplace', but for 'two stanzas which redeem it'. The redeeming stanzas describe the fate of two orphans who have just buried their father, and the quality of human compassion that they inspire moved the critic to pity despite his reservations. He stated that the lines were 'breathed, we fear, in too genuine a tone of feeling'. He had reason to 'fear' the 'genuine' tone of the stanzas because it exposed the hypocrisy of the institutions of charity that conservative critics supported, and the value of which they hoped to find confirmed in Clare's poems. The readers of the *British Critic*, conservative self-styled gentlemen like Lord Radstock, would have done well to be uncomfortable with the ungrateful candour of the stanzas:

Yon workhouse stands as their [the orphans'] asylum now
 The place where poverty demands to live
Where parish bounty scowls his scornful brow,
 And grudges the scant fare he's forc'd to give.

Oh may I die before I'm doom'd to seek
 That last resource of hope, but ill supplied;
To claim the humble pittance once a week,
 Which justice forces from disdainful pride!

These lines threatened conservative notions of altruism by exposing the self-motivated source of charity and its economic inadequacies. The workhouse was exposed as a horrific form of servitude rather than an expression of altruism, and wealthy landowners would not have found the spectacle of their unseemly psychological motives and hypocrisy suitable subjects for poetry. Despite this, the critic included the stanzas because of their affective power, thus trapping himself in a contradiction between his aesthetic response to the poem's emotional resonance and his search for confirmation of his own social values. The review ended by recuperating the social values the critic sought by quoting from 'To Religion', a poem where he could take 'pleasure, from its unaffected piety'.

Other conservative journals praised the poems in less conflicted terms. The reactionary *Antijacobin Review* enthused:

This little volume is the production of a second Burns; a poet in humble life, whose genius has burst through the fetters with which his situation had surrounded it; and astonished the neighbouring villages with the brilliancy of his song.[17]

The anonymous reviewer picked up the vocabulary of natural genius from Taylor's Introduction and re-presented it in class terms. Clare had risen above his station, but what made the poems praiseworthy was the ability of the critic to retain his position of authority over the poet. Genius could 'burst fetters' to a point, but the review itself represented a new social containment of the peasant poet. Conservative readers found comfort in the paternalism occasioned by making an exception for Clare, and by following a cultural version of the Wordsworthian dictum that rural speech should be 'purified of its defects'. The review quoted the final two sections of 'Helpstone', apparently oblivious to the radical analysis of the effects of wealth on the countryside in the previous sections, and ended by calling for greater care in avoiding vulgar diction in future poems. The poems were finally recommended to readers as instances of 'honest simplicity, and natural genius', and for their 'unaffected piety'. Clare was a 'discovery' and capable of improvement via the instruction of the critic in matters of taste.

More liberal publications were cautious in their praise. The *Monthly Review* recapitulated Wordsworth's Preface in refusing to grant Clare the status of a true poet:

> To attempt the sublimer provinces of song, a mind stored with the philosophic treasures of the past and with the wisdom and beauty of antiquity is requisite, as well as a heart that is alive to the sublimity of the highest feelings of our nature; but to achieve a description of the external beauty of the creation requires no knowledge that gazing will not give.[18]

The double bind implicit in Taylor's aesthetic claims strikes home here. Clare could never be a true poet because of the simple fact of his peasant identity. Lack of formal education made philosophic reflection impossible, and Clare was left to write in a lesser poetic mode.[19] The review ends by repeating this premise in an unflattering comparison with Burns. Clare was judged to possess 'but a small share of the acquirements of Burns, whose mind was well stored with much useful knowledge'. Given Clare's class-determined lack of access to sublimity, praise was limited to condescending liberal moralising:

> To extend judicious encouragement, however, to a man who has so laudably displayed the wish for advancement, and the powers and energies which distinguish the writer of these poems, is only an act of justice.

This plea amounts to little more than the aesthetic equivalent to Lord

Radstock's sense of charity.

Not all reviewers were willing to grant Clare charity. Deeply suspicious of the rhetoric of natural genius, the review in *The Guardian* dismissed Clare as 'simply a tolerable versifier' who had 'exhibited nothing of the spirit, feeling, or original views of genius'.[20] Rural subjects were ridiculed, and the reviewer called on Clare's patrons to ensure that Clare remained a peasant, 'the best preservative of his health, humility and happiness'. The equating of 'humility and happiness' underlines the ubiquity of the class judgements that dominated the reviews. J.G. Lockhart's reference to Clare in *Blackwood's Edinburgh Magazine* alluded to *The Guardian* review as the 'best view'[21] of the promotion of Clare. Lockhart, who admitted that he had 'never seen Clare's book', nonetheless dismissed it with the unsolicited advice that 'a respectable peasant is a much more comfortable man, and always will be so, than a mediocre poet'. This fantasy of happy peasants rather confirms the view of Lockhart as an alienated urbanite, and is notable only for the traces of class anxiety that it exhibits, and that found fuller expression in his notorious 'Cockney School' tirades.

The *Eclectic Review* alone resisted Taylor's efforts to shape the reception of the poems. All the other reviews either celebrated Clare's rise through his natural genius, took comfort in his depiction of the pastoral world, or warned against the hollowness of the rhetoric of genius. Either way, they responded directly to the terms of the aesthetic debate Taylor dictated. The reviewer[22] for the *Eclectic* resisted the association of Clare's peasant origins and natural genius. He adhered to a general Romantic definition of genius by quoting from Coleridge's *Biographia Literaria,* chapter four, to the effect that the 'most unequivocal mode of manifestation' of genius was 'so to represent familiar objects as to awaken the minds of others to a like healthy freshness of sensation concerning them'.[23] Coleridge was describing the essence of Wordsworth's genius in relation to the natural world, and this passage followed the warning against the vulgar imitators of Wordsworth's style. The reviewer in the *Eclectic* picked up on both the Wordsworthian aesthetics in the Introduction, and on Coleridge's suspicion of idealised rustic verse in *Biographia Literaria*. More importantly, he challenged the class determinants of Taylor's Introduction by appreciating the poet's gift of awakening fresh sensations on its own terms: '...there can be no hesitation in classing the Author of these poems, to whatsoever rank in society he should prove to belong, among the most genuine possessors of this dangerous gift'. I will take up the dangerousness of Clare's gift in a moment, but first I want to indicate how thoroughly this particular review resisted Taylor. The tone of apology that accompanied the defence of rural speech in the Introduction, and the range of attitudes towards it, from mild condescension to ridicule, of other reviews were replaced by a forthright statement of poetic value:

> Colloquialisms and provincialisms abound in his poems, and attest its substantial originality; but of the grosser vulgarity of affected expression, of all attempt at fine writing, he has steered most commendably clear.

This wonderful inversion of poetic values, citing poetic affectation not idiomatic speech as the source of vulgarity, exploded the class basis of aesthetic judgements of Clare's diction. The review completed the logic of this line of reasoning by asserting the genius of the verse independent of any reliance on making an exception because of Clare's class impoverishment:

> ...instead of thinking them [the poems] *very clever considering they are by a day labourer*, our readers agree with us in conceding to them a high degree of poetical merit quite independent of the circumstances of their Author.

The idea that it was a 'dangerous gift' to be able to provide fresh 'sensations' in relation to familiar objects suggests a political approach to understanding the power of poetic sympathy, Clare's strength of sensibility. The *Eclectic Review* printed the majority of 'Helpstone', including the radical stanza attacking enclosure that the other reviews quoted around. The workhouse passage from 'The Village Funeral' was also quoted. In neither instance was reference made to the explicit political resonances of the passages, but rather attention was called to the poet's power of 'feeling'. His sensibility, his sympathy for the inhabitants and objects of the countryside, was judged to be the essence of his poetic gift. It was made 'dangerous' by what it could show readers about their society and themselves. The response of Lord Radstock and conservative reviewers had been a wilful blindness to the social insights of Clare's 'dangerous gift'. They read in order to find self-confirmation, not to discover potentially dangerous new insights that might threaten their social complacency. That the *Eclectic Review* recognised and promoted the political implications of poetic genius became clear in the following year with a review of Clare's second volume, *The Village Minstrel*. In that review, the attack on enclosure in Clare's poems finally makes an appearance in the public discourse, as lines are quoted to illustrate:

> the Poet's indignant deprecation of that mistaken policy which has pushed the system of enclosure to so vexatious and ruinous an extent. Poets are not always sound political economists ... but it is our firm persuasion, that the changes deplored by Lubin [the poem's protagonist], have, in a large proportion of instances, been decidedly prejudicial.[24]

Clare's poem played a role in persuading the reviewer of the 'prejudicial' nature of enclosure by describing its effects:

> There once were lanes in nature's freedom dropt,
> There once were paths that every valley wound,—
> Inclosure came, and every path was stopt;
> Each tyrant fix'd his sign where paths were found,
> To hint a trespass now who cross'd the ground:
> Justice is made to speak as they command;
> The high road now must be each stinted bound:
> —Inclosure, thou'rt a curse upon the land,
> And tasteless was the wretch who thy existence plann'd.[25]

The specificity of Clare's descriptions of the effects of enclosure on the inhabitants of the countryside doubtless contributed to their power to persuade. The disruption of traditional rural patterns extended to the physical curtailment of liberty as the peasantry were confined to the 'bounds' of public roads. As if to make the point himself that politics and aesthetics were inseparable, Clare characterised this abuse of power ('justice' was a thing owned by tyrants) as 'tasteless'. The disfiguring of the landscape was an assault on beauty itself. In real and aesthetic terms, this destruction was precisely the social and physical force that conservative readers were loath to see in the world around them, or in Clare's poems, and in fact hoped to escape via their nostalgia for an ideal pastoral world.

The final question to address, then, is how did Clare resist the various efforts to 'enclose'[26] his poetry, aesthetically and politically. He reacted with fury at the idea of dropping the 'radical and ungrateful sentiments' from the third edition of *Poems Descriptive* in order to appease Radstock, but relented and allowed the change.[27] Despite resenting 'that canting way of being forcd to please', Clare and Taylor had little power to resist Lord Radstock whose threats to ruin Clare had to be taken seriously. After some initial bravado in which he declared they should 'remain obstinate',[28] Taylor adopted a more pragmatic line whereby they would rely on Lord Radstock's short memory and lazy reading habits. After all, it had apparently taken him two editions to notice the passage. Taylor promised: 'When the Follies of the Day are past with all the Fears they have engendered we can restore the Poems according to earlier Editions'.[29] This shift in Taylor's response caused him to be scorned by some of Clare's supporters at the time. Edward Drury, the Stamford bookseller who had brought Clare to Taylor's attention, quipped that Taylor was 'firm in council but weak in purpose & doing'.[30] Subsequent criticism has been equally harsh. John Lucas, for example, declares in a footnote that he is 'not trying to demonise Taylor',[31] yet his essay on 'Clare's Politics' consistently equates Taylor and Radstock. Lucas follows Johanne Clare in arguing that 'Taylor ... and Lord Radstock ... between them emasculated much of his [Clare's] early work' (p. 150), and suggests that the relationship between publisher and poet was antagonistic: 'Taylor always had the upper hand' (p. 158). While this last statement is doubtless true in a strictly business sense, its tone makes it sound as if Taylor habitually abused his power to Clare's disadvantage, a view that underplays the necessity of a pragmatic approach to publishing, and that inadvertently creates a false impression of Clare as a passive victim.

The real test of Clare's resistance to calls for self-censorship, and of Taylor's attitude towards the radical elements in the poems, came with the publication of Clare's next volume of poems, *The Village Minstrel*. Far from conforming to the political views and wishes of conservative patrons, the long title poem provided detailed realistic views of the happenings in village life during the immediate aftermath of the Napoleonic Wars. Disabled soldiers, homeless and unemployable, pass through the village and make their appearance in the poem. They and the gypsies that pass by appear with a harsh realism that makes them unassimilable to a conventional picturesque landscape. They would have represented jarring and undesirable elements, so far as Lord Radstock was concerned, and clearly violated Hugh Blair's foundational dictum that readers of pastoral should not be subjected to feelings of 'disgust' at the 'mean' employments of 'actual peasants'. Most significantly, attacks on enclosure continued to appear. Stanzas ninety through ninety-seven, in particular, denounced the effects of 'oppression's power'.[32] In Clare's view enclosure created a desert:

> There once were days, the woodman knows it well,
> When shades e'en echoed with the singing thrush;
> There once were hours, the ploughman's tale can tell,
> When morning's beauty wore its earliest blush,
> How woodlarks carol'd from each stumpy bush;
> Lubin himself [the poem's protagonist] has mark'd them soar and sing:
> The thorns are gone, the woodlark's song is hush,
> Spring more resembles winter now than spring,
> The shades are banish'd all—the birds have took to wing. (p. 49)

The destruction of the local landscape, witnessed by the peasant poet Lubin, saw the inherent value of nature betrayed. The outcome was an affront to the very rhythms of nature, spring resembled winter, and the loss was final. The destruction of 'the thorns' would have been a common sight; they would have been considered of no economic value, and were destroyed as the land was 'improved'. The conflict between the economic value of the landscape and its inherent and poetic value came to a head in these stanzas. The 'woodlark's song' was lost, and, as an inhabitant of this landscape, Clare's song was clearly threatened as well. His poetic gift was dependent on the existence of the natural variety of rural scenery, and he was unwilling to falsify the record of economic destruction in order to protect his patrons from discomfort. If they were implicated in this destruction they deserved their share of guilt. And, if they wanted to maintain a paternalistic relationship to this 'Child of Nature', they first must recognise the essential conflict between their economic and aesthetic interests. Clare had promised as long ago as 'Helpstone' that he could 'be content' within the existing relationships of power, provided they truly were benevolent rather than hypocritical and destructive.

Taylor did not attempt to censor this material even though it was certain to anger Lord Radstock. In fact, over time Taylor came to have little use for Radstock, and ceased being interested in appeasing him.[33] Instead, he used the Introduction to the volume to attempt to rationalise Clare's 'vehement' attachment to the objects 'in nature'.[34] He cautiously described the passage as 'some apparently discontented stanzas about the middle of the poem', and claimed that even if the stanzas truly (as opposed to 'apparently') were 'discontented' they should be excused as 'some of the most vigorous and beautiful ebullitions of true poesy that can be met with in our language' (pp. xix-xx). Their political content should be forgiven for the sake of their aesthetic value. This line of reasoning was disingenuous, to say the least, and Taylor constructed a more substantial defence to bolster the aesthetic argument. He appealed to readers' understanding and sympathy in judging Clare's vehemence: 'what allowance ought not to be made for the passionate regard of poor Clare for things which were the landmarks of his life, the depositories of almost all his joys?' (p. xx). The stanzas themselves were unequivocal in denouncing the immorality of enclosure on economic *and* aesthetic grounds, but Taylor buried the 'political economy' in a call for tolerance for the poet's child-like attachments. This was doubtless an astute reading of the psychology of conservative patronage and the public taste, but hardly true to the spirit of the poem. In order to support his construction of the innocent poet grieving over his lost objects of nature, Taylor included an excerpt from a letter from Clare decrying the threatened destruction of his favourite elm trees:[35]

> My two favourite elm trees at the back of the hut are condemned to die—it shocks me to relate it, but 'tis true. The savage who owns them thinks they have done their best, and now he wants to make use of the benefits he can get from selling them. O was this country Egypt, and was I but a caliph, the owner should lose his ears for his arrogant presumption; and the first wretch that buried his axe in their roots should hang on their branches as a terror to the rest. (pp. xx-xxi)

The violence of this outburst seems unlikely to have provided much comfort for any 'improving landlords' among readers, but Taylor included it precisely because Clare was unable to sustain the violent tone and the letter ended in utter deflation:

A second thought tells me I am a fool: were people all to feel as I do, the world could not be carried on,—a green would not be ploughed—a tree or bush would not be cut for firing or furniture, and every thing they found when boys would remain in that state till they died. This is my indisposition, and you will laugh at it. (p. xxi)

Taylor's intention, then, was to comfort conservative readers with the assurance that any 'apparently discontented' sentiments would be moderated by 'the reflection of a wiser head' (p. xx). Radical passages could be explained away as the products of child-like nostalgia. The 'Child of Nature' was finally granted the central poetic power of 'reflection' only as a means of undoing the affective force of his poetry. In fact, Clare's defence of his favourite elms proclaimed the conflict between the intrinsic value of nature, the value that he struggled to preserve in the poems, and the crass economic value of the 'benefits' to be gained from 'selling'. Taylor misrepresented Clare's resignation at his lack of power as the 'wiser head' reflecting on the earlier statements in the letter. The language of absolute power in the letter defined what Clare lacked. He was not a 'caliph', nor was this 'Egypt'. The violence of his temper marked the severity of his sense of powerlessness, and the collapse into a mood of deflation and assumed ridicule ('you will laugh at it') followed from the inability to effect any meaningful change to the exploitative status quo.

Clare's stubbornness in including accurate analyses of the effects of enclosure in his poems, despite the threat it posed to the continuation of his patronage, pointed to more than a fierce political independence under the most difficult of circumstances. His deep commitment to the inhabitants and natural objects of the landscape defined his poetic practice and his aesthetic beliefs. Despite Taylor's belated effort to attribute the power of reflection to Clare, in the form of sentimental nostalgia, the peasant poet deliberately resisted becoming a philosopher of nature. In order to ensure that poetic value remained in the objects of nature he represented, Clare refused to divert aesthetic power into the creation of the poet's philosophic mind. He would not sacrifice nature's intrinsic value in the service of his own poetic self-fashioning. The consistency and vehemence of this belief were evident whether the exploitation he decried was the economic force of enclosure, the act of destroying a tree, or the aesthetic conversion of the landscape into the self.

The aesthetic and political terms of Clare's patronage, and the reliance on them in the reviews, provide us with insight into the powerful cultural forces that surrounded Clare, and which attempted to define the meaning of his poetic gift. Clare's struggle to resist such apparently overwhelming forces throws light on his life-long feelings of isolation, and bears witness to the strength of his aesthetic and political convictions.

NOTES

The author wishes to acknowledge the generous support of the Social Sciences and Humanities Research Council of Canada during the research and writing of this essay.

1. 'Romanticism' is a vexed term, and the history of its use and development is outside the scope of this discussion. In the context of Wordsworth and Coleridge, critics have employed the term to refer to poetry that emphasises philosophical reflection in relation to the natural world. Romanticism of that kind develops from georgic taste, which shared a sense of the country as a place of calm restoration, by de-emphasising classical allusions to an ideal, bucolic golden age in favour of 'the language of real men'. The aesthetic value of rural speech became a crucial debate between Coleridge and Wordsworth, and the theory of Romanticism that followed from that debate placed special emphasis on the inwardness of the poet, the philosophical product of the poetry rather than its materials (nature, rural life and speech, etc.).

2. *Poems Descriptive of Rural Life and Scenery* (London: Taylor and Hessey, 1820, and Stamford: E. Drury), second edition, p. xiv.

3. Clare is in a long line of peasant poets taken up and promoted by the gentry. Such patronage was often competitive, as discriminating gentlemen vied with one another to discover and champion the next literary sensation. Writing about the conditions of the patronage extended to Stephen Duck, E.P. Thompson trenchantly commented: 'Patronage of this order is simply a form taken by the conspiracy of the polite against the poor'. See *The Thresher's Labour by Stephen Duck and The Woman's Labour by Mary Collier: Two Eighteenth-Century Poems*, ed. by E.P. Thompson and Marian Sugden (London: Merlin Press, 1989), p. iv.

4. *Lectures on Rhetoric and Belles Lettres*, 3 vols., 2nd edn. (London: W. Strachan and T. Cadell, 1785), vol. 2, pp. 114-36.
5. Clare had probably not read Blair's lecture before he composed the poems in *Poems Descriptive* and most of those in *The Village Minstrel*, but Blair's *Lectures* was among the first books given to him by his patron Lord Radstock in February 1820. He had read it by 1824, as entries in his Journal make clear. He employed Blair's terms, for example, in dismissing Pope's efforts at pastoral: 'the Pastorals are nick[n]amed so for daffodils breathing flutes beachen bowls silver crooks and purling brooks and such like everlasting sing song does not make pastorals' (Journal, 26 October 1824; *By Himself*, p. 189). The influence of Blair's lecture can be heard as an echo in Wordsworth's use of the word 'disgust' in his Preface, and in Coleridge's attack on Wordsworth's philosophical Pedlar.
6. See Clare's letter to Hessey of 10 July 1820 where he complains of 'false delicasy's seriousness', and the social presumption that demands that 'poor Dolly ... have her artless lamentations shut out', *Letters*, p. 83.
7. Jeffrey attacked Wordsworth's *The Excursion*, for example, because it confused the simplicity of the lower classes and philosophical pretension. He ridiculed the portrait of the Pedlar on precisely those grounds: 'A man who went selling flannel and pocket-handkerchiefs in this lofty diction, would soon frighten away all his customers' (*Edinburgh Review*, 24 (1814), pp. 1-30). Coleridge took a similar line in *Biographia Literaria* when he challenged Wordsworth's claims for the superiority of rural subject matter and diction.
8. See Harold Bloom, 'John Clare: The Wordsworthian Shadow' in *The Visionary Company: A Reading of English Romantic Poetry*, revised and enlarged edition (Ithaca and London: Cornell University Press, 1971).
9. *Lyrical Ballads and Other Poems*, eds. James Butler and Karen Green (London: Cornell University Press, 1992), pp. 744-5. All citations from the Preface are taken from this edition and will be noted in parentheses.
10. *Clare-Markham Sherwill*, 12 July 1820, and *Clare-John Taylor*, 6 December 1821; *Letters*, pp. 85-7 and 221.
11. Quoted in *Early Poems*, I, p. 158.
12. The *OED* definition of 'deficient' emphasises the condition of lack: 'Present in less than the proper quantity; not sufficient of force; wholly or partly wanting or lacking; insufficient, inadequate'. The examples of usage, however, indicate how fickle matters of taste are in determining the poetic qualities that the poet must have in sufficient quantity. The example closest in time (1856) to Clare's career is taken from Emerson's estimation of Hallam's poetic gifts: 'Hallam is uniformly polite, but with deficient sympathy'. This is a complete reversal of the notions of poetic 'deficiency' used to patronise Clare in the

previous thirty-five years.

13. *Biographia Literaria*, eds. James Engell and W. Jackson Bate (Princeton, NJ: Princeton University Press, 1983), II, p. 135.

14. *Poems Descriptive*, p. 9.

15. There has been some confusion in Clare studies concerning which printing of the book Radstock wanted cut. The third edition, from which he demanded the excision of offending lines, was the second printing, being the remainder of the second edition with pages 153 to 164 omitted. The third printing was the fourth edition and appeared the following year. Critics variously have referred to the third edition, the third printing and the fourth edition when identifying the book. I am grateful to Bob Heyes for this useful clarification.

16. *The British Critic* (June 1820), pp. 662-7. I have noted the original publication because the excerpts from the review in *Critical Heritage* do not include the texts of the poems or the note on 'The Village Funeral'.

17. *Antijacobin Review* (June 1820), pp. 348-53, reprinted in *Critical Heritage*, pp. 105-6. The phrase 'and astonished the neighbouring villages with the brilliancy of his song' contains considerable unintended irony. The comparison of Clare's poetry to birdsong followed the general pattern of condescension (the unconscious peasant), but birdsong was one of the natural beauties most under threat from the enclosing of land. Bird habitat disappeared as the countryside was torn up and reshaped. Clare was particularly sensitive to this loss, as witnessed by the stanza from 'The Village Minstrel' in which the 'woodlark's song is hush'. I discuss this stanza in detail later in the essay.

18. *Monthly Review* (March 1820), pp. 296-300, excerpted in *Critical Heritage*, pp. 73-4.

19. This critical view also follows Coleridge's reservations about Wordsworth's claims about rustic speech. See *Biographia Literaria*, ch. 17 (II, pp. 52-7).

20. *The Guardian* (28 May 1820), reprinted in *Critical Heritage*, pp. 100-101.

21. *Blackwood's Edinburgh Magazine* (June 1820), reprinted in *Critical Heritage*, pp. 102-3.

22. Mark Storey considers that the reviewer was almost certainly the poet Josiah Conder, who owned and edited the *Eclectic* from 1814-37. Comparison with Conder's identified prose of the period bears this contention out on both stylistic and cultural grounds. See *Critical Heritage*, pp. 7 and 202.

23. *Eclectic Review* (April 1820), pp. 327-40, reprinted in *Critical Heritage*, pp. 88-92.

24. *Eclectic Review* (January 1822), pp. 31-45, reprinted in *Critical Heritage*, pp. 168-71.

25. *The Village Minstrel, and Other Poems* (London: Taylor and Hessey, and Stamford: E. Drury, 1821), I, p. 50.

26. I use the word 'enclose' here because Clare's resistance to efforts to define him as a simple peasant followed from his resistance to the economic logic of agricultural enclosure. The calls to remove the vulgar language of the rustic from the poems, or the calls to be more philosophical, were efforts to 'enclose' Clare by pulling up his aesthetic weeds and 'improving' his figural landscape. These calls were the aesthetic equivalent to the calls of his conservative patrons for him to be 'content' in the new economic dispensation of the countryside.

27. *Clare-Taylor*, 16 May 1820, *Letters*, p. 69.

28. *Taylor-Clare*, 6 June 1820, *Letters*, p. 69.

29. *Taylor-Clare*, 27 September 1820, *Letters*, p. 98.

30. *Letters*, p. 98, note 2.

31. John Lucas, 'Clare's Politics', in Haughton, *Context*, p. 175.

32. *The Village Minstrel*, I, p. 51. As I have indicated above the explicit political critique in these stanzas was clear enough for the *Eclectic Review* to have referred to them as 'political economy'.

33. At first Taylor had been willing to take Radstock's views into account despite his own inclinations. In a letter to Clare of 12 February 1820, Taylor noted that: 'Lord Radstock wishes that this Poem & Dolly's Mistake shoᵈ both be omitted next Time—So have several other Persons—For my own part I am not so fastidious' (Eg. 2245, f. 37). Taylor was still concerned enough with sales to consider allowing Radstock to censor the bawdy poems from the first volume, as he makes clear later in the letter: 'When you write your Name in Blair's Sermons say "the Gift of Admiral Lord Radstock"—He has taken the greatest pains in promoting the Sale of the Poems—'. By early 1822, Taylor no longer cared about Radstock's opinions and the two had formed antagonistic camps vying to influence Clare. A letter to Clare from Mrs Emmerson (Radstock's friend and ally) of 5 February 1822 shows how far things had deteriorated, to the point where she and Radstock were attempting to persuade Clare to switch publishers for the third book: 'the conduct of certain persons [Taylor], has so thoroughly displeased Lord R. that he cannot take one step to serve you, without feeling he is at the same time serving those who have acted most unbecoming to him—this reflection necessarily abates the ardour of his Lordships exertions' (Eg. 2246, f. 18). Clare resisted these veiled threats, and given the unhappy publication history of *The Shepherd's Calendar*, perhaps to his detriment.

34. *The Village Minstrel*, I, p. xx.

35. The actual letter is lost, so Taylor's printed excerpt in the Introduction is the only record we have.

9. In Place and Out of Place: Clare in *The Midsummer Cushion*

Richard Cronin

It is a very old custom among villagers in summer time to stick a piece of greensward full of field flowers & place it as an ornament in their cottages which ornaments are called Midsummer Cushions

(Clare, headnote to *The Midsummer Cushion*, PMS A54)

There are, and have been for some years, two tendencies evident in the critics of John Clare. One group, led by John Barrell, celebrates Clare as a local poet. For them, Clare's poems are uniquely valuable because through their diction and their syntax they express a mode of perception that would otherwise remain unarticulated. In reading these poems, the argument runs, we are allowed to see the world as it appeared to a particular social group, the agricultural labourers, at a particularly interesting time, the period during which the agricultural industry underwent the process of capitalization, and from a particular place, the village of Helpston in Northamptonshire.[1] Associated with this group are all those critics, many of them, like Seamus Heaney and Tom Paulin, poets themselves, who value above all Clare's use of the language that Helpston gave him, all those words sticky as frog-spawn— 'soodling', 'sloomy', 'gulsh'd', 'crizzling', 'crumping'—that lend the objects in Clare's poems a palpability in comparison with which the natural world as represented by other poets can seem bleached, faded into an idea.[2] A second group of critics, as yet a smaller one,[3] seems anxious that Clare should be marketed by modern critics in a way that so unnervingly recalls the stratagem of his first publisher, John Taylor, who sold Clare's first volume of poems as the work of a peasant poet. For them, the crucial task is to establish John Clare's right to the place that he repeatedly claimed for himself, within the major tradition of English poetry, in 'the eternity of song' ('To a Poet').

Clare was, of course, as the title of the 1994 Clare conference held at the Nottingham Trent University reminds us, a 'self-taught poet', but it is worth pausing for a moment over that phrase. It is used to describe poets who had little or no formal education, and points therefore to a common biographical fact rather than to any shared quality in the poems written by those who have been so described. There is a sense, after all, in which all English poets of the modern period have been self-taught, there being no system of apprenticeship in literature of the kind that obtains in the fine arts. A contemporary of Clare's, who had himself been accused of lacking the education proper to a poet, insisted that 'every man whose soul is not a clod' might claim that title 'if he had loved / And been well nurtured in his mother tongue',[4] and if this is the education proper to a poet then Clare, like Keats, might claim to be rather well-educated, well-nurtured not only in his mother tongue but in its poetry. Byron and Shelley had access to classical literature and to the literature of a number of modern European languages, but I do not think that either had the wide and deep familiarity with English poetry from the sixteenth century to his own time that Clare could claim. When, in 1831, Taylor sent him Southey's selections of the British poets 'from Chaucer to Jonson', Clare was pleased to find Surrey, the two Fletchers and Wither represented, and especially pleased by Browne's *Britannia's Pastorals*, but he was disappointed by the volumes: 'where is Suckling & where is Herrick & twenty more that ought to have been there'.[5] It is the response of an unusually well-read man.

Clare read for pleasure, but he read, too, because he had since his early youth bound himself apprentice in the craft of poetry. It was at precisely the time of this letter, 1831, that Clare was compiling the manuscript that, though it remained unpublished until 1979, constitutes his most substantial single volume, *The Midsummer Cushion*, and the poems collected here are those of a man who has mastered his craft. Let me give three, brief examples, chosen almost at random. In the sonnet 'Field Thoughts' Clare praises, as he often does, wild flowers, which move him because their beauty is not produced by a gardener's care, and because they are tended by nothing 'But dews & sunshine & impartial rain...' (*Middle Period*, IV, p. 311). It is a quiet line raised into monumental finality by its single epithet, a technique that in English poetry is much more commonly associated with poets steeped in the classics than with poets in the self-taught tradition. Or take a couplet from 'Pleasures of Spring':

How beautiful the wind awakes and flings
Disordered graces o'er the face of things (ll. 321-2; *Middle Period*, III, p. 61)

As John Barrell, among others, notes, Clare was fond of invoking an aesthetics of disorder, but in this couplet what strikes is how gracefully the enjambment disorders the pentameter lines. Or take the final line of 'St Martins Eve', a rural idyll in the tradition of poems such as Burns's 'The Cotter's Saturday Night', but written in Spenserian stanzas. The poem closes as the revellers walk home: 'While every lanthorn flings long gleams along the snow'. Keats has very often been praised for his handling of the final alexandrine of the Spenserian stanza—'And the long carpets rose along the gusty floor'—but Clare finds a way to register in the sense of the line its metrical extension in a manner that makes Keats's effect seem in comparison a little studied.

The confident expertise so repeatedly evident in *The Midsummer Cushion* is on the face of it an uncomplicated good. The presiding pathos underlying Gray's *Elegy* is that Gray, the super-educated don, fastidiously literate in several languages, must himself step forward to tell the 'artless tale' of the rural poor, for the poor cannot adequately, in the 'uncouth rhymes' on the churchyard stones, memorialise their own lives. In the rural villages there are only those who might have been poets, Miltons who, for lack of education, must remain 'mute' and 'inglorious'. Clare, it might be said, by the mid-1820s had broken down the barrier that Gray mourns between the experience of the rural poor and the eloquence necessary to articulate it.[6] But Clare repeatedly indicates that, however heartening such a view might be, it fails to convince, for it may be that the experience of Gray's villagers is not simply hidden by their inability to articulate it, waiting to be revealed by someone like John Clare who had miraculously learned to master the arts of eloquence, but rather that theirs is an experience that is constituted by their inarticulacy, by their muteness, and therefore an experience that is falsified precisely by virtue of its being spoken.

The crucial matter for Clare is literacy. 'Both my parents was illiterate to the last degree', he writes, and goes on to catalogue his father's reading with unusual precision: the Bible, penny broadsheets, *Nixon's Prophecy, Mother Bunch's Fairy Tales,* and *Mother Shipton's Legacy* (*By Himself*, p. 2). It is an attentiveness that is reproduced in the poems, as when the 'Village

Doctress' pores over 'Culpeppers Herbal' and 'Westleys Physic', and on Sundays reads 'Bunyan's Pilgrim' or

> seeks her ancient prayer book wrapt with care
> In cotton covers lest her hands should soil
> The gilded back full loath is she to spoil
> A book of which her parents took such heed (ll. 192-5; *Middle Period*, III, p. 341)

The 'Cottager' has his prayer-book and Bunyan, too, and also Tusser's *Husbandry* and *The Death of Abel*.[7] The 'Shepherd', when he sits by his fire after work, sometimes 'takes up a book full of stories and songs', and in the sonnet 'A Awthorn Nook' the nook is occupied by a shepherd who 'on his elbow lolls to read / His slip of ballads bought at neighbouring fair'.[8] When Clare records a house like the 'Shepherd's Lodge' in the poem of that title, that is entirely without books, he pauses to ponder the fact. Its tenant is

> To books unknown he never knows
> What they to thinking minds supply
> & yet his simple knowledge shows
> Much wiser men might profit bye (ll. 103-6; *Middle Period*, III, p. 541)

Clare notes, then, the reading habits of his neighbours, but he also notes his own, not just in his autobiographical writings, as in the twice-narrated story of how his reading of Thomson's *Seasons* made him a poet,[9] or in his Journal, in which he planned to set down his 'opinion' of the books that he read, but in the poems themselves. In fact, Clare, more frequently than any of his contemporaries, more frequently even than Keats, presents himself in his poems as a reader, as a man who, when he returns home from a walk, is apt to 'reach down a poet [he] love[s] from the shelves', a copy of Thomson or Cowper ('The Holiday Walk'), who spends his evenings 'bending oer [his] knees', reading by the light of the fire, and, when he worked in the fields, would often wish for rain so that he might get back to his books ('Labours Leisure').[10] Clare is happy to confess, as Wordsworth would never have done, to feeling the excitements of bookishness, 'cutting open with heart beating speed' the leaves of a 'brother poets' long-sought volume ('The

Pleasures of Spring').[11] When he takes his walks, he takes a book with him, and if the scenery is 'delicious' enough to persuade him to 'shut & put the volume bye', it is a fact worth noting ('On Visiting a Favourite Place').[12] Readerly habits are dear to him, especially the habit of marking a passage by turning down the corner of a page. Reading out of doors some 'pocket poet' a plucked primrose serves 'Instead of doubling down to mark the place' ('The Pleasures of Spring'),[13] and the same habit gives Clare a metaphor to define his own poetic purpose:

How many pages of sweet natures book
Hath poesy doubled down as favoured things ('Nature')[14]

My first point is the obvious one: that Clare himself in his poems repeatedly acknowledges that, if he is an expert reader of the book of nature, then he owes that expertise in some part to his habitual reading in other books, and especially the books of his brother poets. My second point is that Clare's reading complicates his relationship both with the natural world that he describes and with the community with which he shared it; both with his landscape and with his neighbours. I will begin with the neighbours. Clare's lifelong love of Helpston did not prevent him either from feeling or on occasion from forcefully expressing his contempt for his fellow-villagers. He wrote to Taylor in 1822:

I live here among the ignorant like a lost man in fact like one whom the rest seems careless of having anything to do with—they hardly dare talk in my company for fear I shoud mention them in my writings & I find more pleasure in wandering the fields than in musing among my silent neighbours who are insensible to every thing but toiling & talking of it & that to no purpose (*Letters*, p. 230)

Once again, this is a disposition that informs the poems. In 'Pleasures of Spring' there is an entirely characteristic distinction between the 'man of taste', an accomplished naturalist who takes with him on his springtime walks a 'pocket poet of some favoured muse', and the 'Hind' who scans his Bible 'wrapt in baize to keep the covers clean' for texts appropriate to the season, and the poem is characteristic too in that Clare's evident identification of himself with the man of taste underwrites his—in this case fond—detachment from the 'Hind'. Even John Barrell notes this tendency, but he tends to discount it. For him, Clare's introduction into his poems of figures such as 'Hodge', 'the swain', and 'the hind' is evidence only of a lingering contamination by the conventions of eighteenth-century landscape poetry, and he chooses to stress rather all those other characteristics of Clare's poetry that identify him with rather than detach him from his community: the use of dialect words, of a grammar of speech rather than of writing, the refusal to place the objects in his poems within any framing hierarchy.[15] But it seems fairer to accept that Clare's poems are not characterised by one or other of these habits, but by both, and to accept, too, that they are contradictory.

Clare will sometimes claim that poetry has an existence independent of language, so that the title of poet might justly be claimed by the illiterate, and even by the inarticulate:

> True poesy is not in words
> But images that thoughts express
> ('Pastoral Poesy', ll. 1-2, *Middle Period*, III, pp. 581-4)

The image, unlike the word, is common to all, available even to the 'simplest'. In the same poem Clare suggests that poetry 'sings & whistles' before it ever 'talks aloud' (ll. 57-8, p. 583). He is haunted here by a dream that Keats and Shelley also entertained, that a poem might be as natural, as untaught and unpremeditated, as birdsong, but for Clare the thought has an urgency not evident in his contemporaries. It prompts him in 'The Progress of Ryhme' to write poetry not about, but out of the nightingale's song:

> 'Wew-wew wew-wew chur-chur chur-chur
> 'Woo-it woo-it'—could this be her
> 'Tee-rew tee-rew tee-rew tee-rew
> 'Chew-rit chew-rit'—& ever new
> 'Will-will will-will grig-grig grig-grig'
> (ll. 251-5; *Middle Period*, III, pp. 492-503, p. 500)

This looks like a proto-modernist experiment, but it expresses a deep nostalgia for a lost time when the language of poetry was uncontaminated by the social and educational distinctions from which our ordinary language cannot be disentangled. But even in these lines Clare cannot fully assimilate language to birdsong, and in other moods he is willing to entertain the notion that for a poet to aspire to a language that evaporates, leaving no barrier between the reader and the natural world it represents, is to pursue an impossible dream. It may be, Clare sometimes recognises, that language, and in particular writing, cannot simply record the natural world, for to know a language, and to be able to read and write, is to have acquired a knowledge that informs every act of perception by which the natural world is known. Clare twice describes youngsters watching skeins of wild geese. In 'Schoolboys in Winter' the boys are 'Watching the letters that their journeys make' (*Early Poems*, II, p. 586, l. 5). The thought is expanded in 'March' in *The Shepherd's Calendar*, when the shepherd boy:

> marks the figurd forms in which they flye
> And pausing follows wi a wondering eye
> Likening their curious march in curves or rows
> To every letter which his memory knows (ll. 109-12; *Middle Period*, I,
> p. 42)

The flight of geese becomes a test case for Clare, marking his sense of how literacy cannot simply allow one to record pre-existing perceptions, because a knowledge of reading and writing informs the perception itself.[16] Yellowhammers' eggs prompt the same thought. In the sonnet sequence, 'A Walk', a cowboy triumphantly carries off a nest, excited by the mysteriously potent writing on the eggs, and in 'The Yellowhammers Nest' the 'pen-scribbled' eggs prompt a more literate observer to think of the 'scrawls' as 'natures poesy & pastoral spells'.[17] The conclusion is clear: that when the hind and the man of taste look into a yellowhammer's nest they do not see the same eggs, and not even the cowboy sees the eggs as a member of a pre-literate culture would do. And a further conclusion follows. Clare was not only socially isolated in his village by his fame as a poet. His ability to articulate his world of itself rendered the world in which he lived crucially different from the world that his neighbours inhabited, and the more Clare developed his craft the more different the two worlds became.

Clare found, as had Robert Bloomfield, the poet with whom he most closely identified, that the role of the peasant poet was a lonely one, a role that in itself served to isolate the poet from the communal village life that he celebrated.[18] Like Bloomfield, Clare found himself occupying a position neither within the world of the village, nor within the literary world that both men associated with London, but somewhere between the two, at a remove equally from literary society and the community of the village. Clare was a greater poet than Bloomfield because he did not simply suffer this predicament, rather he allowed it to inform a substantial group of poems, which, for that reason, represent Clare's greatest achievement.

Clare, as Tom Paulin remarks, is 'both the poet of place and displacement',[19] and he is at his best when he is both at once. This is most obviously the case in the most widely discussed group of poems that Clare wrote, the poems named by Johanne Clare the 'enclosure elegies'.[20] Inevitably, and properly, the bulk of commentary on these poems has been historical and political in its bent, but it is worth remarking that contemplating the enclosed landscape of Helpston brought together for Clare with peculiar intensity the two contradictory emotions the coincidence of which seems the condition of his finest poetry. First, there is the object intimately known and deeply loved, and then there is that same object withdrawn from him, become blankly unfamiliar. Clare is, of course, pre-eminently the poet of familiar things, but he is also a poet who counts among the most potent items in his vocabulary the word 'strange'. It is the object at once familiar and strange that most excites him, and the enclosed landscape of Helpston is for him the most extreme example of such an object. This will seem a chilling remark to those, like E.P. Thompson, who prize Clare because he 'conveys with extraordinary sensitivity the ways in which the psychic landscape of the village was savagely transformed by the enclosure of commons and open fields',[21] but I want for the moment to incur the risk of that response, and even to increase it. After all, Clare's best critics have themselves been apt to treat his hostility to enclosure as a metaphor—John Lucas, for example:

> The hundred years between 1750 and 1850 is the century of dictionaries, of grammatical rules, and of the standardizing of pronunciation. As I have elsewhere remarked this is, in short, the period when language is being enclosed.[22]

For Lucas, Clare's hostility to orthographic and grammatical conventions, and to 'that awkward squad of pointings called commas colons semicolons' (*Letters*, p. 421) is of a piece with his hostility to the enclosure of the open fields of Helpston, and in both cases it is a hostility that marks Clare's solidarity with the ordinary villagers, unlanded and uneducated. But the metaphor opens more complex possibilities. The century that Lucas nominates is, after all, also the century in which the laws of copyright were gradually formulated, in which published writings were, to extend the metaphor, enclosed. Clare's father who 'could sing or recite above a hundred' ballads (*By Himself*, p. 2) lived in an unenclosed literary landscape, but Clare, as his troubled relations with Edward Drury, Taylor and Hessey indicate, tried staunchly, if with little success, to establish his own title to his poems.[23] For Clare's father, ballads and songs were the property not of an individual but of the community. His skill as a ballad-singer earned him social prestige, not an income. But, for his son, literature, like the enclosed landscape of Helpston, had undergone the process of capitalization. Edward Drury put the matter bluntly:

My view of these poems is to consider them as wares that I have bought which will find a market in the great city. I want a broker or a partner to whom I can consign or share the articles I receive from the manufacturer...[24]

Clare often expressed his contempt for the notion that the value of poetry might be determined by market forces,[25] but he could not afford to ignore in practice the new status of poetry as a market commodity.

Clare, then, was at once an agricultural labourer and a manufacturer of wares that found their market in 'the great city', and those two, scarcely consistent roles produced the complex position out of which Clare's poems are written. In the great poem that records his removal from Helpston to Northborough, 'The Flitting', he writes:

I sit me in my corner chair
That seems to feel itself from home
(ll. 17-18; *Middle Period*, III, pp. 479-89, p. 480)

The chair is an old possession, its contours and Clare's frame comfortably
adapted one to the other by the habit of long years, but it becomes for Clare
a poetically charged object at the moment when a disconcerting strangeness
is superimposed on its familiarity, when it feels itself 'from home', 'at loss',
'ill at ease'.[26] It is at this moment that it becomes the appropriate chair on
which to imagine Clare sitting as he writes his strongest poems.

As almost all his readers have noticed, Clare never writes better than
when he writes about birds, and in particular about bird-nests. Clare claims:

I found the poems in the fields
And only wrote them down
('Sighing for Retirement', *Later Poems*, I, pp. 19-20, ll. 15-16)

He found the poems, then, as he took his daily walks, in precisely the same
way that he found the bird-nests, the discovery of which these poems record,
and the poems, Clare must want us to notice, are like the nests, woven together
from humble natural materials, and like the eggs that the nests contain they
own a fresh perfection of form that delights us when we come across them.
These are, then, amongst Clare's most natural poems, but they are also
amongst his most literary, for it is in writing these poems that Clare most
fully articulates his sense of his own distinctive place amongst the poets of
the Romantic period. He begins his sonnet 'The Wren' by addressing them:

Why is the cuckoos melody preferred
& nightingales rich song so fondly praised
In poets ryhmes Is there no other bird (ll. 1-3; *Middle Period*, IV, p. 164)

His first response here is to point to the thin selection of birds that do service
in the poems of his contemporaries—Wordsworth's cuckoo, the skylark that
Wordsworth shares with Shelley, and the nightingales of Coleridge and
Keats—and respond with a flock of poems that mocks, in the very variety of
birds celebrated, the meagreness of the symbolic imagination.[27]

The selection of British birds that the Romantic poets make is thin, but it
is not arbitrary. They choose birds that can be heard without being seen: the
cuckoo hidden in the leaves, the nightingale lost in the gathering gloom, and
the skylark that sings from a height at which, as Shelley puts it, one 'feels'

rather than 'sees' its presence; and in doing so they celebrate the possibility that poetry might free itself from the merely temporal circumstances, the 'weariness, the fever, and the fret', out of which it was produced. Just as the cuckoo's invisibility renders it for Wordsworth not a bird but simply a 'wandering voice', so poetry is offered as a 'mystery' through which the constraints of earthly life may be transcended, in which it is possible to leave behind all the limiting material weight of ordinary existence in order to experience what Shelley calls 'unbodied joy'. Even mortality itself may, in this view of things, be transcended by the song of the bird or the art of the poet: 'Thou wast not born for death, Immortal Bird!'

Clare is characteristically hostile to such claims. For him, the action of even the simplest of flowers, the daisy, has more power to withstand time than the poet ('The Eternity of Nature'). But it is in his poems on birds and bird-nests that Clare most fully adumbrates his own dissenting position. His first and crucial tactic is his refusal to listen contentedly to the song of an unseen bird. The music of the nightingale prompts Clare to go 'Creeping on hands and knees through matted thorns' until he finds a spot from which he can watch the nightingale as it sings, and 'marvel that so famed a bird / Should have no better dress than russet brown' ('The Nightingale's Nest').[28] Clare is willing to agree with his contemporaries that birds may be 'poet-like' ('The Yellow Hammer's Nest'),[29] but poets, in Clare's view of things, are not released from their bodies by their music any more than the nightingale is freed from its russet brown feathers. Whatever Keats might have thought, the nightingale is not 'viewless': it is just that he did not know where to look for it, or did not look hard enough. Clare's insistence on finding and describing the birds' nests works still more strongly to ground song in the material facts of life: the need for food and shelter, and the over-riding obligation to feed and to protect one's offspring. When Clare inspects a nest with that delighted exactitude of his, noting how the pettichap builds its nest from 'small bits of hay / Pluckt from the old propt-haystacks pleachy brow' and 'withered leaves' that 'from the snub-oak dotterel yearly falls / & in the old hedge-bottom rot away', fashioning the materials into a shape like an 'oven', lining it with 'feathers warm as silken stole', and contriving a 'snug entrance... Scarcely admitting e'en two fingers in', he is doing more than paying the natural world the tribute of his rapt attention.[30] In such passages he is making his own eloquent plea against an aesthetics of transcendence. He works out in these poems a view of his own craft in terms of which the more exalted claims of his contemporaries appear childish, like the boys who think that if they could fly so high as a skylark they would build their dwellings 'on nothing but a passing cloud', and live there

> As free from danger as the heavens are free
> From pain & toil—there would they build & be
> & sail about the world to scenes unheard
> Of & unseen ('The Sky Lark', *Middle Period*, III, pp. 523-5)

But the lark itself rests content with its 'low nest', built amongst 'the russet clods' and hidden in the corn.

Song, as Clare well knew, offers no magical escape from a world of 'pain and toil', and these poems quietly rebuke any such claim. But they do more. By repeatedly tracing the song-bird to its nest, Clare articulates his recognition of the intimate connection between his poetry and his village, between his song and the material conditions of his life. Hence, in this group of poems Clare might be thought to reconcile the apparent contradictions that I began by addressing. He appears in them as a poet aware of, and responsive to, the work of his peers, and yet a poet fully conscious of his own distinctive place amongst them, and thus more than able to sustain the modest claim that he makes in 'The Progress of Ryhme': 'My harp though simple was my own'.[31] And he also appears in these poems as a countryman, and as a writer whose authority is grounded in his intimate familiarity with a locality; with its language and with its landscape. To refuse either of these aspects of Clare's poetry is, it might be thought, to make the mistake that Clare seems to imply was too often made by his fellow-poets: it is to suppose that the bird might be separated from its nest. Clare was both a poet and a man of Helpston, and in him these two identities were inseparable.

This is a heartening view, but for all that it remains unconvincing. Its defectiveness is best indicated by pointing to another characteristic of this group of poems. Clare repeatedly represents the boys of Helpston, himself among them in his remembered boyhood, as pathologically addicted to bird's-nesting. The cowboy singing in triumph as he carries off in his hat his trophy, the 'stubbly nest' of a yellowhammer in 'A Walk', is not monstrous, but at most a case of arrested development.[32] Schoolboys, Clare tells us in the sonnet

'Sedge Birds Nest', are 'In robbing birds & cunning deeply skilled'.[33] All summer long they patrol the fields 'In their bird's-nesting rounds' ('The Landrail'), and a nest, once seen, is safe from them only if their approach to it is barred by an enraged bull ('The Wild Bull'), or if the climb to the nest is so difficult that 'down they sluther' before they have reached it ('The Raven's Nest').[34] But it is ground-nesting birds that most move Clare; birds such as the lark, the fern owl, the peewit or the pettichap:

> Its nest close by the rut gulled waggon road
> & on the almost bare foot-trodden ground
> > ('The Pettichaps Nest', *Middle Period*, III, pp. 517-19, ll. 3-4)

He is affected by the apparent vulnerability of these nests, that somehow survive though 'horses trample past them twenty times a day', and that remain even though built on open ground so hard to see that

> > you and I
> Had surely passed it on our walk today
> Had chance not led us to it (ll. 9-11)

In the sonnet, 'The Meadow Hay' Clare represents himself as just such a bird, stretched in 'the new mown swath' only 'a minute from the path', and humming a song which prompts a passer-by to pause wonderingly as he passes, and then move on,

> Unthinking that an idle rhymester lies
> Buried in the sweet grass
> > (*Middle Period*, IV, p. 253, ll. 7-8)

It is a pleasantly relaxed sonnet, lacking the tense alertness that characterises Clare's nesting birds and his own best poems, and it is the tension that offers the strongest indication that he and the birds share the same landscape, a landscape intimately known, and a landscape to which they are supremely adjusted, and yet nevertheless a landscape in which both Clare and the birds remain vulnerable, and under threat.

My point in the end is a simple and a sad one. It is not possible to understand Clare as an English poet amongst other English poets, distinguished from them only by a knowledge of the English countryside that they could not match, and neither is it possible to understand him as a villager amongst his fellow villagers, remarkable amongst his neighbours only in that he, unlike them, was able to articulate their common experience. Clare on occasion strikes each of these attitudes. He may sometimes claim a place in the literary community, as when he begins a sonnet to an admired fellow writer, 'Friend Lamb', and, rather more often, he may claim a place in the village community, as one of the 'merry folks' 'circling round the fire' ('St Martins Eve'). But his true place, and the place from which he writes his most compelling poems, is neither of these, but an uncomfortable position in which familiarity and estrangement coincide, a place in which, as Clare puts it in 'I Am',

Even the dearest that I love the best
Are strange—nay rather stranger than the rest

NOTES

1. See Barrell, *The Idea of Landscape and the Sense of Place, 1730-1840: An Approach to the Poetry of John Clare* (London: Cambridge University Press, 1972). Amongst those in broad agreement with him is John Lucas in his *John Clare* (Plymouth: Northcote House, 1994), though Lucas may be more properly placed in between the two groups of critics that I distinguish.
2. Seamus Heaney, 'John Clare's Prog', in his *The Redress of Poetry* (London: Faber, 1995), pp. 63-82; Tom Paulin, 'John Clare in Babylon' in his *Minotaur: Poetry and the Nation State* (London: Faber, 1992), pp. 47-55.
3. See in particular Kelsey Thornton, 'The Complexity of John Clare' in *John Clare: A Bicentenary Celebration*, ed. by Richard Foulkes (Northampton: University of Leicester, Department of Adult Education, 1994), pp. 41-56; Paul Chirico, 'Writing Misreadings: Clare and the Real World' in *The Independent Spirit: John Clare and the Self-Taught Tradition*, ed. by John Goodridge (Helpston: The John Clare Society and The Margaret Grainger Memorial Trust, 1994), pp. 125-38; and Eric Robinson, 'John Clare's Learning', *JCSJ*, 7 (July 1988), 10-25.
4. John Keats, 'The Fall of Hyperion', ll. 11-15.
5. *Letters*, p. 550. For Clare's own collection of books, see David Powell's

Catalogue of the John Clare Collection in the Northampton Public Library (Northampton: Northampton Public Library, 1964), pp. 23-34.

6. On the relation between Clare's poems and Gray's 'Elegy', see R.J. Ellis, '"Plodding Plowmen": Issues of Labour and Literacy in Gray's "Elegy"', in *The Independent Spirit*, pp. 27-43; John Goodridge, '"Three cheers for mute ingloriousness!": Gray's *Elegy* in the poetry of John Clare', *Critical Survey*, 11, no. 3 (2000), 11-20.

7. *Middle Period*, III, pp. 414-18.

8. *Middle Period*, IV, pp. 138-9, 309.

9. *By Himself*, pp. 10-11, and Mark Storey, 'Edward Drury's "Memoir" of John Clare', *JCSJ*, 9 (1992), 15.

10. *Middle Period*, III, p. 397; IV, p. 331.

11. *Middle Period*, III, pp. 48-68 (ll. 27-9, p. 50).

12. *Middle Period*, III, pp. 561-5 (l. 68, p. 563).

13. *Middle Period*, III, pp. 48-68 (l. 295, p. 60).

14. *Middle Period*, IV, p. 163 (ll. 1-2).

15. John Barrell argues powerfully that Clare's growing maturity as a poet is evidenced by his becoming 'more able to emancipate himself from the influence of Goldsmith, and to discover a language of his own' (p. 120). Similarly, for John Lucas, such expressions are merely 'linguistic traps', *John Clare*, p. 46.

16. I am indebted to Paul Chirico's discussion of this passage in his 'Writing Misreadings: Clare and the Real World', in *The Independent Spirit*, pp. 125-38. Clare may well be recalling the story of Palamedes, who is reputed to have invented the alphabet when watching the flight of a flock of cranes, which suggested to him the possibility of letters.

17. *Middle Period*, IV, pp. 311-14 (pp. 313-14, ll. 62-70); *Middle Period*, III, pp. 515-17 (p. 516, ll. 13-15).

18. On the relationship between the two poets, see John Lucas, 'Bloomfield and Clare' in *The Independent Spirit,* pp. 55-68.

19. Tom Paulin, 'John Clare: A Bicentennial Celebration', in Foulkes, *John Clare: A Bicentenary Celebration*, pp. 69-78 (p. 74).

20. Johanne Clare, *John Clare and the Bounds of Circumstance* (Kingston and Montreal: McGill-Queen's University Press, 1987).

21. E.P. Thompson, [Bicentenary Thoughts], *JCSJ*, 12 (1993), 31.

22. John Lucas, 'Clare's Politics' in Haughton, *Context*, p. 211.

23. Drury's relationship with Clare is described by Edward Storey in *A Right to Song: The Life of John Clare* (London: Methuen, 1982), especially pp. 121-31. Clare's publishers, Taylor and Hessey, particularly Taylor who edited Clare's first three books, have been much maligned by Clare's admirers for their treatment of him. They are ably and in many ways persuasively defended

by Zachary Leader in his *Revision and Romantic Authorship* (Oxford: Clarendon Press, 1996), pp. 206-61.

24. Quoted in Storey, *A Right to Song*, p. 128.

25. Most movingly perhaps in the triple sonnet, 'To the Memory of Bloomfield', *Middle Period*, IV, pp. 181-4.

26. The first two phrases are from 'The Flitting', ll. 18, 27, the third from 'The Mores', l. 50; *Middle Period*, III, pp. 479-89 (pp. 479, 480); II, pp. 347-50 (p. 349).

27. Amongst the birds celebrated by Clare are the blackcap, the bumbarrel, chiff-chaff, crow, fern-owl, firetail, hedge-sparrow, heron, kingfisher, landrail, lark, missel thrush, moorhen, nightingale, nuthatch, peewit, pettichap, quail, raven, redcap, reed-bird, robin, sand-martin, snipe, swallow, wagtail, woodpecker, wryneck and yellowhammer. Many of the bird poems are collected in John Clare, *Bird Poems,* introduced by Peter Levi (London: The Folio Society, 1980), and *John Clare's Birds*, ed. by Eric Robinson and Richard Fitter (Oxford: Oxford University Press, 1982). Wordsworth is more various than the other poets in his bird observations, and he, like Clare, on occasion, finds their nests. See, for example, his 'A Wren's Nest'.

28. *Middle Period*, III, pp. 456-61 (ll. 13, 20-1, p. 457).

29. *Middle Period*, III, pp. 515-17 (l. 17, p. 516).

30. 'The Pettichaps Nest', *Middle Period*, III, pp. 517-19 (ll. 14-21, p. 518).

31. *Middle Period*, III, pp. 492-503 (l. 135, p. 496).

32. *Middle Period*, IV, pp. 311-14 (ll. 63-5, p. 313).

33. *Middle Period*, IV, p. 153, l. 6.

34. *Middle Period*, III, pp. 553-4, 520-3, 559-61 (l. 9, p. 560).

10. Of Birds and Bards: Clare and His Romantic Contemporaries

P.M.S. Dawson

My point of departure is provided by some interesting remarks by David Constantine, in an essay on Clare's descriptive poetry. Constantine is concerned with certain ethical issues that he sees as involved in the attitude of Romantic writers to the natural world:

> At the core of Romanticism, as its glory and its curse, is the revolutionary re-assessment of how the mind works, 'the Copernican revolution in epistemology': that the mind functions not like a mirror but like a lamp; that all perception is unavoidably subjective; that we see not *data* but *facta*, things made in part by us, their natural integrity unavoidably interfered with by our imaginative minds. This establishes a frightful series: subjectivity, egocentricity, solipsism. We project ourselves upon our surroundings, inflict ourselves on innocent Nature, impose our sense upon an indifferent reality...
>
> Imposition of the self upon landscape may be thought of as a logical and fateful extension of that anthropocentrism established theologically in Genesis: 'And God said, Let us make man in our image, after our likeness: and let them have dominion over the fish of the sea, and over the fowl of the air, and over the cattle, and over all the earth, and over every creeping thing that creepeth upon the earth.' The Pathetic Fallacy is an equivalent in the imaginative life of the subjugation and exploitation represented by Enclosure. Subdue the earth, have dominion over it. Perceive all things in your own image.[1]

Constantine's account of Clare sets him against this 'Romantic' attitude and involves a defence of Clare against criticisms of him made by contemporaries who applied 'Romantic' criteria to his work:

> It was, and perhaps still is, a common criticism of Clare's poems that 'they abound too much in mere description and are deficient in

Sentiment and Feeling and Human Interest'. What makes poems more or less interesting, by that standard, is the degree to which the natural world has been exploited for the expression of personal life. The more anthropocentric, the better. I certainly don't deny that such self-interest is perfectly natural and that much great poetry gets written on the axiom that the proper study of mankind is me. But Clare is most himself, and most moving, when his own 'mere complexities' are subsumed in one steady feeling for the landscape before him: love. It is both a humility and a heroism to manage to override the demands of an unhappy self with admiration of beauty. (p. 194)

There are some difficulties with the view that Constantine expresses, not least the fact that having made us sensitive to issues of domination and exploitation he is himself open to the charge that he is exploiting Clare as a positive counter-example to attitudes about which he has, to say the least, reservations (just as I am exploiting his remarks for my own purposes). His account of these attitudes also raises problems. His main intention is to contrast Clare's characteristic poetry with that of his famous Romantic contemporaries, but the characteristics that he locates are hardly specifically Romantic, as can be seen when he cites Genesis and notes that contemporary criticisms of Clare may still be current today, and when he remarks that 'Clare's eighteenth-century predecessors' also considered 'the natural world at their disposal' (p. 198). For all that, one cannot help feeling that he has indeed pointed to a significant problematic that is central to Romanticism—the relationship between the mind and the world—and one that is very relevant to our understanding and evaluation of Clare's poetry. To know what Clare is we must appreciate that in some significant sense he is not (or not always) a Romantic poet. The weakness that I find most salient in Constantine's account is that he sees the relationship between Clare and the values and practice of Romanticism as one simply of difference, which allows him to defend Clare against a Romantically inflected critique, but does not allow him to recognise that Clare himself may have been perfectly well aware of the difference and capable of offering his own critique of Romanticism.[2] Constantine offers us the 'naive' Clare to set against his 'sentimental' contemporaries, to use terms from Schiller that have been applied to Clare by Juliet Sychrava.[3] In this essay I shall argue that not only was Clare commendably free of certain potentially dominating and exploitative attitudes to the natural world which can not unfairly be ascribed to Romanticism, but that he also had a critical but sympathetic understanding of them that can be traced in some of his best poetry.

For the purposes of this essay I shall focus primarily on Clare's knowledge of and attitude to Keats—and Keats's attitude to Clare. Their mutual if rather wary interest in each other is at least partly explained by the fact that they shared a publisher. Clare sent his 'sincere Respects' to Keats via John Taylor with the message that 'I like his first vol of Poems much'.[4] He also knew *Endymion*, commenting, again to Taylor, 'think as you will I begin to like it much' (*Letters*, p. 51). Clare received complimentary copies of Keats's poems from his publishers, and there survive some notes that he wrote on the 1820 volume, consisting of extracts underlining expressions that struck him.[5] Clare's admiration and sympathy for Keats extended to an elegiac sonnet, printed in *The Village Minstrel*.[6] But Clare's strengths and Keats's were not the same, and Clare's response to Keats includes a critical component. He produced a brief fragment on his brother poet, possibly intended for eventual publication, and probably prompted by Keats's 1820 volume:

He keeps up a constant alusion or illusion to the grecian mythology & there I cannot follow—yet when [he] speaks of woods Driads & Fauns & Satires are sure to follow & the brook looks alone without her naiads to his mind yet the frequency of such classical accompaniments make it wearisome to the reader where behind every rose bush he looks for a venus & under every laurel a thrumming appollo—In spite of all this his descriptions of senery are often very fine but as it is the case with other inhabitants of great cities he often described nature as she appeared to his fancies & not as he would have described her had he witnessed the things he describes—thus it is he has often undergone the stigma of Cocknyism & what appears as beauties in the eyes of a pent up citizen are looked upon as consciets by those who live in the country—these are merely errors but even here they are the errors of poetry—he is often mystical but such poetical liscences have been looked on as beauties in Wordsworth & Shelley & in Keats they may be forgiven[7]

The issue of Clare's attitude to Keats's classical 'alusion or illusion' is a large one that cannot be explored here.[8] His claim that Keats is often 'mystical' is of particular interest, particularly as he associated him with Wordsworth and Shelley in this respect. 'Mystical' and 'mystery' are the imprecise but revealing terms that Clare characteristically uses of his Romantic contemporaries, with, one suspects, reference to precisely their most 'Romantic' characteristics, almost as if, in the absence of 'Romantic' as a critical term at the time he had coined 'mystical' to serve the same function.[9]

The points at issue between Clare and Keats can be illuminated by considering what the latter said of the former, brief though it is. The critical verdict quoted by Constantine above, to the effect that Clare's poems 'abound too much in mere description and are deficient in Sentiment and Feeling and Human Interest', was actually made by Hessey, Taylor's publishing partner, but it is little more than an amplified statement of the pithier judgment of Keats that Taylor passed on to Clare. 'When I read Solitude to him', Taylor reported on 16 March 1820, 'he observed that the Description too much prevailed over the Sentiment', going on to give his own rather cryptic view that this was 'a good Fault'—perhaps Taylor had no desire to see Clare attempt to imitate Keats.[10] Keats's view is amplified in a later letter from Taylor:

If he [Keats] recovers his Strength he will write to you. I think he wishes to say to you that your Images from Nature are too much introduced without being called for by a particular Sentiment.—To meddle with this Subject is bad policy when I am in haste, but perhaps you conceive what it is he means: his Remark is only applicable now & then when he feels as if the Description overlaid & stifled that which ought to be the prevailing Idea.[11]

It is a pity that we only have Keats's view at second-hand, but Taylor's capitalization suggests that 'Description', 'Sentiment' and 'Idea' were the actual terms that Keats used, contrasting the first to the latter two (and the fact that Keats seems to have used Sentiment and Idea interchangeably is itself revealing). The language that Taylor ascribes to Keats—'prevailed', 'overlaid & stifled', 'prevailing'—suggests that in Keats's mind at least some kind of power struggle was at issue. Hessey delicately uses a less confrontational language ('abound', 'deficient') to make much the same point.

For Hessey it was a question of getting the balance right between description and sentiment; for Keats what was at issue was rather who was to be the master. If we substitute Nature or World for Description and Mind for Sentiment or Idea then we can see that Keats is expressing precisely that dominating and exploitative attitude that Constantine denounces as typically Romantic and distinguishes from Clare's.

We do not have Clare's response to Keats's critique of his poetry, and it is unlikely that he would have had much interest in debating the issue on the level of the abstractions to which the more theoretically-minded Keats chose to raise it. His reply comes not in the form of a theoretical discussion but in his poetry. It is certainly true, as Constantine argues, that Clare's poetry is of a different kind from Keats's and must be understood and judged differently. But Clare's poetry also shows itself aware of the difference between itself and that of Keats and other Romantics, though it sees this difference not so much in terms of a struggle for power as in terms of an illusion which it simultaneously comprehends and exposes. To make this case I shall consider in detail one poem, 'The Sky lark', which Clare included in his manuscript collection *The Midsummer Cushion* and which was published in *The Rural Muse* (1835). Clare was of course fond of writing about birds, a subject on which he produced many of his finest poems. But it is not I think accidental that a poem which is essentially a critique of Romanticism should choose this subject. The skylark, he remarked drily in his bird list, is 'a bird that is as of much use in poetry as the Nightingale'.[12] Clare almost certainly has in mind some famous bird poems by his contemporaries, most obviously Keats's 'Ode to a Nightingale' but also Shelley's 'To a Skylark'. It is appropriate ground (a way of putting it that will turn out to be peculiarly apt) on which to engage them, as will become clear if we consider why there are so many famous Romantic poems about birds.[13]

Birds are an obviously attractive subject for poets because the 'song' of birds can serve as a figure for poetry. Thus Keats refers to the song of the nightingale as a 'plaintive anthem' (l. 75), and Shelley is very explicit about his own attempted self-identification with the skylark.[14] In an Aesopian fable referring to his treatment by his publishers Clare himself encodes poets as songbirds, modestly casting himself as the thrush.[15] Another aspect of avian behaviour that is attractive to poets (and not, as Clare recognises, only to them) is their ability to fly, to escape from the constraints of gravity. In his sonnet 'Written on the Day that Mr. Leigh Hunt Left Prison' Keats claimed that even while in prison Hunt was 'as free / As the sky-searching lark' and 'To regions of his own his genius true / Took happy flight' (ll. 3-4, 12-13). Keats was thinking of Hunt's activities as a poet as much as of his political integrity. The flight of birds is a figure peculiarly appropriate to poetry, which invests so much in its own flights of fancy, undertaken on what Keats calls 'the viewless wings of Poesy' ('Ode to a Nightingale', l. 33). This trope has its ethical dimension, in that such flights can easily be condemned as escapist, and Keats is very frank about his desire to 'Fade far away, dissolve, and quite forget / What thou among the leaves hast never known' ('Ode to a Nightingale', ll. 21-2). The further danger in all this is that the bird is appropriated by the poet for his own purposes, in the kind of gesture about which Constantine has well-founded reservations. Shelley is admirably frank in his address to the skylark: 'Bird thou never wert—' ('To a Skylark', l. 2). Clare is no stranger to enthusiasm and no naive literalist, but it is hard to think of him addressing a bird in those terms. Part of his criticism of Keats is that 'he often described nature as she appeared to his fancies & not as he would have described her had he witnessed the things he describes', and it is difficult not to believe that he had Keats's famous ode in mind in the following passage:

> your Londoners are very fond of talking about this bird & I believe fancy every bird they hear after sunset a Nightingale I remember when I was there last \while/ walking with a friend in the fields of Shacklwell we saw a gentleman & lady listning very attentive by the side of a shrubbery & when we [*del.* passd] came up we heard them lavishing praises on the beautiful song of the nightingale which happend to be a thrush but it did for them ... such is the ignorance of nature in large Citys that are nothing less then over grown prisons that shut out the world & all its beautys[16]

Another cancelled passage suggests that poets can be as ignorant as townies (and Keats was both), or at least disregardful of fact in spinning their fancies:

Nightingale

A naturalist must not always look into a poets fanciful descriptions for facts for when the poet happens to fall in love with a pastoral chloe <or> Phillis &c the devoted nightingale is addressd by them as a lover also <& of> course their songs like those of the poets are to be made up of hop<es> & <wishes> &c to its featherd Phillises & chloes if the poets mistress frown on his pastoral why then to be sure the poor nightingales mistress must frown likewise & its song must spring from dissapointments & sorr<ows> be melancholy of course cloud must obs[c]ure the sun & tempests discomfort the landscape but if his mistress happen to smile why then all nature is told to be gay & flourishing these are the expanses of fancy & in poetry they are all very well but nature is not so changable she cares as much for the poets invoctaions [sic] & his mistress as the weather does for an almanack
(PMS A34, p. R14)

The tone in both passages is indulgent rather than denunciatory, but it is clear that Clare himself would not choose to be so cavalier about the facts of natural history for the sake of a poetical fancy. The second passage focuses on what was to become known as the Pathetic Fallacy, which Constantine describes as 'an equivalent in the imaginative life of the subjugation and exploitation represented by Enclosure'. Clare, though, seems less concerned with subjugation and exploitation than with the way in which such deluded reactions to the natural world show those who indulge them as imprisoned, whether within the cultural confines of the city or within their own personal concerns. His own view is both larger and truer, and this is demonstrated in 'The Sky Lark' not so much by attacking less adequate views but by including them within it.

The contrast I am suggesting between Clare and Romantic poets like Keats and Shelley involves issues of literary form, or at least mode, as well as overt opinion. Romantic poems concerning birds are typically lyrics, addressed to rather than written about the bird who is the ostensible subject, and the fervent apostrophes, by their evidently figurative nature, draw attention to the large measure of self-identification involved in such addresses. These poems, we readily understand, are about the poets or speakers themselves, and appropriate their apparent subjects as pretexts for self-expression. Clare's poem, despite its relative brevity, should not be mistaken for a lyric. As Margaret Grainger notes, 'He is no Keats or Wordsworth using reference to a bird as a springboard for exploration of his own "mysterys" or emotions...'[17] The poem is descriptive, or more accurately perhaps a description developed by means of narrative; or even more accurately, a description developed by narrative that has lyric embedded within it. The lyric here is not so much the self-expression of the poet or speaker (there is no overt first-person reference to the speaker, the usual mark of the lyric) as that of characters within the narrative, who are framed in a way that allows us to inspect rather than simply share the feelings expressed. These feelings are prompted by and directed to the skylark, though, of course, they tell us more about the boys than about the bird. The boys, we are told, are flower gatherers, vying with each other 'to pluck the prize', and probably potential bird's-nesters: that is, they are already engaged in pursuits that we could regard as dominating and exploitative (if these were not rather too severe a criticism to ascribe to Clare, who himself engaged in both activities; there is of course a whole other essay to be written on poesy and poseys). Their misunderstanding of the lark can be seen as extending these other activities into the imaginative realm, in a way that supports Constantine's ethical reservations about Romantic attitudes.

The boys are 'far from home', but there is no reason to think they are Cockneys. They know enough about birds to know a skylark when they hear one and they know that it is a famously high-flying bird ('fine warbling song in towering flight', as my field guide puts it).[18] Not being poets they are less desirous of appropriating the bird's song than its powers of flight, at least imaginatively. But in so doing they remain unaware of or forget another crucial fact of natural history. If skylarks habitually fly higher than most songbirds they also nest and spend much of their time lower, on the ground itself in fact, where, as a video guide puts it, 'their earthy colours blend superbly with their surroundings'.[19] The boys' failure to recognise this actually frustrates any acquisitive projects they may have; they will not find the nest, despite its vulnerability, where they will not think to look for it. Their reaction to the bird is a dream, or rather a daydream, of freedom. They refuse to accept that a bird with such powers of flight would ever come down to earth; they imagine it in their own image: 'had they the wing / Like such a bird themselves would be too proud / & build on nothing but a passing cloud'. Like Shelley, they assume that the skylark must be a 'Scorner of the ground' ('To a Skylark', l. 100). As my use of the phrase 'come down to earth' might suggest the boys' behaviour is framed by implicit allusion to various proverbial phrases, allusions that would be considered intertextual were they to Shakespeare (as in Keats's allusion to *Hamlet* in 'dissolve') or to Milton, but which Clare himself would probably describe as common sense. The boys have their heads in the clouds (a way of putting it that is positively witty in this context); they are building castles in the air. The recourse to proverbial expression is in itself a way of bringing the high-flown fancies of the boys down to earth. The poem as a whole makes clear that earth is the skylark's medium as much as air. It begins and ends looking down at 'the russet clods', the natural habitat of the skylark and of the hare who is herself 'like some brown clod the harrows failed to break', vulnerable and yet miraculously untouched, like the skylark's nest. The return at the end associates the lark's nest with the leveret, the soaring bird with the squatting hare. And even when it is at its highest point, so high as to be virtually invisible, the bird is significantly described as 'a dust spot'.[20]

In the context of other Romantic bird poems—if we consider for a moment the possibility that Clare too is a Romantic—we might argue that 'The Sky Lark' is actually a concealed lyric. The bird, in this reading, is a figure for the poet, mindful of his lowly origins but confident in his ability to soar— and sing. I would not reject this 'Romantic' reading because I do not think that Clare himself rejects Romantic aspiration or even illusion. He does not present the boys' fancies scornfully or dismissively. He is fully aware of why they feel as they do—it is natural to do so, however unrealistic such aspirations may be. But at the same time as he is willing to indulge illusions, he is determined to recognise that they are illusions. They are only part of the whole story and the poem firmly and delicately reconstructs the whole in order to place and frame the boys' partial apprehension of it.

I would hazard that a consistent and rather comprehensive account could be given of the whole *Midsummer Cushion* collection by tracing the theme of illusion. Certainly 'Pleasures of Spring' could be read as a virtual compendium of illusions, which we are invited to participate in sympathetically while still recognising their illusory status, from the shepherd seeing shapes in the clouds (ll. 101-36) to the boy who tries to run a race with the moon (ll.

418-63).[21] Clare's distance from a full-blown participation in Romantic illusions can be gauged from his fondness for the word 'fancy'. He uses this word and its cognates far more frequently than he does 'imagination', and when he does use the latter word it is with a sense of its unreliability rather than of its creative power. The creative power in Clare is indeed the Fancy, but it is a power whose provisional status is always recognised. Keats's fondness for the same term suggests perhaps that there might be more common ground between the two than my tactical counterposition of them would suggest. Keats's conclusion that 'the fancy cannot cheat so well / As she is fam'd to do, deceiving elf' ('Ode to a Nightingale', ll. 73-4) would I think have drawn a wry smile of recognition from Clare. David Constantine's desire to distinguish Clare from Romanticism proper (if there is such a thing as 'proper' Romanticism—perhaps in this context it is more fitting to speak of 'High Romanticism') is critically illuminating, but can lead us into serious error if we do not recognise that Clare himself was fully aware of what was at issue, and this awareness itself qualifies the absoluteness of the distinction. The interrogation of Romantic illusion could be defined as a central strand in Romanticism itself, in which case Clare could be claimed as a Romantic with as much justice as, say, Byron. It was of course Byron's mantle that Clare was to claim in his most extended asylum poems. In viewing Clare as a mad poet readers have chosen to regard as merely an illusion or rather delusion what could be considered a literary fancy (or allusion) and one with considerable validity (like Blake's claim to reincarnate Milton). Again the mistake is to underestimate Clare's own awareness of what was at issue, as if he imagined he really was Byron, where it might be better to say that he was deliberately exploring the fancy that he was. Like his skylark, Clare is not simply up in the air or down on the ground but characteristically both.

NOTES

1.	David Constantine, 'Outside Eden: John Clare's Descriptive Poetry', in J.R. Watson (ed.), *An Infinite Complexity: Essays in Romanticism* (Edinburgh: Edinburgh University Press/University of Durham, 1983), pp. 181-201.
2.	For accounts of Clare that suggest a more conscious resistance to Romantic attitudes, see James C. McKusick, 'Beyond the Visionary Company: John Clare's Resistance to Romanticism' in Haughton, *Context*, pp. 221-38, and L.J. Swingle, 'Stalking the Essential John Clare: Clare in Relation to his

Romantic Contemporaries', *Studies in Romanticism,* 14 (1975), 273-84.

3. See Juliet Sychrava, *Schiller to Derrida: Idealism in Aesthetics* (Cambridge: Cambridge University Press, 1989).
4. *Letters*, pp. 36-7.
5. PMS A5, p. 58.
6. 'To the Memory of Keats', in *Early Poems*, II, p. 476-7.
7. PMS A49, p.10; published with some errors in *Prose*, p. 223.
8. Though an obvious case in point is Keats's address to the nightingale as 'light-winged Dryad of the trees' ('Ode to a Nightingale', l. 7).
9. He commented on Wordsworth's 'The White Doe of Rylstone' that it contained 'some of the sweetest poetry I ever met with tho full of his mysterys' (Journal, 29 October 1824; *By Himself,* p. 190). For Clare's use of this word elsewhere and his evident awareness of its ambiguities, see Louise Sylvester, '"The Misterys Of His Art": A Moment of Ambiguity in Clare's Autobiography', *JCSJ*, 17 (1998), 35-40.
10. Eg. 2245, f. 62r, quoted in *Letters*, p. 38, note 4.
11. Eg, 2245, ff. 225v-226r.
12. *Natural History*, p. 139.
13. Tom Paulin and Richard Cronin, in their papers at the 1998 Trent conference, pointed to Clare's interest in birds as builders of nests, bricoleurs (as Paulin put it) with whom Clare as 'naive' artist could identify; an interest not, significantly, shared by many other poets. See Richard Cronin's essay, above.
14. Clare too can address the skylark as 'of each grassy close ... the poet and guest' and as 'thou feathered poet' ('The Skylark'; *Later Poems*, I, p. 316).
15. See P.M.S. Dawson and David Powell, 'Clare and His Publishers: An unpublished prose work', *JCSJ*, 18 (1999), 65-9, which reprints Clare's 'Fable of the animals in partnership'.
16. *Natural History*, p. 37.
17. *Natural History*, p. 120.
18. John Gooders, *Field Guide to the Birds of Britain and Ireland* (London: Kingfisher Books, 1986), p. 192.
19. *A Guide to British Birds*, Vol. 1, Country Birds, written and directed by Peter Double (Castle Vision video, CVB 1092, n.d.).
20. In a more conventional later poem 'To the Lark' (where Clare follows Shelley in attempting a metrical imitation of the bird's song) he compares it to 'a speck upon the sky / Small as those clods that crumble where I lye' (*Later Poems*, I, p. 310).
21. The shepherd actually wishes for 'the larks wings that whistles oer his head / To realize his glowing dreams & flye / To the soft bosom of that sunny sky' (ll. 128-30).

But what the Lord showeth me that will I seek
And it my God biddeth me that will I speak
And now Lord I go to my people again
Come & I'll show thee — their language more plain
What this people here which my blessings must praise
Shall do to thy people in strifes latter days
& he took up his parable justly & clear
saying Balaam the prophet the offspring of Beor
He fell in a trance & yet having his eyes
open to visions that gleamed in the skies
Do I not speak the most high in my voice
Are they not the almighty his chosen & choice
I shall see him anon but not now with my eyes
& I shall behold him anon but not now is nigh
out of Jacob a star shall illumine the skies
A sceptre from Israel shall flourish & rise
& smite all the corners of moab into strife
& destroy all the children of sheth to the life
& Edom shall be a possession & heir
Shall be a possession for enemies near
& Israel shall do valiant deeds for their dower
Out of Jacob comes he with dominion & power
To destroy him that get in the city remains
& prosper the freedom of mountains & plains
& then he led looked over Amalek — he
Took up his parable justly & free
Amalek first of all nations — the given
Of life dooms they and that then perish forever
& he looked on the Kenites not ceasing to mock
saying strong is thy place like a nest in the rock
song of Balaam

For mankind and his prison'd solitude
the winds candle in its narrow ———

"If where thou art I may not dwell
"I will sooth to be where thou hast been
                                    Byron

"They shall dig for death as for hid
treasures & shall not find it "
                              Job

Nature says "May" but my pen denies
to write the truth & so it lives in sighs

—O! would it were my lot
To be forgetfull as I am forgot—"
                              Byron

Honesty & good intentions are
So moved & hampered in with evil lies
she hath not room to stir a single foot
nor even strength to break a spiders web

"I've now turned ... into a common of nature
Of all freedom & mocking all
                              Dryden

—so lies keep climbing round I loves sacred stem
Blighting fair truth whose leaf is evergreen
Whose roots are the hearts fibres & whose own
The soul that cheers & smiles it into bloom
Till heaven proclaims that truth can never die

continued
Nevertheless Kenites shall fail in that day
& Ashur shall carry them captives away
& he took up his parable nothing to miss
Alas who shall live when my God doeth this
Ships come from Chittim in what & riven
T'afflict ashur — & Ebor shall perish for ever
& Balaam arose to his place on that day
& Balak he also rejoined on his way

11. Byron, Tasso, and John Clare's *Child Harold*

Cathy Taylor

I.

On page 22 of Northampton MS 6 (reproduced opposite), Clare has interrupted his pearaphrase of 'Balaam's Parable, Numbers, Chapter 24' to write six two-line quotations and one nine-line stanza in keeping with the mood and content of those earlier stanzas clearly attributed to his own poem, *Child Harold*. Two quotations are taken from Byron's poem 'The Lament of Tasso':[1]

> Imputed madness prison'd solitude
> & the minds canker in its savage mood[2]

and:

> —O! would it be my lot
> To be forgetfull as I am forgot—[3]

One other quotation is taken from Byron's 'Stanzas To Florence':

> If where thou art I may not dwell
> "T'will sooth to be where thou hast been".[4]

The two lines which follow appear to be Clare's own:

> Nature says "Mary" but my pen denies
> To write the truth & so it lives in sighs

Another quotation is taken from the Book of Job, chapter three:

> They shall dig for death as for hid
> treasures and shall not find it.

The final reference is from Dryden's *All For Love*:

I've now turned wild a commoner of nature
of all forsaken & forsaking all[5]

Two things strike the reader who encounters these references. Firstly, the incongruity of the quotations in the middle of a biblical paraphrase (unique to this particular page of NMS 6). Secondly, there is the undisputed preoccupation with the experience of exile, confinement, separation, dislocation and loss of identity. Clare's own stanza explores the lack of truth and honesty in a corrupt, deceiving society:

Honesty & good intentions are
So mowed & hampered in with evil lies
She hath not room to stir a single foot
Or even strength to break a spiders web
—So lies keep climbing round loves sacred stem
Blighting fair truth whose leaf is evergreen
Whose roots are the hearts fibres & whose sun
The soul that cheers & smiles it into bloom
Till heaven proclaims that truth can never die

These lines not only prefigure the themes of 'Don Juan A Poem', fair copied sixteen pages later, but they also echo the main theme of the material of NMS 6 as a whole—the power and essential truth of Love which acts as a stabilising force in the face of change, mutability and corruption. Such truth is centred, in this instance, on a benign God also referred to in the discontinued 'Balaam's Parable'. Clare's paraphrase begins[6] with a direct reference to the type of continuity and sanctuary found only in the location of home (where coincidentally Mary also resides). Balaam perceives familiar place as a refuge where:

...he sought not enchantment or spell
But he turned to the wilderness loved in his youth
Where nature & God live in silence & truth

Clare's decisive 'ruling off' of the middle of page 22 marks a clear distinction between his personal response to Byron's work and the more formal biblical paraphrase. What is revealing about Clare's use of lines taken from 'The Lament of Tasso' and 'Stanzas to Florence', in particular, is his obvious identification with the poet's expression of loss, madness, separation, incarceration and denial. A sequence of parallel relationships begins to make itself evident: Byron—Augusta, Tasso—Leonora, Clare—Mary Joyce.[7] What might have prompted the disruption to the paraphrase precisely at this point in the manuscript is unclear but there is no evidence of the same quotations breaking the continuity of an earlier draft of 'Balaam's Parable' in the smaller notebook, NMS 8. The fact that Clare also includes two of his own lines alongside those of his more celebrated and notorious contemporary suggests the degree to which Byron's presence shadowed his first confinement at High Beech. Similarities between the voices of Byronic prototypes and Clare himself are also unmistakable. Byron, Byron's Tasso,—John Clare, Clare's 'Child'— *all* are outsiders. What is more, they are trapped by potent memories of a lost woman located *elsewhere*. Byron's fictional speakers, together with Byron and Clare himself, are victims of a self-perpetuating 'emotional thraldom' in which they find themselves not only in physical confinement but also held in psychological bondage. Separation from the beloved, either by physical distance or by the gulf of social and moral constraint, binds Clare to Byron and Byron to Tasso.

Byron in *Childe Harold* articulates the compulsive power of love outside the jurisdiction of conventional marriage. Canto III of *Don Juan* also draws a distinction between the positive experience which develops through a relationship described as 'true love' and the negative, emotional sterility synonymous with legal contract. The *Don Juan* Canto examines the polarity between spontaneous affection and the deadening effect of conjugal habit: 'There's doubtless something in domestic doings, / Which forms, in fact, true love's antithesis'.[8] Again, in Canto III of *Childe Harold*, though on this occasion in more sombre, lyrical and confessional mood, Byron touches on the very subject which would appear to haunt Clare as he fair copied the material of NMS 6:

And there was one soft breast, as hath been said,
Which unto his was bound by stronger ties
Than the church links withal; and, though unwed,
That love was pure, and, far above disguise,
Had stood the test of mortal enmities
Still undivided and cemented more
By peril, dreaded most in female eyes;
But this was firm, and from a foreign shore
Well to that heart might his these absent greetings pour![9]

Tasso, in Byron's poem, is equally defiant in the face of moral and social laws, refusing to acknowledge the sin associated with coveting a socially superior woman. Ironically, the weakness which shuts 'him from mankind' by imposing physical confinement creates in turn the condition of isolation necessary for the imagination to take flight. Imprisonment nourishes a particular type of creative freedom:

But let them go, or torture as they will,
My heart can multiply thine image still:
Successful Love may sate itself away;
The wretched are the faithful; 'tis their fate
To have all feeling, save the one, decay,
And every passion into one dilate,
As rapid rivers into Ocean pour;
But ours is fathomless, and hath no shore.[10]

It is worth considering a third echo of a similar refrain which Clare would seem to be employing in *Child Harold*. On page 10 of NMS 6, Clare's speaker declines to accept that in loving Mary he has committed any sin at all. He argues that their love was 'heaven's own choice' and that fate has exercised a hand in nurturing the relationship. Neither distance nor absence can destroy pre-ordained love and commitment:

I loved her in all climes beneath the sun
Her name was like a jewel in my heart
Twas heavens own choice—& so Gods will be done

Love ties that keep unbroken cannot part
Nor can cold abscence sever or desert
That simple beauty blessed with matchless charms
Oceans have rolled between us—not to part
E'en Icelands snows true loves delirium warms
For there Ive dreamed—& Mary filled my arms

This quotation appears to be a fusion of the quotation from Byron's *Childe* and the general mood and tone of 'The Lament of Tasso' while ostensibly modifying what appears to be, (in Byron's work at least), a disregard for fundamental religious tradition.

Apart from the more obvious identification with Byron's thwarted lovers, it was possibly Byron's dislike of cant and hypocrisy that Clare identified with most, as the speaker in 'Don Juan A Poem' testifies. While Byron opened *Don Juan* with a reference to the want of a 'true' hero, Clare commences his own version with reference to social and moral hypocrisy: '—in these canting days / Women of fashion must of course be ladies'. Clare's nine-line stanza on page 22, where the opening two lines—'Honesty & good intentions are / So mowed & hampered in with evil lies'[11]—reiterate what is being suggested in most of the remaining quotations: there is a discrepancy between what is being said and done. Ambiguity and inconsistency may also be heard in the following couplet: 'Nature says "Mary" but my pen denies / To write the truth & so it lives in sighs'. Here, the speaker reveals that the very act of writing can 'undo' or contradict intention. The act of putting pen to paper affirms what Clare's lines suggest he cannot do: write and speak of Mary. Revelation and assertion of love for Mary Joyce are passionately expressed even while Clare's pen is ostensibly in denial.

Notions of 'seeming', deception, and more obviously, self-beguilement, surface and resurface throughout the pages of NMS 6. While Clare openly borrows from Byron's *Childe Harold* throughout the composition of his own poem, he would also appear to set out consciously to contradict or subvert lines from the original poem, obscuring or changing their meaning. A specific case of such blatant adaptation may be found in three lines on page 6 of NMS 6. In the fifth stanza, Clare has written:

> —change cannot constant prove
> The south is bright—but smiles can act contrary
> My guide star guilds the north—& shines with Mary

Byron's lines in Canto III of *Don Juan* suggest a completely different interpretation of the reliability or constancy of Clare's North Star, as the following lines reveal: 'His polar star being one that rather ranges / And not the fix'd'.[12]

The reader of NMS 6 becomes easily entangled in Clare's shifting and teasing discourse on truth or honesty. Inconsistency and vulnerability—both essential characteristics of Byron's hero—become transferred to this manuscript's 'Child'. Clare's perception of what is *true* appears to be dependent upon how effectively he accommodates the truth of Mary's absence and death at a given point in his manuscript.[13] Clare's hold *on* and perception *of* truth is as unstable as it is complex. It is significant that by the time he fair copied 'Balaam's Parable' onto page 22 he had already arrived home after his escape from High Beech, to discover that Mary Joyce was not only absent from the landscape with which he had associated her while in confinement; she was also dead, literally and figuratively. On the opening page of the Northborough notebook and again on page 17 (though the verb 'sojourning' in the first song is altered to 'returning' in the second version), Clare fair copied a number of stanzas which record in a spare, nihilistic mood his acceptance of Mary's death. A series of recurrent lines serve to endorse the immediacy of the absence of 'loved woman' (a phrase Clare uses in his notebooks): 'Mary never once was seen', 'But Mary's abscent everywhere', and 'Sweet Mary she is absent still'. The *truth* behind his own two-line reflection on page 22 may be that Clare's pen refuses to write what he acknowledges is, in effect, a lie.

What is interesting about this page, coming as it does after the lyrical, elegiac autumnal sequence of stanzas which Clare wrote immediately on his return to Northborough after his escape from High Beech,[14] is Clare's strong identification with Byron's work and his fictional characters as opposed to believing himself to *be* Byron. During his second hospitalisation at Northampton a fellow patient, William Jerom, in his 'Reminiscences of Clare By a Fellow Patient'[15] describes Clare's obsession with the poet. The speakers in both Clare and Byron's poems (Tasso especially) are not only in denial of the loss of 'loved woman' but they are also both writing through a shared experience of exile—Clare reflecting on his confinement retrospectively after his escape and Byron exiled in Italy where his Tasso stanzas were composed in 1817.

Both Byron and Clare associated loved woman with home and while in exile it was necessary to keep such memories alive. If nourishing the poetic presence of loved woman sustains the memory of 'home' and freedom in exile, then the act of commemoration is to be upheld at all costs even when *remembering*, in the words of Tasso, incites 'strange tumult and soft pain'. On occasions, memory and fantasy threaten the possession and control of daily routine, blocking out all rational response to 'impotent' reality with an overwhelming sense of thwarted desire:

And with my years my soul began to pant
With feelings of strange tumult and soft pain;
And the whole heart exhaled into One Want...[16]

Anticipation and blind wish-fulfilment are preferable to the crushing emotional sterility of everyday life. If beguilement or lying to oneself brings about temporary solace, then both Byron and Clare, and their speakers, are not above complying. In an editorial note to Byron's 'The Lament of Tasso' even Ernest Hartley Coleridge draws a distinction between poetic licence or fiction and historical evidence, throwing doubt on the veracity of Tasso's love for Leonora:

It is highly improbable that Tasso openly indulged or secretly nourished a consuming passion for Leonora d'Este and it is certain that the 'Sister of the Sovereign' had nothing to do with his being shut up in the Hospital of Saint Anna. That poet and princess had known each other for over thirteen years, that the princess was seven years older than the poet and in March, 1579, close upon forty-two years of age are points to be considered; but the fact that she died in February 1581, and that Tasso remained in confinement for five years longer, is a stronger argument against the truth of the legend. She was a beautiful woman, his patroness and benefactress and was the subject of sonnets and canzoni but it was not for 'her sweet sake' that Tasso lost either his wits or his liberty.[17]

In this essay I want to explore the ways in which John Clare used Byron's poems of confinement and exile in his Northborough notebook to underpin and make 'imaginative sense'[18] of his own experience of hospitalisation. It is highly improbable that Clare had read Tasso's *Gerusalemme Liberata* in the original Italian, John Hoole's translation of 1763[19] or Edward Fairfax's earlier translation of 1600, published under the title *Godfrey of Bulloigne*.[20] Clare *had* read H. F. Cary's translation of Dante, however.[21] Edward Fairfax's translation of the whole of Tasso's epic was known to many Romantic writers, extremely critical as regards translations. John Payne Collier in his edition of *Seven Lectures on Shakespeare and Milton by the late S. T. Coleridge* has left a revealing account of a conversation between Wordsworth, Coleridge, Hazlitt and Charles and Mary Lamb in which they discussed Fairfax's translation, though he gives no indication of the year in which it took place. Apparently when the celebrated literary group met in Lamb's rooms in The Temple, the conversation turned to a discussion of Tasso's *Jerusalem Delivered*, particularly Spenser's obligations to the Italian poem and the translation of *Godfrey of Bulloigne or The Recoverie of Jerusalem Done into Englishe Heroicall Verse by Edwarde Fairfax*. Lamb reacted ambivalently when pressed about his views on Fairfax's translation:

> Lamb mentioned the translation of Tasso by Fairfax of which Wordsworth said he had no copy and was not well acquainted with it. Lamb gave it as his opinion that it was the very best yet the very worst translation in English, and being asked for an explanation of his apparent paradox he stammered a little and then went on, pretty flowingly to say that it was the best for the air of originality and ease which marked many of the stanzas and the worst as far as he was able to judge (and he had been told the same by competent Italians) for literalness and want of adherence to the text.[22]

Mary Lamb obviously admired the translation, 'averring to the amazing pains and polishing Fairfax had bestowed upon his work'. In a letter to H. F. Cary of 15 April 1797, her brother, on this occasion, openly celebrated the purchase of a copy of the edition: 'By the way, I have lit upon Fairfax' *Godfrey of Bullen* for half a crown. Rejoice with me!' Clare may have read

Fairfax's or Hoole's translation of Tasso but there is no evidence of this in his Journal where he frequently kept a record of his reading. Clare's familiarity with Tasso's life and poetry may well have been diffused through reading Byron. Leigh Hunt, Scott, Byron and Shelley regarded Tasso's work and life highly. Sir Walter Scott specifically alludes to Tasso when Flora compliments Waverley 'as a man, so gentle, so well informed that he can admire the moon and quote a stanza from Tasso' (*Waverley*, ch. 52). John Payne Collier also described Wordsworth's growing admiration for Tasso's work, even referring to a 1600 edition given to him by Collier himself but lost without trace after the poet's death. Collier, in the following quotation, draws attention to the first page of the translation in which he informs us that there were three variations of an opening stanza:

> Soon afterwards I had the pleasure of giving Wordsworth a copy of Fairfax' *Godfrey of Bulloigne*, as he entitles his translation, of the date 1600, in which the whole of the first leaf had been reprinted, with several variations, in order that the translator's third attempt at an opening stanza might be inserted. What became of the book on the death of the poet I do not know, but I never saw another copy with this peculiarity.[23]

Leigh Hunt made his own translation of Tasso's *Aminta*. Byron and Shelley, who visited Ferrara in April 1817, became more deeply involved with the idea of the poet's incarceration and it is this personal identification with Tasso that Clare appears to have absorbed. Shelley's visit to Ferrara is recorded in a letter to Peacock on 7 November 1818, where he notes that both he and Byron had seen Tasso's original manuscripts and had been moved by the subject matter. Shelley, who had been contemplating a poetic drama on the subject of Tasso's confinement and madness,[24] prised off a splinter of wood from the door of the grated prison. Shelley in particular was struck by the poet's personality represented through calligraphy:

> the hand writing, (in contrast to Ariosto's) is large free and flowing except that there is a checked expression in the midst of its flow which brings the letters into smaller compass than one expected from the beginning of the word. It is the symbol of an intense and earnest mind exceeding at times its own depth and admonished to return by the chilliness of the

waters of oblivion striking on its adventurous feet.—You know I always seek in what I see the manifestation of something beyond the present and tangible object.[25]

Later in the same account Shelley dwells on the tragic nature of Tasso's script written in confinement: 'There is something irresistibly pathetic to me in the sight of Tasso's own handwriting moulding expressions of admiration and entreaty to a deaf and stupid tyrant'.[26] A year after the visit to Tasso's cell, while living at the Casa Bertini,[27] Shelley had sketched one or two scenes for his drama, including a 'Song' about Tasso's love for the princess Leonora:

Sometimes I see before me flee
A silver spirit's form like thee,
O Leonora, and I sit
...still watching it,
Till by the grated casement's ledge
It fades, with such a sigh, as sedge
Breathes o'er the breezy streamlet's edge.[28]

The mood and tone of the following lines from Byron's 'The Lament of Tasso' demonstrate the degree to which the two exiled poets shared the same poetic impulse:

But Thou, my young creation! my Soul's child!
Which ever playing round me came and smiled,
And wooed me from myself with thy sweet sight,
Thou too art gone—and so is my delight.[29]

Byron, who had begun writing 'The Corsair' in December 1813, four years prior to his visit to Ferrara, chose the following motto for his poem from Tasso's *Gerusalemme Liberata*: 'I suoi pensieri in lui dormir non ponno' ('his thoughts cannot sleep with him'). At the head of his First Canto he also quoted from Dante's *Inferno,* Canto V, 'nessun maggior dolore / Che ricordasi del tempo felice / Nella miseria' ('The greatest of all woes is to remind us of our happy days / In misery'). It is easy to see why Clare would have found such reflections so emotionally potent. Byron would go on to describe the events leading to the composition of his poem, 'The Prophecy of Dante', as a result of a suggestion by the Countess Teresa Guiccioli. She had reminded Byron of the association between Tasso's confinement and Dante's exile. Clare would surely have appreciated the plight of both poets and the relevance of their situation as regards his own in 1841. Although 'The Prophecy of Dante' is not directly referred to on page 22 of NMS 6, Clare is not above 'borrowing' entire lines from this poem elsewhere in the manuscript. On page 7 of NMS 6 for example, in the third stanza, the opening line, 'How servile is the task to please alone,' is lifted from the third canto of Byron's poem.[30] The material which makes up NMS 6 is characterised by a poet/ singer who comprehends the tension between the joys and pains associated with remembering one's past.

Byron's interest in Dante as well as Tasso also appears to have been assimilated by Clare. Historically, both Italian poets were engaged in voyages or journeys, and the metaphorical and physical implications of 'journeying' were something that Clare knew all about. NMS 6 documents not only Clare's physical journey out of Essex (on pp. 1-4) but also a psychological voyage of bereavement at the loss of Mary Joyce. Equally, the material of NMS 6 mirrors the preoccupations of these two earlier writers and recalls Byron's own self-imposed exile begun in July 1816 and his subsequent journey of 'self-discovery'. On page 22 of NMS 6 Clare appears, tacitly at least, to be questing, like Dante, Tasso, and Byron, in what David Nolan describes as 'finding the way'.[31] Lanfranco Caretti's favourite adjective for Tasso, 'generoso',[32] may also be applied to Byron and Clare. They are all engaged in psychological journeys producing a 'corpus of writing' which reveals intimate, confessional self-portraits, even if, on occasion, they take refuge behind a series of poetic masks when unrelenting self-exposure becomes too much.

While Clare repeatedly referred in his letters of 1841 to his confinement as a form of terrible imprisonment (the words 'separation', 'miseries', 'shutting me up', 'Hell of a Madhouse', 'prisoner' and 'keepers' surface in most of the correspondence of this period), he romanticised his predicament in NMS 6 by strongly identifying with the Byronic poet/lovers created by Byron in poems such as 'The Prisoner of Chillon',[33] 'The Prophecy of Dante' (whose influence is felt most strongly in the opening stanzas of *Child Harold*), and 'The Lament of Tasso'. It is helpful to hear the change in register and mood as Clare moves from the contents of a letter addressed to Mary Joyce written in May 1841, where we witness more of the indignant rage associated with Byron's prisoner, and the lines of the ballad which opens up his own *Child Harold* in NMS 6. In the letter, written but never posted, and found in his earlier notebook NMS 8, Clare complains about the slow drag of time in hospital: 'No one knows how sick I am of this confinement possessing two wives that ought to be my own & cannot see either one or the other if I was in Prison for felony I could not be served worse then I am'.[34]

In his ballad written on page 5 of NMS 6, however, Clare, on this occasion through the persona of his 'Child', describes confinement as being tempered by a quintessential Romantic belief in Nature's enduring power to regenerate and sustain:

Nature's love is eternal
In forest & plain
Her course is diurnal
To blossom again

There are, too, some subtle differences in Romantic perception between Byron and Clare. In Byron's 'The Prisoner of Chillon' there is less of the poet as pilgrim and more of the gothic hero. In 'The Lament of Tasso' Byron describes his speaker as being 'a beast of prey', 'Sullen and lonely, couching in the cave / Which is my lair and—it may be—my grave'. Here Byron's prisoner is fiercer in despair, battling with his agony which has given him wings 'to overfly / The narrow circus of my dungeon wall' (Section I). Clare's speaker, in contrast, particularly in the early pages of NMS 6, clings to the consoling love of God, like Bunyan's pilgrim:

True love is eternal
For God is the giver
& love like the soul will
Endure & forever[35]

Whether Gothic revenger or stoic pilgrim, their creations share the same survival instinct. It may have been Byron's heroes and their very struggle for existence and recognition that appealed most to Clare in captivity. Dante's moving claim, at the close of Canto I in 'The Prophecy of Dante', is that the worst part of confinement is not only the separation from family—'Ripped from all kindred, from all home, all things / That make communion sweet, and soften all pain'—but the indignity of having to reduce his mind and its 'own infinity' to a narrow cell shared with 'little men'.[36] Clare's 'Child' shares the same distrust of a society with which he feels no spiritual or creative affinity and which:

> locks me in a shop in spite of law
> Among a low lived set & dirty crew
> Here let the muse oblivions curtain draw
> & let man think—for God hath often saw
> Things here too dirty for the light of day[37]

Imprisonment separates the poet/lover from all that is most important to him, but it cannot entirely break the human spirit, as Dante states in Byron's poem. Life:

> hath taught
> A bitter lesson; but it leaves me free:
> I have not vilely found, nor basely sought,
> They made an Exile—not a Slave of me.[38]

II.

Anne Barton in her article 'John Clare Reads Lord Byron' (1996)[39] draws attention to Clare's imitation of Byron's *Don Juan* and *Childe Harold*, and Mark Storey, in 'Byron and Clare: "Childe Harold" and "Child Harold"' (1987),[40] considers Clare's preoccupation with Byron, particularly during his first confinement, as an attempt by Clare to 'vie for the laurel' with the more illustrious poet. I shall argue that although I agree with the view that Byron's influence upon Clare throughout his life was substantial, four years into his confinement at High Beech Clare appeared to be moving towards a more *separate* existence[41] by the time he had begun fair copying his work into NMS 6. After page 23 of this manuscript Clare has clearly identified more with the various voices of the biblical paraphrases in their apocalyptic view of the universe as opposed to the Byronic twins *Don Juan* and *Childe Harold*. Job, Jeremiah, and Isaiah in their self-denial, self-doubt, and continuing exile tend to replace the Romantic quester and poet/exile. It is significant that in the very last years of Clare's second and final hospitalisation, in Northampton Asylum, the Byronic imitation would cease altogether, and Clare reverted to composing a series of repetitive songs, more in the Scottish tradition of Burns, and dedicated to a procession of unidentified women.

I now want to trace the growth and development of Clare's preoccupation with Byron from his early career to 1841, culminating with his use, in his Northborough notebook, of the Byronic prisoner-exile who is also the poet/lover. Clare positions and repositions himself into different narratorial positions, a number of which sound like Byron's representations of Dante and Tasso, not merely to mask his own identity (as has been suggested by Anne Barton, Lynne Pearce,[42] Mark Storey and Clare's earliest biographer Frederick Martin in 1864), but to enhance and reveal his purposeful autobiographical presence in NMS 6 more effectively. Despite what Anne Barton describes in her article as 'a yawning gap' between the two poets in terms of social rank, education, longevity, and fame, Clare remains closest to Byron in his healthy disrespect for critics and critical reviews. In his essay on 'Popularity in Authorship' Clare describes his admiration for Byron's ability to look upon critics as 'the countryman does on a magistrate he beheld them as a race of petty tyrents that stood in the way of genius ... & he treated them accordingly he let them know there was another road to parnassus without taking theirs' (*Prose*, p. 209).

If there *is* a yawning gap between the two poets, it is possibly in their experience of, and attitude to, travelling or voyaging. While Byron set sail from Falmouth in 1816 to travel throughout Europe and Greece in self-imposed exile, Clare became panicky and disorientated when he was forced to move beyond a three-mile radius from home, as his move from Helpston to Northborough in 1832 would testify. Clare compensated for his lack of experience in the style of a Grand Tour by travelling in his mind instead, questing in 1841 (despite physical confinement) towards a location peopled with memories and inhabited by one significant woman and muse—Mary. In this respect, he became bound up in a self-created existence of wish fulfilment more compulsive than reality. Byron in *Childe Harold*, particularly in Canto III, which Clare admired most, described the power of the mind to imagine itself out of incarceration and exile, together with its ability to conjure absent places and most importantly loved woman, almost at will:

'Tis to create, and in creating live
A being more intense, that we endow
With form our fancy, gaining as we give
The life we imagine, even as I do now... (III, vi)

Bereft of family and friends, isolated, without conjugal visits, Clare turned more and more to attempting to write his own long poems *Child Harold* and 'Don Juan A Poem'. Clare's sense of isolation is palpable as his hospitalisation continued. In the same letter to Mary Joyce I quoted earlier, he describes the therapeutic value of writing, and importantly writing *like* as opposed to *as* Byron:

to get myself better I went a few evenings on Fern hill & wrote a new Canto of Child Harolde & now I am better I sat under the Elm trees in old Mathews Homestead Leppits Hill where I now am—2 or 3 evenings & wrote a new Canto of Don Juan—merely to pass the time away but nothing seems to shorten it in the least & I fear I shall not be able to wear it away—nature to me seems dead & her very pulse seems frozen to an iceicle in the summer sun (*Letters*, p. 646)

While Byron's presence haunted Clare's apprenticeship as a poet from the moment he fair copied part of a journal kept by a seaman brother of a Helpston neighbour, and was struck by the observation of 'a odd young man lame of one foot on which he wore a cloth shoe who was of a resolute temper fond of bathing in the sea' (*By Himself*, p. 65), to his first glimpse of Byron's work 'The Giaour' in 1818, when Edward Drury first showed him the poem, Byron intersected Clare's own life. In early January 1820, as his 'Sketches' describe, Clare was lent two volumes of Byron's *Childe Harold* by Gilchrist, as a consequence of which Clare begged to 'keep it longer wishing to read it a second time', so enamoured was he with Canto III in particular. Even Byron's ghost passed Clare when he was not actively looking for it. While walking down Oxford Street on his third visit to London in 1824 Clare came across the funeral cortege, made up of aristocracy comparatively uninterested in either Byron's work or his physical remains, making its final journey to Nottingham. Clare observed that the streets were lined with ordinary people, who 'stood in proufond silence till it passd ... and they mournd in saddend silence' (*By Himself*, p. 157).

Clare's interest in Byron increased steadily throughout the 1820s and 1830s as his library at Northampton demonstrates. This collection contains the 1823 edition of *Don Juan* presented by Clare's friend Henderson, the 1828 Galignani edition of *Byron's Works Including The Suppressed Poems* presented by Eliza Emmerson, Volumes I, II and IV of Murray's four-volume edition published in 1828, and an 1816 edition of *Poems on his Domestic Circumstances*. We know from Clare's Journal that by 1824 he had read most of *Don Juan*, waiting seventeen years before writing his own version while in confinement at High Beech. And this is the crux: it was only while in confinement that Clare was able to draw upon his familiarity with Byron and his work, most particularly *Don Juan* and *Childe Harold*, and actively to make full use of his knowledge of Byron's poetry to feed and nourish his own.

Significantly, Byron and Clare shared very similar methods of composition. The most striking similarity, one feels (if Clare's *Child Harold* is read alongside Byron's poem), is their tendency to rely upon poetry to document and order intense personal experience. Emotional trauma and personal adversity are used to advantage as Byron's 'Childe' articulates in Canto III of *Childe Harold*:

> There is very life in our despair,
> Vitality of poison,—a quick root
> Which feeds these deadly branches; for it were
> As nothing did we die; but Life will suit
> Itself to Sorrow's most detested fruit,
> Like to the apples on the Dead Sea's shore[43]

Byron, in a quotation from Moore which leads his poem 'The Giaour', encapsulates what would appear to have motivated both himself and Clare in exile, while nourishing their creative survival. Before writing his advertisement for 'The Giaour', Byron's use of Moore's lines draws attention to an obsession he shares with Clare:

One fatal remembrance—one sorrow that throws
Its bleak shade alike o'er our joys and our woes—
To which Life nothing darker nor brighter can bring,
For which joy hath no balm—and affliction no sting.[44]

Both Clare and Byron, as Anne Barton explains, composed rapidly, in an open-ended form dependent often upon 'powerful Old Testament style verbs'. Both poets were ambivalent about editorial interference. Both men comprehended the creative possibilities which emerge from isolation and withdrawal from family, friends, and a fickle literary public. One is tempted to ask whether Clare's two long poems of 1841 would have existed at all without the experience of confinement and exile. There is also the importance of the timing of Clare's escape from High Beech, and the effect this had upon the development of *Child Harold* in particular. What is intriguing about the consequences of Clare's hospitalisation is that while the pages of NMS 8 would suggest that he was having difficulty in distinguishing his own identity from that of Byron, the later manuscript Clare used after his escape to Northborough in the late summer of 1841, NMS 6, would indicate that he had already begun to move towards what Anne Barton maintains was 'an entirely rational awareness that Lord Byron is somebody else and dead'.[45]

I want to suggest that in the Northborough notebook of 1841 in particular, Clare is speaking entirely as himself while using a number of Byronic creations to mirror and reconstruct his own predicament. In the course of this discussion I hope to demonstrate that while the earlier notebook belonging to the year 1841 reveals a number of unstable identities and voices dominated by the Byronic presence, the later manuscript which Clare was using to fair copy material he had written at High Beech reveals him manipulating the Byronic heroes of exile, captivity and thwarted love to emphasise his personal circumstances in this eventful, fertile, creative year. I will look in particular at the surfacing of Byron's poem 'The Lament of Tasso' in the middle pages of NMS 6, as it appears that Clare clearly identified with Byron's representation of Tasso together with the poem's narrative of madness and thwarted love.

It is appropriate that Clare responds to a Byronic scenario constructed around the love of the poet for a woman beyond his social reach. Tasso confronts his own social station in Section V of Byron's poem, conceding that his love for Leonora challenges the social order:

> I knew thy state, my station, and I knew
> A Princess was no love-mate for a bard;
> I told it not, I breathed it not, it was
> Sufficient to itself, its own reward... (ll. 122-5)[46]

Clare's autobiographical account of his early life recalls his love for Mary Joyce, and recounts why they separated: 'When she grew up to woman hood she felt her station above mine at least I felt that she thought so ... tho I felt a hopeful tenderness one that I might one day renew the acquaintance and disclose the smotherd passion'.[47] Clare would appear to be using *Child Harold* together with the remaining contents of NMS 6 to both renew his acquaintance with Mary Joyce and to disclose his obsessive love for her.

What are the differences, then, between Clare's attitude and response to Byron in his earlier notebook of 1841, NMS 8, and the later manuscript used at Northborough, NMS 6? What evidence is there in NMS 6 to suggest that Clare has a stronger hold on his own identity and that as a result of this the Byronic presence in his creative and personal life has undergone a sea change? The contrast between the fluid, unstable identities which inhabit NMS 8, and the more clearly accessible unitary ego of NMS 6, is striking. In NMS 8, Clare appears to be unable to sustain one specific voice for any length of time. On page 1 of the earlier notebook, the Byronic twins who speak in 'Don Juan A Poem' and *Child Harold* interchange their narratives within the space of a few lines. John Clare as his autobiographical self writes to Eliza Phillips on page 13 of NMS 8 complaining about the conditions of his 'madhouse', which are likened to Hell: 'Having been cooped up in this Hell of a Madhouse till I seem to be disowned by my friends & even forgot by my enemies for there is none to accept my challanges which I have from time to time given to the public' (*Letters*, p. 647). Clare appears unable to sustain his own narrative and halfway through the letter he slips entirely into the persona of a prize fighter: 'It is well known that I am a prize fighter by profession'. By the end of this short letter Clare signs himself John Clare once more though the letter is addressed to a woman called Eliza and not Mary who dominates NMS 6.

Later, on page 25 of NMS 8, the confused voice of the stereotypical madman speaks through what appears to be part of John Clare's autobiographical account of his escape from High Beech. This voice believes himself to be the father of the Queen of England: 'His daughter is the queen of England & is now sitting on a stone heap on this highway'. Later still, on page 42, the voice is that of another boxer, the pugilist Jack Randall, who challenges the world to a fight in the ring. On the opposite page to this challenge, the autobiographical voice intrudes briefly with an observation on an authentic location—Buckhurst Hill, its church and the forests near High Beech. Pertinently, at the bottom of this account, Clare has signed himself as Byron, deleted the name, and punned instead: Byron—'made of Iron'. Is Clare referring to Byron's sense of irony here? Jack Randall, Byron, a champion boxer, the satirical Don Juan or the poet lover Child Harold— where *is* John Clare of Northborough amongst this procession of speakers who threaten to overwhelm him in NMS 8?

After Clare's arrival home at Northborough it would seem that there was a period of readjustment where the Byronic presence remained important in terms of marking Clare's own experience of exile, but was no longer subsuming his own identity. Once at home, he picked up his Galignani edition of *Byron's Works Including the Suppressed Poems* and wrote three stanzas of his own *Child Harold* on the back cover. In a shaky hand, he documented his recent ordeal, revealing the relief he felt to be once more 'at home':

Friend of the friendless from a host of snares
From lying varlets & from friendly foes
I sought thy quiet truth to ease my cares
& on the blight of reason found repose
But when the strife of nature ceased her throes
other hearts would beat for my return
I trusted fate to ease my world of woes
Seeking loves harbour—where I now sojourn
—But hell is heaven could I cease to mourn[48]

Is Byron the 'Friend of the friendless' or does Clare imagine Mary's welcome? Does Clare write to Byron on the most appropriate paper he can find immediately on his return home to sustain the continuity of the one identity who has never let him down? Byron, who like himself had experienced alienation, social rejection and exile: who else better to understand his predicament? What is important here is that if indeed Clare is referring to Byron in these stanzas (they are not written in NMS 8) he is speaking *to* and not speaking *through* him as appears to be the case in NMS 8.

In NMS 6, Clare's autobiographical presence is unmistakable. I want to suggest that Clare is using Byron's fictional creations as opposed to the Byronic persona itself as reconstructions of his own story. Whereas the Byronic persona amongst others threatens to consume John Clare of Northborough in NMS 8, in NMS 6 Byron's poet/lovers—Dante in 'The Prophecy of Dante', Tasso in 'The Lament of Tasso', and the speaker in 'The Prisoner of Chillon', all companions in physical confinement as well as in unrelenting emotional thraldom—are lined up by Clare to identify with and to console him under duress. It is interesting to observe that it is only *after* Clare has escaped from confinement that he can make sense of it. When Clare left High Beech he was not only attempting to rationalise the truth of his love for Mary but he was also slipping the chains of his reliance upon Byron.

The journey up the Great North Road, recorded haltingly and erratically in NMS 8, where Clare writes three or four lines of his account interspersed with biblical paraphrases and stanzas from *Child Harold*, appears to be a space where Clare was able to regain a grasp of who he really was. Three stanzas of a song written, it seems, during the eighty-mile trek home, first on page 23 of NMS 8 and then on page 1 of NMS 6, which begins with the line 'I've wandered many a weary mile', is resonant with the autobiographical presence of John Clare of Northborough. Clare's obsession with Byron would seem to have been exorcised to a degree on his arrival home.

III.

How *does* Clare make use of the Byronic poet/lover to mirror and endorse his own story in NMS 6, and what in particular did he find to identify with in Byron's 'The Lament of Tasso'? Although Clare's use of Byron's 'The Prisoner of Chillon' surfaces throughout the manuscript, for example on p. 4 of NMS 6, there is an indication that Byron's poet/lovers—the singers of truth in confinement—cease to be as important. It is useful, perhaps, at this point to draw attention to the presence of songs in NMS 6. Although there are songs in NMS 8, it is clear that the Romantic notion of questing told through a narrative of song and ballad is important to Clare. With this in mind it is easier perhaps to understand why Clare is so engaged with the plight of the poet/lover who sings of his loved one both to console himself and to reconstruct the events which led to his particular confinement and exile. In the case of Tasso there is the obvious parallel of Byron's narrative of Tasso's madness and confinement combined with the biographical details of Tasso's life—his alleged love for Leonora (though as we have seen Ernest Hartley Coleridge is quick to point out that this is not corroborated by history), and his confinement over the course of seven years at the hospital for the insane, Saint Anna. Clare's love for Mary Joyce, their social incompatibility, and his use of songs to tell his story of thwarted love, overlaps Tasso's narrative. This trinity of experience is important, both to the way Clare learnt to live independently of the Byronic presence in his life after his escape from High Beech, and in Clare's utilisation of the central motif of confinement as a background for his own story.

It is not difficult to see why Clare in 1841 identified with Tasso's predicament. What is less obvious is why he interrupted his biblical paraphrase to quote the Italian poet at this particular point in his manuscript. We may attach some importance to Clare's first quotation from 'The Lament of Tasso': 'Imputed madness prison'd solitude / the minds canker in its savage mood'. To impute is to ascribe or attribute: in this instance, insanity. The fact that Clare consistently rejected the notion of his own madness is borne out time and again in the letters written at High Beech. Clare believed his mind to be a disappointment to himself and others, as a letter written to George Reid in November 1841 bears out: 'I am very well that is as well as middling for my mind is as it always has been from a boy—a disappointment'.[49] On page 21 of NMS 6 Clare meditates on precisely the same notion, observing briefly before going on to paraphrase 'Balaam's Parable', that 'The word middling gennerally denotes somthing of a casuality—if the character of a woman is reckoned middling & she's a pretty woman the world genneraly looks upon her as above the middling but if she once gets below public opinion her character soon stinks and dies rotten'.

Tasso in Section III of Byron's poem summarises the mighty error of those who have hospitalised him:

they call me mad—and why?
Oh Leonora! wilt not *thou* reply?
I was indeed delirious in my heart
To lift my love so lofty as thou art;
But still my frenzy was not of the mind[50]

Like Tasso in Section III of Byron's poem, who differentiates his own delirium from the maniac's cry, Clare's 'Child' in the early stanzas of *Child Harold* draws a distinction between his delirious love for Mary and the corruption and defilement of the nineteenth-century madhouse. Tasso encapsulates the horror of being mad 'in love' while imprisoned with those whose insanity excludes them from an understanding of moral and social law:

Above me hark! The long and manic cry
Of minds and bodies in captivity.
And hark! the lash and the increasing howl,
And the half-inarticulate blasphemy!
There be some here with worse than frenzy foul
Some who do still goad on the o'er laboured mind
And dim the little light that's left behind
With needless torture...[51]

Clare's 'Child', on page 7 of NMS 6, also dwells on the lawlessness of the madhouse:

Here let the Muse oblivions curtain draw
& let man think—for God hath often saw
Things here too dirty for the light of day
For in a madhouse there exists no law
Now stagnant grows my too refined clay
I envy birds their wings to flye away.

Another similarity between Tasso's narrative and Clare may be seen in the issue of forgetfulness. Both Clare and Byron's Tasso, and indeed Byron himself, are bound in a complex chain of 'remembrance' where the act of commemoration brings consolation but also pain. On page 23, immediately following the Byron quotations, Clare writes a meditative fragment of prose on 'Self Identity'. Clare's exploration of the notion of forgetfulness is directly in keeping with Tasso to whom he has referred on the previous page: 'A very good common place counsel is *Self Identity* to bid our own hearts not to forget our own selves & always to keep self in the first place lest all the world who always keeps us behind it should forget us all together'. Byron's Tasso foreshadows the negative aspects of having a mind *unable* to forget, stating that he:

> ...had forgotten half I would forget
> But it revives Oh would it be my lot
> To be forgetful as I am forgot.

NMS 6 is resonant with the notion of forgetfulness, together with an understanding of what it is to be forsaken. Clare's 'Child' describes himself in similar terms, on page 16 of the manuscript: 'So on he lives in glooms and living death / A shade like night forgetting & forgot'. A line from a paraphrase of 'The Lamentations of Jeremiah' on page 50 of NMS 6 expresses a similar mood, 'Like a desolate being I sorrowed & mourned'.

In what would become Appendix 8 of Clare's Journal, which is headed 'Coincidences', Clare set out to note the similarities between Byron's work and his own. Two poems written before 1841, 'Superstitions Dream' and 'The Nightmare', owe a great deal to Byron. Although interestingly he acknowledges the influence of De Quincey's 'Opium Eater' he does not mention Byron's 'Darkness', composed in 1816. In 1841, Clare is, however, openly attributing quotations to Byron on page 23 of NMS 6. There are other similarities to 'The Lament of Tasso' in *Child Harold*, even to the point where particular lines take on the same mood and imagery. In Section VI of 'The Lament of Tasso' Tasso lies under the shade of overhanging trees to dream of the outside and liberty or indeed a past life, 'Where I did lay me down within the shade / Of waving trees and dreamed uncounted hours'. Clare's 'Child' in the Byronic stanzas on page 9 of NMS 6 is equally at home in the consoling presence of the forest:

> I love to stretch my length 'tween earth & sky
> & see the inky foliage oer me wave

Though shades are still my prison where I lie
Long use grows nature which I easy brave

I will conclude on a final point of coincidence that appears to represent Clare's relationship with Byron. In his advertisement to 'The Lament of Tasso' Byron describes the existence of the original manuscripts of Tasso's *Gerusalemme* as well as Guarini's *Pastor Fido*.[52] He goes on to observe that he also saw some of Tasso's letters, one from Titian to the poet, though he fails to describe the details. Byron was obviously profoundly affected by the poet's cell, his inkstand and his chair. In the same advertisement Byron comments ironically on posterity's unhealthy interest in the misfortune of poets, not their success or happiness: 'But as misfortune has a greater interest for posterity, and little or none for the contemporary, the cell where Tasso was confined in the hospital of St. Anna attracts a more fixed attention than the residence or the monument to Ariosto—at least it had this effect on me'. Dante reiterates the same observation in Canto IV of Byron's 'The Prophecy of Dante': 'Despair and Genius are too oft connected'. Clare would have appreciated the irony behind both observations, particularly as history has shown that critical commentators have appeared to be much more concerned with the details of Clare's own madness and despair, as opposed to the astonishing range and brilliance of the poetry composed and fair copied into NMS 6 in the summer and autumn of 1841.

NOTES

1. Ernest Hartley Coleridge (ed.), *The Poetical Works of Lord Byron* (London: John Murray, 1905), pp. 415-18.
2. *Works of Lord Byron*, 'The Lament of Tasso', Section I, ll. 4-5, p. 415.
3. *Works of Lord Byron*, 'The Lament of Tasso', Section II, ll. 80-1, p. 416.
4. *Works of Lord Byron*, 'Stanzas To Florence', stanza ii, p. 243.
5. *All For Love*, Act l, p. 197, in Montague Summers (ed.), *Dryden: The Dramatic Works* (New York: Gordian Press, 1968).
6. 'Balaam's Parable' commences on page 21 of NMS 6, after six lines of prose which discuss the word 'middling'.
7. Clare refers to Mary Joyce as 'loved woman' throughout NMS 6, despite the fact that their relationship was broken off when Clare was about seventeen. The last time he saw her she was twenty-four.

8. Jerome McGann, *Byron: The Oxford Authors* (Oxford and New York: Oxford University Press, 1986), Canto III, stanza 8, ll. 57-8, p. 489.
9. *Byron: Oxford Authors*, 'Childe Harold', Canto III, stanza 55, ll. 486-92, p. 119.
10. *Works of Lord Byron*, 'The Lament Of Tasso', Section II, ll. 56-64, p. 416.
11. *Later Poems,* p. 69, ll. 795-803.
12. *Byron: Oxford Authors*, Canto III, stanza 80, ll. 636-7, p. 507.
13. For a more detailed account of this argument see Cathy Taylor, 'The Resurrection of *Child Harold*: A Transcription of Nor, MS6 And A Reconsideration of John Clare's *Child Harold* and Related Writings.' (unpublished doctoral thesis, York University, 1998).
14. NMS 6, pp. 17-22.
15. PMS G5. There are two drafts of this account held at Peterborough.
16. *Works of Lord Byron*, Section VI, ll. 166-8, p. 417.
17. *Works of Lord Byron,* pp. 416-17.
18. This is Tim Chilcott's expression. I am indebted to him for a number of invaluable conversations concerning Clare's poetry of 1841.
19. John Hoole was a protégé of Samuel Johnson's, producing a translation of Tasso's *Gerusalemme Liberata* in 1793 which was to become the standard edition for half a century. Some critics favoured Hoole's translation due to the fact that his translation was written in rhyming couplets.
20. Torquato Tasso, *Godfrey of Bulloigne: A Critical Edition of Edward Fairfax's Translation of Tasso's Gerusalemme Liberata, Together with Fairfax's Original Poems*, ed. by Kathleen Lea and T. M. Gang (Oxford: Clarendon Press, 1981).
21. *Letters*, p. 551.
22. Tasso, *Godfrey.*
23. Tasso, *Godfrey*, p. 15.
24. On 20 April 1818, Shelley told Peacock: 'I have devoted this summer, and indeed the next year to the composition of a tragedy on the subject of Tasso's madness, which, I find upon inspection, is, if properly treated, admirably dramatic and poetical'. Cited in Tasso, *Godfrey*, p. 33.
25. F. L. Jones (ed.), *The Letters of Percy Bysshe Shelley*, Vol. II (Oxford: Oxford University Press, 1964), p. 47.
26. *Letters of Shelley*, p. 47.
27. Richard Holmes, *Shelley: The Pursuit* (London: Quartet, 1974), pp. 414-38.
28. Holmes, p. 425.
29. *Works of Lord Byron*, 'The Lament of Tasso', Section II, ll. 5-8, p. 415.
30. *Works of Lord Byron*, 'The Prophecy of Dante', Canto The Third, l. 86, p. 449.
31. David Nolan, 'Dante and Tasso' in *Dante Comparisons: Comparative Studies*

of *Dante and Montale, Foscolo, Tasso, Chaucer, Petrarch, Propertius and Catullus*, ed. by Eric Haywood and Barry Jones (Dublin: Irish Academic Press, 1985), pp. 98-108.

32. Michael Sherberg, *Rinaldo: Character and Intertext in Ariosto and Tasso* (Saratoga: Anma Libri, 1993, Stanford French and Italian Studies, 75), p. 153.

33. On page 4 of NMS 6, at the end of his account of his 'Reccolections etc of journey from Essex', Clare quotes two lines from Byron's 'Sonnet on Chillon': 'May none those marks of my sad fate efface / For they appeal from tyranny to God'.

34. NMS 8, p. 18; *Letters*, p. 646.

35. NMS 6, p. 5.

36. *Works of Lord Byron*, 'The Prophecy of Dante', Canto I, ll. 164-9, p. 445.

37. NMS 6, p. 5.

38. *Works of Lord Byron,* 'The Prophecy of Dante', Canto I, ll. 172-8.

39. Anne Barton, 'John Clare Reads Lord Byron', *Romanticism*, 2, no. 2 (1996), 127-48.

40. Mark Storey, 'Byron and Clare: "Childe Harold" and "Child Harold"', in *Byron: Byronism—Liberalism—Philhellenism*, Proceedings of the 14th International Symposium, Athens (6-8 July 1987), pp. 42-52.

41. See also Mark Minor, 'Clare, Byron and the Bible: Additional Evidence from the Asylum Manuscripts', *Bulletin of Research in the Humanities*, 85, no. 1 (1982), 104-26.

42. Lynne Pearce, 'John Clare and Mikhail Bakhtin: The Dialogic Principle. Readings from John Clare's Manuscripts 1832-1845', (unpublished doctoral dissertation, University of Birmingham, 1987). Pearce's argument is encapsulated in an article written in 1989, 'John Clare's "Child Harold", a Polyphonic Reading', *Criticism,* 31, no. 2 (Spring, 1989), pp. 139-57.

43. *Byron: Oxford Authors*, 'Childe Harold', Canto III, stanza 34, ll. 298-301.

44. *Byron: Oxford Authors*, 'The Giaour', p. 207.

45. Barton, p. 134.

46. *Works of Lord Byron*, Section V, p. 113.

47. *By Himself*, p. 87.

48. NMS 6, p. 10.

49. *Letters*, p. 652.

50. *Works of Lord Byron*, Section II, ll. 48-52, p. 416.

51. *Works of Lord Byron,* Section II, ll. 65-72. p. 416.

52. *Works of Lord Byron*, p. 415.

12. Masculinity, Misogyny and the Marketplace:
Clare's 'Don Juan A Poem'

Simon Kövesi

On one face of John Clare's gravestone in the churchyard of St Botolph's in Helpston, are carved the words 'A POET IS BORN NOT MADE'.[1] In 1841 Clare wrote two poems which overtly react to the work of Byron, his own *Child Harold* and 'Don Juan A Poem'.[2] The latter begins: '"Poets are born"—and so are whores'. Clare is clearly referring to, and undermining, the proverb that was ironically to end up labelling his buried remains. In his early career Clare was marketed by John Taylor as a 'Peasant Poet', as a natural genius, as a Wordsworthian 'Child of Nature',[3] a policy which was to make its mark on the other face of Clare's gravestone in the chiselled words 'NORTHAMPTONSHIRE PEASANT POET'. If Clare's feelings about such marketing were always ambivalent, by 1841 they had become terribly problematic, to the point where he could conflate the making of a poet with that of a prostitute. Attacking the proverb which ended up on his gravestone and marked and marketed him for life, Clare suggests that a poet is no more 'born' a poet than a woman is born a whore; both are formed by circumstance, by society and by money.

This essay considers the ways in which 'Don Juan A Poem' represents poets and women, and how each representation informs the other. As Clare's poem is an explicit reaction to Byron's, I will also look at Byron's poem of the same name. The first rhyming word of Byron's *Don Juan* is 'cant':

I want a hero: an uncommon want,
  When every year and month sends forth a new one,
Till, after cloying the gazettes with cant,
  The age discovers he is not the true one;
Of such as these I should not care to vaunt,
  I'll therefore take our ancient friend Don Juan,
We all have seen him in the pantomime
Sent to the devil, somewhat ere his time.[4] (I, 1)

Try and rhyme 'want', 'cant' and 'vaunt' and another word, less palatable even than cant, appears as an imposition on the rhyme sounds of this first stanza. It is an aural trick: Byron deliberately forces the reader to hear the word 'cunt' in the first rhyming word, especially when we back-track after hearing the longer vowel sound of vaunt.[5] Clare, it seems, picks up on this subtle aural complexity, and makes it a more explicit and central topic of his own 'Don Juan A Poem':

> Childern are fond of sucking sugar candy
> & maids of sausages— larger the better
> Shopmen are fond of good sigars & brandy
> & I of blunt— & if you change the letter—
> To C or K it would be quite as handy
> & throw the next away—but I'm your debtor
> For modesty—yet wishing nought between us
> I'd hawl close to a she as vulcan did to venus (ll. 33-40)[6]

Clare's cynicism here is staggering. As Vulcan (the outcast blacksmith god of fire, and Milton's architect of Pandemonium) the speaker sexualises the eating habits of children, and implies the hungry fellatory needs of women. He denigrates the decadence of 'shopmen' (who could be pimps) and then openly admits, via some crude linguistic trickery, that his desire for sexual gratification is reducible to the desire for cunt, and equal to a desire for 'blunt', which was the current slang for money. Women are thus reduced to voracious genitalia and associated, via the speaker, with an equally powerful hunger for money. This is an association that is supported by the frequency of the word 'whore' in the poem as a whole. The first stanza sets this theme:

> "Poets are born"—& so are whores—the trade is
> Grown universal—in these canting days
> Women of fashion must of course be ladies
> & whoring is the business—that still pays
> Playhouses Ball rooms—there the masquerade is
> – To do what was of old—& now adays
> Their maids—nay wives so innocent & blooming
> Cuckold their spouses to seem honest women (ll. 1-8)

The appearance of 'canting' has to have the underlying sound of 'cunting' implicit in it, as the subject here is whoring. Clare's narrator is open about the nature of writing verse in his day; he implies that he himself is a poet-whore, willing to sell his verse for money, and that writing poetry is cheap, commonplace, corrupt and diseased. The act of cutting off the proverb 'Poets are born, not made' highlights this poem's virulent opposition to Coleridge's conceptualising of 'natural genius'. As I have already said, Clare was marketed in his early career as a natural genius. But 'Don Juan A Poem' repeatedly asserts the significance of material effects upon the poet, who in material need is no different from anyone else in society. That economic conditions and conditioning have such a profound effect upon poets, turning them into materialist and commercial negotiators, is presented as a terrible shame. The impoverishment of contemporary poetry is reflected in the following stanza, as the narrator begs the reader for cash. Clare is clearly condemning himself as one of these poet-whores:

> Now i'n't this canto worth a single pound
> From anybodys pocket who will buy
> As thieves are worth a halter I'll be bound
> Now honest reader take the book & try
> & if as I have said it is not found
> I'll write a better canto bye & bye
> So reader now the money till unlock it
> & buy the book & help to fill my pocket (ll. 263-70)

Like a thief bound by the noose of the rope which will hang him, Clare is bound by the wishes of his audience. And like Byron, he acknowledges the power of his audience to make him or break him, while simultaneously portraying his relationship with the public as corporal punishment, as public humiliation, and as poetic death. The word 'canto' here is also caught up in the complex of sounds and meanings which echo through the poem—cant, canting, can't, cunt, cunning, coney—the implication being that each division of the poem, each canto, is available for sale to the highest bidder, who will be fooled into purchasing a disease-ridden exercise in empty cant. Byron's narrator is ironically open about the 'trade' of selling cantos; like Clare, he sells his poem as he goes along:

Love, war, a tempest—surely there's variety,
  Also a seasoning slight of lubrication,
A bird's-eye view too of that wild, society,
  A slight glance thrown on men of every station.
If you have nought else, here's at least satiety
  Both in performance and in preparation,
And though these lines should only line portmanteaus,
Trade will be all the better for these cantos. (XIV, xiv)

The following stanza of Clare's (which concludes the poem in Tim Chilcott's edition *The Living Year 1841*) complicates yet further the 'canto' sound complex:

Love worse then debt or drink or any fate
It is the damnest smart of matrimony
A hell incarnate is a woman-mate
The knot is tied—& then we loose the honey
A wife is just the protetype to hate
Commons for stock & warrens for the coney
Are not more tresspassed over in rights plan
Then this incumberance on the rights of man (ll. 295-302)

This concluding stanza is the high bile-mark of Clare's poem, vented at woman and the institution of marriage. Twisting the normative associations, the speaker suggests that love is in fact the greatest root of pain in marriage. A wife is a 'protetype' (an original model) of hatred: she is hatred's prime example, perhaps its prime source. The editors of the *Later Poems* interpret the line beginning 'Commons...' in this way: 'i.e. women are often "trespassed" upon as unenclosed land is by farm animals or rabbit colonies by people in search of rabbits'.[7] This interpretation is not entirely right. The language does indeed suggest the idea of territory and 'rights', but the colloquial origins of 'warrens for the coney' include it in the 'cant/cunt/canto/can't' sound complex. Clare includes the idea of the countryside in this territorial version of female sexuality, reducing it again to the pudenda: the word 'coney' meant rabbit and the female genitals.[8] The wife is therefore the territory ('commons' and 'warrens') which is encroached upon by others: the wife's 'stock'– her value, or use—is her cunt. As in *Hamlet*,[9] the 'countryside' is twisted into the '*cunt*ryside' of woman; the territory of the woman is an infringement upon the 'rights of man'. Her sexuality is an 'incumberance': it threatens because it is available to be 'tresspassed over'. Female sexuality, as it is represented here, embodies a threat because it allows any trespasser, and in doing so trespasses upon the rights of masculinity to define borders. The image of the rabbits is particular to this metaphor: they are popularly known for their procreative energies. The editors of *Later Poems* also omit the vital fact that the word 'warren' signified a brothel (and a boarding-school), and that the term 'cunny-warren' also signified a brothel. Another text is playfully referred to, Thomas Paine's *The Rights of Man* (1791): women, in or out of wedlock, infringe upon the sexual and political rights of manhood. The model of marriage being the antithesis of love which Clare adopts in the above stanza is straight from Byron. The latter writes 'love and marriage rarely can combine' (*Don Juan,* III, v, line 3).

Byron's 'Dedication' to his *Don Juan* is characterised by contempt for other poets. The narrator attacks the celebrated lake-poets of his day (Southey, Coleridge and Wordsworth) implying specifically that they write verse for cash:

> I would not imitate the petty thought,
>   Nor coin my self-love to so base a vice,
> For all the glory your conversion bought,
>   Since gold alone should not have been its price.
> You have your salary–was't for that you wrought?
>   And Wordsworth has his place in the Excise.
> You're shabby fellows–true–but poets still,
> And duly seated on the immortal hill. (Dedication, 6)

Clare seems to have picked up on this portrayal of the famous poets of his day and the problems all poets face in their mediations with the marketplace. For the aristocratic Byron, the English Parnassus is inhabited by poets who are incapable of writing verse without writing to the order and desire of the buyer, with money as their muse: they have no financial freedom to do otherwise, and if they do take a position to provide themselves with security, they are to be condemned, like Wordsworth. Clare, like Wordsworth and

Coleridge, was well aware of the problems of having patrons, and of the volatility of the marketplace. The impossibilities of the negotiations the poet has to undergo to maintain a relationship with the marketplace bring us to the other possible reading of 'cant' in Clare, and that is the conflated 'can not' or 'can't', especially in Clare's manuscripts which so often lack punctuation. In Clare's 'Don Juan A Poem', a negation of ability, or a lack of possibility, has a very relevant implication for the narrator: the inability to write to the order of the marketplace. Back in 1822 Clare wrote to John Taylor of disappointing sales of *The Village Minstrel*:

> the old Vol had gone thro 2 editions ere this & I think a notice in the london agen of a New vol of Poems preparing is nessesary as a stimulant to revive the flattness of these for I am jealous of their ill sucess   at least I feel somthing that tells me they dont go off like the others & I prevent that feeling as much as ever I can from damping my further exertions but I cannot help it doing so at some times—still Im determind in the teeth of vexation to surmount dissapointment by unwearied struggles—
> 10

From the start of his career Clare was thus desperately vexed with—and sensitively aware of—a fickle marketplace. In the same letter he blames his 'fickle Hussey' of a Muse for not stimulating him to write. All of his artistic frustration with a neglectful marketplace, and its effects upon his writing power, informs 'Don Juan A Poem'. The third stanza is full of such frustrations and tensions:

> I wish—but there is little got bye wishing
> I wish that bread & great coats ne'er had risen
> I wish that there was some such word as 'pishun
> For ryhme sake for my verses must be dizen
> With dresses fine—as hooks with baits for fishing
> I wish all honest men were out of prison
> I wish M.P.'s. would spin less yarn—nor doubt
> But burn false bills & cross bad taxes out (ll. 17-24)

The speaker suggests here that his verses need 'dresses fine', as if his poetry were a prostitute in need of tarting up, as it were, to catch the eyes, and cash, of the punters, thus forging a palpable link with the letter of 1822. The poet-whore has to put the bait of 'dresses fine' on his hook to provide a 'stimulant to revive the flatness' of sales.

The image of the prostitute wearing 'dresses fine' is linked with the M.P.s' 'spinning yarn' who are therefore implied as 'dressing up' their speeches; in other words, of talking fashionable rubbish, or cant. Clare's attacks on politicians are in some ways similar to Byron's, in that he shows no particular allegiance to any party: he writes, 'I wish the Whigs were out of office' and 'I'm weary of old Whigs' but also 'Ive seen a Whig & Tory / Turn imps of hell—& all for Englands glory' (ll. 66, 103 and 111-12). His reaction to political parties, and attacks upon individuals such as the shortly-to-resign Prime Minister Melbourne, suggest that Clare is attempting to write a poem situated very much in the hub of urban and capital life. Lord Melbourne—as plain William Lamb in 1812—had been made into a cuckold by his wife Caroline Lamb's celebrated affair with none other than Byron; Clare would have been well aware of this controversy.[11] Historical accounts confirm Melbourne's fawning intimacy with Queen Victoria, his passion for the royal court, and his fluid political allegiances.[12] Clare makes much of these popular views:

Me-b-ne may throw his wig to little Vicky
& so resign his humbug & his power
& she with the young princess mount the dickey
On ass milk diet for her german tour
Asses like ministers are rather tricky
I & the country proves it every hour
W-ll-gt-n & M-lb–n in their station
Coblers to queens—are phisic to the nation (ll. 81-8)

This stanza might indicate that one of the reasons for the attack on women in general in this poem is that the leading men of the day are seen by the narrator to be subservient to a woman, and a young one at that. Her reign is cast as incapacitation for man. The potency of the patriarchy is usurped by the governing matriarch, dismissed as 'little Vicky'. The 'phisic' that Wellington and Melbourne bestow upon the nation is undermined by its slang meanings of sexual coition, gambling losses, hard punching and strong drink.[13] All of these meanings make sense in the context of the politicians' serving the nation, bizarrely enough, as they are all vice- or violence-oriented. The overall sense is clear: politicians do no good whatsoever for the state. They are as corrupt as the subjects they represent.

The recurrent image of the poet-prisoner is arguably as significant in this poem as the poet-whore. Somehow the poet-prisoner is both deeply embedded within society—understanding its mostly feminine core corruption from Queen Victoria through to whores—while being also alien to it, left out, locked up and not a participant in the masquerade of decadent and prurient society. The implication in 'Don Juan A Poem' is that corruption begins at the top. Queen Victoria becomes the lead in Clare's feminine figuration of corruption, which could be indicative of a broader criticism of the nation state itself. The fragility, deceptivity and sheer liability of female sexuality as represented in 'Don Juan A Poem' characterises the nation. In the matriarchy, the corrupt mother figure 'little Vicky' is implicated when the speaker asserts that the very word 'woman ... implies a whore' and is 'mans ruin'. If the head of state is ruinous, and her politicians 'withered stinking dead and rotten' (l. 96), the only authority the speaker might pin his hopes on is God. But the narrator links the nobility ('noble bastards', l. 64), the government, the Queen, Prince Albert, the devil and God in a way which implies they are all equally decrepit and culpable. The many hollow lines which begin 'I wish' are a parodic undermining of Byron's opening desire 'I want a hero'; the speaker of Clare's poem wants one too, but he has given up hope of finding one.

Clare's poem suggests that there isn't anyone who could be called a hero in 1840's England. Even God warrants some indirect criticism (see ll. 78, 92, 104). The politicians contrive a canting language which 'few can understand'; the implication is that they are criminals who could be punished by 'some good atorney' (l. 67). They undermine personal property and personal liberties. In abusing the nation's purse ('Whigs strum state fiddle strings until they snap', l. 57), they symbolically defile the queen. In defiling the queen, they cuckold every man in the state—destroying the possession a man (by implication) should have over the procreation in his marriage. The final words of the poem 'the rights of man'—of masculinity—are worthless.

The poem seems to suggest that if everything is for sale, then everything has the objective of deceit and misrepresentation: be it sexuality, literature, gambling, medicine or politics, every aspect of society is diseased, corrupted and unoriginal. The next stanzas make it clear why Clare chose to adopt the work of another poet to continue: in contemporary society everything bears the stain of misuse and the tawdry, tatty quality of being second-hand and unoriginal. The poem's origins, in being openly unoriginal, reflect that society. The repetition of 'new' in the first line of the following stanza forms a double negative; the second 'new' is old—it is a copy of the first—and its appearance proves that the first 'new' is a sham. The half-rhyming consonance of 'Now' is old by the end of the line.

> Now this new poem is entirely new
> As wedding gowns or money from the mint
> For all I know it is entirely true
> For I would scorn to put a lie in print
> —I scorn to lie for princes—so would you
> & ere I shoot I try my pistol flint
> —The cattle salesman—knows the way in trying
> & feels his bullocks ere he thinks of buying (ll. 151-8)

The poem is likened by its narrator to objects associated with dependable honesty and security: a virgin-white wedding dress and newly coined money. The poem itself has already offered opposing versions of the intrinsic 'value' of both: the 'road to marriage is—"the road to ruin"' while marriage itself is a 'driveling hoax / To please old codgers' and an 'incumberance on the rights of man' (ll. 294, 287 and 302); and bills of payment can be 'false' (l. 24). The speaker duplicitously defends himself, after a fashion, colloquially suggesting both the limits of his ability and insight in saying 'For all I know', and hammering home that he 'would scorn to put a lie in print'. He suggests that, perhaps unlike other writers 'in print', he would be loath to write for royalty or riches. The first two lines of Byron's 'Dedication' to his *Don Juan* attack a poet whose status is built upon doing exactly what Clare's narrator claims he would never do: he works for royalty. 'Bob Southey! You're a poet, poet laureate, / And representative of all the race.' Southey was still laureate in 1841.[14]

Clare's speaker evokes a very Byronic image—the preparing of pistols—

but the image's association with a rich patron and print can only mean that before he publishes he makes sure his weapon is ready to spark. The word 'pistol' was colloquial slang, verging on euphemism, for the penis. The verb 'to shoot'[15] was available to Clare as a colloquial expression referring to the male orgasm. It is therefore a thoroughly masculine sexual image, and this interpretation is supported by the subsequent farcical punning image of a salesman feeling 'his bullocks' before a sale. The preparation then, before publication—before the sale—is a strutting and posturing of reassuringly masculine similes. The phallic 'pistol' is prepared, and the bullock is fondled. Either Clare is undermining by parody the pomposity of the Romantic-period writer (specifically the aristocratic Byron), or the poem reveals a problem for the male writer with performing in print. As the animal which is for sale is not a potent bull but a castrated 'bullock', it could be that the anxiety of going into print is an anxiety which affects the poet's masculinity. Although the pun made available to the reader via 'feels his bullocks' is 'feels his bollocks', in actual fact the bullock has none. This suggests that the poet is not only a whore for entering into negotiations with the marketplace via a 'cattle salesman', but also that he is a castrato because he is a poet. The image of the cattle-market returns us to the dominating figure of the poet-whore. The poet-whore is at the beck and call of the marketplace; the poet who writes for princes is patronised out of his artistic freedom; the bull without testicles is just live meat—he will not procreate—he is manufactured into sterility. The poet-whore is a prisoner of the public. In Clare's poem the whore is an image of powerlessness and degradation. If the image of the whore does have any power over the speaker, he is always repulsed by the attraction, and is violently misogynist as a result. She represents the manufactory of desire—a lie, an untruth, a deception of love. She is functionality without spirituality—she is castrated of love. As is the poet who writes verse 'to fill his pocket'.

Sonia Hofkosh considers Romantic masculinity's anxiety about authorship to be the result of that domain becoming increasingly feminised, and she traces the image of the prostitute in other poets' work, particularly that of Byron:

...the difficulty of being a writer in this culture repeatedly takes the form of prostitution. The prostitute figures the writer who depersonalizes the self-expression by marketing it; even more, her promiscuity, her failure to distinguish among men, vexes to its depths the foundation of self-expression—the logic of personality and property by which men determine what they are and what they own.[16]

Clare's poem parodies a poet explicitly seeking to foster interest from a buying public; as such it becomes a parody of poetry which is 'made' or determined by market forces. He makes us aware of the materiality of the work in the title; his only addition to Byron's title are the words 'A Poem', which maybe appear to reassure the reader that this is indeed literature, and worth buying. But like the prostitute, the poem's existence, and even its value, depend upon that same purchasing interest of the public; in this sense the poet and whore are both 'made' or *un*-made by the attention or neglect of the consumer. Byron makes it plain. The possibility of his continuing his poem is in the readership's hands:

> ...but whether
> I shall proceed with his adventure is
> Dependent on the public altogether.
> We'll see, however, what they say to this;
> Their favour in an author's cap's a feather,
> And no great mischief's done by their caprice,
> And if their approbation we experience,
> Perhaps they'll have some more about a year hence. (I, cic)

Byron is teasing his readership as if it were a child: be nice, and you can have more. His admission that the power is really in the market, not with the author, is significant. In a marketplace glutted with female authors, the male poet is threatened by enormous competition from a gender previously excluded from authorial property.[17] In representing women and poets as prostitutes, Clare is admitting not only that his gendered position as a male poet is under threat, but also that it has been disastrously compromised by market forces. The poem repeatedly forces the point that in such circumstances artistic endeavour can have no integrity. In asserting a continual parallel between the state of poetry and the state of society, the poem goes further to suggest that without meaning and integrity in its art, society is itself a meaningless drudge of production and consumption. The repeated intertextual allusions to other poets and poems and the act of adoption of someone else's poem becomes a commentary on the state of the poetic product. The materiality of the poem—captured succinctly in the begging call to 'fill [the] pocket' (l. 270) of the writer—is a construct designed to portray poetry at its lowest ebb. And it seems that women are largely to blame.

Byron attacks literary women throughout *Don Juan*, for example:

> Oh ye, who make the fortunes of all books,
>   Benign ceruleans of the second sex!
> Who advertise new poems by your looks,
>   Your imprimatur will ye not annex?
> What, must I go to the oblivious cooks,
>   Those Cornish plunderers of Parnassian wrecks?
> Ah, must I then the only minstrel be
> Proscribed from tasting your Castalian tea?
>
> What, can I prove a lion then no more?
>   A ballroom bard, a foolscap, hot-press darling?
> To bear the compliments of many a bore
>   And sigh, 'I can't get out', like Yorick's starling?
> Why then I'll swear, as poet Wordy swore
>   (Because the world won't read him, always snarling),
> That taste is gone, that fame is but a lottery,
> Drawn by the bluecoat misses of a coterie. (IV, cviii and cix)

For Byron, women are the arbiters of fortune and fame for a male writer. The power they have is exercised in their triple roles of audience, critic and author. Women infringe upon the classically male territory of the inspirational Mount; so the male literary 'lion' king of poetry feels his power, and his masculine authority, is undermined. Clare's poem expresses similar concerns:

> I wish I had a quire of foolscap paper
> Hot pressed—& crowpens—how I could endite
> A silver candlestick & green wax taper
> Lord bless me what fine poems I would write

The very tailors they would read & caper
& mantua makers would be all delight
Though laurel wreaths my brows did ne'er environ
I think myself as great a bard as Byron (ll. 247-54)

The speaker wants the decadent and expensive trappings of a middle-class writer in order to write. These trappings are perhaps characteristic of the vain world which Byron parodies: Byron's narrator fears becoming a 'ballroom bard, a foolscap, hot-press darling'. In other words, he fears becoming the darling of the fashionable, and the female. Clare's speaker is critical of fashion too, but by pretending to nurse a desire to court the same fashionable readership—he calls them 'tailors' (possibly a pun on [John] Taylor's marketing policies) and 'mantua makers'. The vanities of fashion, which seem to have infected the manner of poetic production, can be flattered if the writer has the right equipment. In Clare's poem, it seems almost as if the writing equipment, or the paper on which the work is published, is more significant to the readership than the words written. This fear is expressed in Byron's words: 'taste is gone ... fame is but a lottery'. Clare's parodic poet also points to the whimsy of blind fame: after attributing the writing of great verse to the quality of the pen, the paper and the candle of the writer, the poet casually assumes Byron's status. And he is right to pick Byron for a poem about the degraded status of poetry: the latter had been incredibly famous, but his posthumous reputation by 1841 had dwindled dramatically. Clare's poem suggests that the deplorable state of contemporary poetry is represented in the vanity of believing that a good writing set will be enough; therefore the actual writing itself is of no importance. Byron writes that the bluestockings 'advertise new poems by [their] looks'; vanity, display and fashion are seen to be the significant factors in the contemporary degradation and feminisation of poetry. Both Clare and Byron had seen the enormously famous poet Wordsworth become embittered '[b]ecause the world won't read him'. Fashion turns away without any reason: 'fame is but a lottery'. If anyone does have control over the modern marketplace, it is the women both poets attack. The power of the new readership and authorship of women challenges, undermines and usurps both poets' sense of authorial masculinity. Perhaps, then, both poems point to the failure of masculine Romantic poetry to adapt to the feminisation of literature.

NOTES

For help with this essay I am grateful to Richard Cronin, Bob Cummings, Jane Stabler, Nicola Trott and Susan Wolfson. A longer version appears in my PhD thesis (Nottingham 1999).

1. Discussing the origins and use of this proverb, William Ringler writes: 'the earliest appearance, in any recognizable form, of the expression *poeta nascitur non fit* is in a commentary on Horace which now goes under the name of *Pseudo-Acro* ... Coleridge cited it when discussing the marks of "a natural poetic genius" in chap. xv of his *Biographia Literaria*.' William Ringler, '*Poeta nascitur non fit*: Some notes on the History of an Aphorism', *Journal of the History of Ideas*, 2, no. 1, 1941 (College of the City of New York), 497-504.

2. The most extensive study of Clare's *Child Harold* appears in chapters five and six of Lynne Pearce's unpublished doctoral thesis, 'John Clare and Mikhail Bakhtin: The Dialogic Principle. Readings from John Clare's Manuscripts 1832-1845' (University of Birmingham, 1987). See also chapter 11, above. For a historical and biographical consideration of Byron's influence on Clare, see Anne Barton, 'John Clare Reads Lord Byron', *Romanticism*, 2, no. 2 (1996), 127-48. Edward Strickland's article 'Boxer Byron: A Clare Obsession', *Byron Journal*, 17 (1989), 57-76, on Clare's fascination with Byron adds to this historical criticism. Perhaps the most theoretically sensitive work on the literary relationship between the two poets is by Philip Martin, 'Authorial Identity and the Critical Act: John Clare and Lord Byron', in *Questioning Romanticism*, ed. by John Beer (Baltimore and London: Johns Hopkins University Press, 1995).

3. See Taylor's Introduction to *Poems Descriptive of Rural Life and Scenery* (London: Taylor and Hessey, Stamford: E. Drury, 1820).

4. All references to Byron's *Don Juan* refer to Volume V of *Lord Byron: The Complete Poetical Works*, ed. by Jerome J. McGann (Oxford: Clarendon Press, 1986).

5. I am indebted to Robert Kirkpatrick of the University of North Carolina at Chapel Hill for this interpretation of the rhyme sounds of this opening stanza.

6. All references to Clare's 'Don Juan A Poem' are to *John Clare, The Living Year 1841*, ed. by Tim Chilcott (Nottingham: Trent Editions, 1999), recto pages 37-57. Chilcott's edition of the poem supersedes all previous editions in its chronological and textual accuracy. The order of the stanzas contrasts significantly with previous editions of the poem.

7. *Later Poems*, I, p. 90, note 38.

8. Eric Partridge, *A Dictionary of Slang and Unconventional English*, ed. by Paul Beale (London: Routledge and Kegan Paul, 8th edn., 1984), used throughout this essay.

9. *Hamlet*, ed. by T. J. B. Spencer, (London: Penguin Books, 1980), III. ii. 125.

10. *Clare-John Taylor*, 8 February 1822; *Letters*, pp. 229-30.

11. Not only did Clare own a copy of Medwin's *Conversations*, but also *Lord Byron and Some of His Contemporaries*, by Leigh Hunt (London: Henry Colburn, 2nd edn., 1828) and William Hazlitt's less than favourable criticism of Byron in his *Lectures on the English Poets, Delivered at the Surrey Institution* (London: Taylor and Hessey, 1819).

12. See chapter 24 of *Melbourne* by Philip Ziegler (London: Fontana/Collins, 1976), pp. 336 ff.

13. Partridge, *Dictionary of Slang*.

14. Clare had criticised Southey for writing for Royalty long before. In his 1820s portrait of contemporary literary life 'The Bards & their Doxeys' he writes:
    While Southys old nurse of a doxys so tame
    & so fond of shoving her nose into fame
    That shed een nurse a monkey to prove her self loyal
    & sing him an ode if his title was royal (*Middle Poems* II, p. 91, ll. 19-22)
    A 'dox(e)y' is a beggar's wench.

15. Partridge, *Dictionary of Slang*.

16. Sonia Hofkosh, *Sexual Politics and the Romantic Author* (Cambridge: Cambridge University Press, 1998), p. 44.

17. Catherine Gallagher, 'George Eliot and *Daniel Deronda*: The Prostitute and the Jewish Question' in *Sex, Politics, and Science in the Nineteenth-Century Novel*, ed. by Ruth Bernard Yeazell (Baltimore: Johns Hopkins University Press, 1986), p. 43:
    Thackeray identifies two reasons for this historical conjuncture [of poet and whore]: the development of cheap serial publication (in which authors were often paid by the line) and the growth of a massive popular readership in the 1830s and 1840s. These conditions most directly affected what we now call popular literature, but the decreasing cost of publication, advances in education, and changes in copyright law made it impossible for any professional writer to claim to be independent of the marketplace ... The author, moreover, does not go to market as a respectable producer with an alienable commodity, but with himself or herself as commodity ... This combination puts writers in the marketplace in the position of selling themselves, like whores.

FURTHER READING:
A CHRONOLOGICAL SURVEY OF CLARE CRITICISM, 1970-2000

John Goodridge

Introduction

This list of modern critical responses to Clare is designed to supplement, with a generous overlap, the existing bibliographies, which are listed below. (The most important are those by Crossan, Dendurent, and Estermann. Dawson is the most useful guide to recent criticism.) Since the emphasis here is on critical writings, supplemented by biographical and historical scholarship, I have not attempted to list editions, stray publications, creative, journalistic, personal or autobiographical responses. These areas are sampled where they appear to have significant critical content or contribute to general Clare scholarship. Introductions to editions are included. Review essays are normally included, and the more important reviews (others are cited selectively under the reviewed book's entry). Citations to reference volumes are by no means exhaustive.

A comprehensive bibliography of Clare, though, is not attempted here, partly because it would demand an unreasonably large amount of space, but also because, as Greg Crossan has noted, such a thing serves no purpose. Some of the excluded areas noted above would be best served by having their own dedicated bibliographical resources (a listing and discography of the proliferating musical responses to Clare, for example, would be very useful). The particular purpose of the present list is to enable readers to see how Clare criticism has developed over three decades. It is therefore arranged chronologically, by year, with separate sections for bibliographies and sources of manuscript and archival information at the beginning. There are four sub-sections for each year: (a) books, (b) articles, chapters and short pamphlets, (c) scholarly theses, and (d) *John Clare Society Journal* (from 1982), the latter separately listed in order to enable readers to assess the contents of each annual number. Material of value from the *John Clare Society Newsletter* (mainly notes and queries), is included under (b). Where (as is usual) no date is given for an item, the year of publication is the one under which it is filed.

The index was developed for the *John Clare Page* on the internet, where it will continue to be updated and corrected. The 1993-2000 part of it has also been published in the *John Clare Society Journal*, nos. 18-19 (1999-2000), and new publications will continue to be listed in the *Journal*.

Thanks are due to Celia Coates and Mary Dawson (Library and Information Services, Nottingham Trent University) for invaluable database searching, to Bob Heyes for generously supplying copies of bibliographical materials and extensive general assistance, to Simon Kövesi for putting things into shape for the website, and to Paul Chirico, Stephen Colclough, John Coletta, Greg Crossan, Tim Fulford, Bob Heyes, Bridget Keegan, Simon Kövesi, John Lucas, Jim McKusick, Scott McEathron, Simon Sanada, John Wareham and Sarah Zimmerman for their contributions.

Bibliographies

A Check List of Books By and About John Clare (chiefly from a private collection) (Wilbarston, Northamptonshire: Pilgrim Publications, 1970), 20 page pamphlet.

Crack, F. N., 'Nature Poet John Clare', *The Book and Magazine Collector*, 113 (Aug 1993), 50-7.

Crossan, Greg, 'John Clare: A Chronological Bibliography', *Bulletin of Bibliography*, 32 (1975), 55-62, 88.

— 'John Clare: a Bibliography of Commentary on the Poems, to 1982', *Bulletin of Bibliography*, 41 (Dec 1984), 185-200.

— 'Some Fugitive John Clare Items 1820-1977', *Notes and Queries*, 231 (n.s. 33) (June 1986), 167-70.

Dawson, P.M.S., 'John Clare', in *Literature of the Romantic Period: A Bibliographical Guide*, ed. by Michael O'Neill (Oxford: Clarendon Press, 1998), pp. 167-80.

Dendurent, H. D., *John Clare, a Reference Guide* (London and Boston: George Prior Publishers and G. K. Hall, 1978), reviewed in *Notes and Queries*, 225 (n.s. 27) (Aug 1980), 378; and by John Barrell in *Review of English Studies*, 32 (1981), 114-15.

Estermann, Barbara H., *John Clare: an Annotated Primary and Secondary Bibliography* (New York: Garland, 1985), reviewed in *Notes and Queries*, 232 (n.s. 34) (June 1987), 286-9; *Keats-Shelley Journal*, 36 (1987), 203-5; *JCSJ*, 6 (1987), 50-1. Based on a dissertation: see *Dissertation*

Abstracts International, 46 (4), 988A.

Musty, John, 'Collecting Country Writers 6. The Labouring Poets: Stephen Duck, Robert Bloomfield, and John Clare', *Antiquarian Book Monthly Review*, 13 (1) (Jan 1986), 4-15, includes a basic first editions checklist to 1981.

Romantic Movement Bibliography (annually, from 1979; formerly in *ELN)*, a listing and selective review of Clare material, mainly by Mark Minor (whose summary reviews are incisive and useful).

Storey, Mark, 'John Clare', in Joanne Shattock (ed.), *The Cambridge Bibliography of English Literature, Volume 4, 1800-1900, Third Edition* (Cambridge: Cambridge University Press, 2000).

Todd, Janet M., 'John Clare: a Bibliographical Essay', *British Studies Monitor*, 4 (Winter 1974), 3-18.

Note: there are useful bibliographies in many of the books listed below, notably Crossan (1976), Chilcott (1985), Goodridge (1994), and Haughton, Context (1994).

Manuscripts and archival materials

Grainger, Margaret, *A Descriptive Catalogue of the John Clare Collection in Peterborough Museum and Art Gallery* (Peterborough: printed for the Earl Fitzwilliam, 1973), reviewed in *Notes and Queries*, 218 (n.s. 21) (Sep 1974), 354.

[Powell, David], *Catalogue of the John Clare Collection in the Northampton Public Library* (Northampton: Northampton Public Library, 1964; with inserted loose-leaf *Supplement*, 1971).

— 'The John Clare Collection in Northampton Public Library', *Library World*, 65 (May 1964), 362-3.

Rosenbaum, Barbara, 'John Clare (1793-1864)', *Index of English Literary Manuscripts, Vol. IV (1800-1900), Part 1 (Arnold-Gissing)*, ed. by Barbara Rosenbaum and Pamela White (London: Mansell, 1982), pp. 421-58, 828-9.

Sutton, David C., *Location Register of English Literary Manuscripts and Letters: Eighteenth and Nineteenth Century* (London: British Library, 1995), I, pp. 203-5.

1970

(b)

Adlard, John, 'John Clare: the Long Walk Home', *English*, 19, 85-9.

Brill, Barbara, 'Conservation and the Poet', *Library Review*, 22 (8), 412-15.

Evans, George Ewart, *Where Beards Wag All* (London: Faber), pp. 169-70.

Fraser, Angus M., 'John Clare's Gypsies', *Northamptonshire Past and Present*, 4 (5), 259-67, reprinted in *Journal of the Gypsy-Lore Society*, 3rd ser., 50 (1971), 85-100.

Pinsky, Robert, 'That Sweet Man, John Clare', in *The Rarer Action: Essays in Honor of Francis Ferguson*, ed. by Alan Cheuse and Richard Koffler (New Brunswick, New Jersey: Rutgers University Press), pp. 258-74.

Powell, David, 'Northamptonshire's Own Poet', *Northamptonshire Life*, Feb-March, pp. 33-5.

Storey, Mark, 'Clare's "Love and Beauty"', *Explicator*, 28 (March), item 60.

Watson, J. R., *Picturesque Landscape and English Romantic Poetry* (London: Hutchinson), pp. 22-3, 187-8.

Williams, Raymond, 'Ideas of Nature', *Times Literary Supplement*, 4 Dec, p. 1421.

(c)

Minor, Mark George, 'The Poet in his Joy: a critical study of John Clare's poetic development', PhD dissertation, Ohio State University; *Dissertation Abstracts International*, 31, 4784A.

1971

(a)

Blunden, Edmund, *John Clare: Beginner's Luck* (Wateringbury, Kent: Bridge Books/Kent Editions); reprinted with corrections in *JCSJ*, 15 (1996), 5-10.

(b)

Fowles, John, 'The Blinded Eye', *Animals*, January, pp. 388-92, reprinted in *Second Nature*, ed. by Richard Mabey with Susan Clifford and Angela King for Common Ground (London: Jonathan Cape, 1984), pp. 77-89, and in Fowles's *Wormholes: Essays and Occasional Writings* (London: Jonathan Cape, 1998), pp. 259-68.

Frosch, Thomas R., 'The Descriptive Style of John Clare', *Studies in Romanticism*, 10, 137-49.

Jones, Leonidas M. (ed.), *The Letters of John Hamilton Reynolds* (Lincoln, NA: University of Nebraska Press), Appendix 1, pp. 71-2, prints an incomplete draft of a pre-publication notice of *The Village Minstrel* by Reynolds.

Storey, Edward, *Portrait of the Fen Country* (London: Hale), pp. 191-202.

Storey, Mark, 'Edwin Paxton Hood (not the Rev. Romeo Elton) and John Clare', *Notes and Queries*, 216 (n.s. 18) (Oct), 386-7.

Wade, R.A.R., 'An Introduction to John Clare', *Journal of the Gypsy Lore Society*, 3rd ser., 50, 82-5.

(c)

Barrell, John, 'The Idea of Landscape and the Sense of Place, 1730-1840: An Approach to the Poetry of John Clare', PhD dissertation, University of Essex (published as a book in 1972).

Bush, Eliot Jarvis, 'The Poetry of John Clare', PhD dissertation, University of Wisconsin, Madison; *Dissertation Abstracts International*, 32, 3295A.

Gillin, Richard L., 'In that so ungentle sky: A Study of John Clare's Sonnets', PhD dissertation, Bowling Green State University; *Dissertation Abstracts International*, 32, 6374A-75A.

Todd, Janet, 'In Adam's Garden; a Study of John Clare', PhD dissertation, University of Florida; *Dissertation Abstracts International*, 33, 768A (published as a book in 1973).

1972

(a)

Barrell, John, *The Idea of Landscape and the Sense of Place, 1730-1840: An Approach to the Poetry of John Clare* (London: Cambridge University Press), reviewed in *Times Literary Supplement*, 9 June, p. 654; *Connoisseur*, 181 (Oct), 139; *English*, 21 (Autumn), 111-13; *Anglo-Welsh Review*, 22 (1) (1973), 197-208; *Critical Quarterly*, 15 (Summer 1973), 188-9; *Notes and Queries*, 218 (n.s. 20) (Sep 1974), 353-4.

Tibble, J. W. and Anne, *John Clare: a Life* (London: Michael Joseph), revised
edition, reviewed in *Times Literary Supplement*, 13 Oct, p. 1216; *The
Scotsman* (24 June).

(b)

'Celebrating the *is*', *Times Literary Supplement*, 9 June, p. 654.

Chilcott, Tim, *A Publisher and His Circle: The Life and Work of John Taylor,
Keats's Publisher* (London: Routledge), esp. pp. 86-128; reviewed in
Times Literary Supplement, 27 Oct; *Review of English Studies*, 24 (1973),
225-6; *Notes and Queries*, 218 (n.s. 20) (Sep 1974).

Church, Richard, 'A Poet and His Landscape', *Country Life*, 151 (23 March),
732.

Donoghue, Denis, 'Clare and Country', *Spectator*, 228 (25 March), 481-2,
a review of Barrell.

Grigson, Geoffrey, Introduction to J.W. and Anne Tibble, *John Clare: a
Life*, pp. xvii-xxi.

Todd, Janet, 'Mary Joyce in the Poetry of John Clare', *Mary Wollstonecraft
Newsletter*, 1 (July), 12-18.

Wainwright, Judith, 'The Particular Place', *Stand*, 14 (3) (1972-3), 42-9.

(c)

Masson, Louis Joseph, 'The Fearful Vision: The Poetry of John Clare', PhD
dissertation, University of Syracuse; *Dissertation Abstracts
International*, 33, 279A.

Russell, Charles Anthony, 'Experience and Relationship: a Context for the
Poetry of John Clare', PhD dissertation, University of Pennsylvania;
Dissertation Abstracts International, 33, 6883A-4A.

1973

(a)

Storey, Mark (ed.), *Clare: the Critical Heritage* (London: Routledge & Kegan
Paul), reviewed in *Times Literary Supplement*, 27 July, p. 856; *English
Studies*, 55 (1974), 367-8; *Victorian Periodicals Newsletter*, 3 (3) (Sep
1974), 32-4.

Todd, Janet, *In Adam's Garden: a study of John Clare's pre-asylum poetry* (Gainesville: University of Florida Press), University of Florida Humanities Monograph no. 39, reviewed by Mark Storey, *Essays in Criticism*, 24, 399-406.

(b)

'An unsuitable case for treatment', *Times Literary Supplement,* 27 July, p. 856.

Gregory, Horace, 'The Sight of Nature in the Poetry of John Clare', in his *Spirit of Time and Place* (New York: W.W. Norton), pp. 25-32.

Humfrey, Belinda, Review of Barrell (1972), *Anglo-Welsh Review*, 22 (1), 197-208.

Ishii, Shonosuke, 'John Clare no Shizen-shi' [John Clare's nature poems], *Eige Seinen [The Rising Generation]* [Tokyo], 119, 258-9, 332-3.

Jordan, John E. (ed.), *De Quincey as Critic* (London: Routledge & Kegan Paul), pp. 356-60, reprints De Quincey's 1840 comment on Clare and Allan Cunningham.

Kirkup, James, 'Clare the Bird Watcher', in *Birds Nest: Twenty Poems by John Clare*, ed. by Anne Tibble (Ashington: Mid-Northumberland Arts Group), pp. 10-16, and in *Eigo Seinen [The Rising Generation]* [Tokyo], 118, 634-7.

Stanford, Derek, 'Poetry', *Books and Bookmen*, 19 (Nov), 106.

Storey, Mark, 'A "Missing" Letter from John Clare to John Taylor', *Notes and Queries*, 217 (Feb), 54-7.

Tibble, Anne, 'The Provenance of the Poems', in *Birds Nest: Twenty Poems by John Clare* (Ashington: Mid-Northumberland Arts Group), pp. 7-10.

— 'John Clare and His Doctors', *Charles Lamb Bulletin*, n.s. 4 (Oct), 77-81.

Wade, Stephen, 'John Clare's Use of Dialect', *Contemporary Review*, 223 (Aug), 81-4.

Wainwright, Judith, 'The Particular Place', *Stand*, 14 (3), 42-9.

Williams, Raymond, *The Country and the City* (London: Chatto and Windus), pp. 132-41.

(c)

Dennehy, Frederick J., 'The Broken Charm: A Study of John Clare's Poetry', PhD dissertation, University of Virginia; *Dissertation Abstracts International*, 34, 1854A-5A.

Fletcher, C. V., 'The Poetry of John Clare: with particular reference to poems written between 1837 and 1864', MPhil dissertation, Nottingham University.

Rapf, Joanna, '"The Constellation of the Plough": The Peasant Poets, John Clare and his "Circle," a study of their relationship to some major Romantic writers', PhD dissertation, Brown University; *Dissertation Abstracts International*, 34, 6603A-4A

1974

(a)

Storey, Mark, *The Poetry of John Clare: a Critical Introduction* (London: Macmillan), reviewed in *English*, 24 (1975), 62-3; *Choice*, 12 (April 1975), 224; *English Studies*, 56 (1975), 436-7; *Dalhousie Review*, 55 (Summer 1975), 387-9; *Critical Quarterly*, 17 (Summer 1975), 186-7; *Library Journal*, 100 (15 Jan 1975), 132; *Criticism*, 17 (Fall 1975), 371-3; *Review of English Studies*, 27 (1976), 90-1; *Notes and Queries*, 221 (n.s. 23) (March 1976), 135-7; *Victorian Studies*, 20 (Autumn 1976), 96-8; *Yearbook of English Studies*, 6 (1976), 300; *Charles Lamb Bulletin*, n.s. 13 (Jan 1976), 101-4.

(b)

Crossan, G. D., 'John and Thomas Clare', *Times Literary Supplement*, 1 March, p. 212.

Grigson, Geoffrey, 'Visions of Freedom', *Country Life*, 156 (17 Oct), 1150.

Hatley, Victor A., 'The Poet and the Railway Surveyors, an Incident in the Life of John Clare', *Northamptonshire Past and Present*, 5, (2), 101-6.

Luckin, Bill, 'The Pathology of the Past', *Times Literary Supplement*, 22 March, p. 294, a reply to Macalpine and Hunter, below.

Lupini, Barbara, '"An Open and Simple Eye": The Influence of Landscape on the Work of John Clare and Vincent Van Gogh', *English*, 23, 58-62.

Macalpine, Ida and Richard Hunter, 'The Pathography of the Past', *Times Literary Supplement*, March, pp. 256-7.

Nye, Robert, 'John Clare: Poet of Nature', *Books and Bookmen*, 19 (10), 54-5.

Porter, Peter, 'John Clare (1793-1864), in *The English Poet: from Chaucer to Edward Thomas* (London: Secker and Warburg), pp. 221-4.

Rapf, Joanna E., Review of Barrell and Tibble (both 1972), *Studies in Romanticism*, 13 (Winter), 79-84.

Robinson, Eric, 'A Note on John Clare', *British Studies Monitor*, 5 (Fall), 36-8.

Storey, Mark, 'Some Previously Unpublished Letters from John Clare', *Review of English Studies*, 25 (May), 177-85.

Tibble, Anne, 'Written by Clare', *Times Literary Supplement*, 10 May, pp. 502-3.

— 'John Clare: a Tribute', *Countryman*, 79 (Summer), 113.

Todd, Janet M., '"Very Copys of Nature": John Clare's Descriptive Poetry', *Philological Quarterly*, 53 (Jan), 84-99.

1975

(a)

Levi, Peter, *John Clare and Thomas Hardy* (London: The Athlone Press), The John Coffin Memorial Lecture, 1975, reviewed in *Modern Language Review*, 73 (1978), 175-7.

(b)

Blythe, Ronald, 'The Dangerous Idyll: Sweet Auburn to Akenside', *Essays by Divers Hands*, n.s. 38, 15-20, collected in his *From the Headlands* (London: Chatto & Windus, 1982), pp. 144-61, and in his *Talking About John Clare* (Nottingham; Trent Editions, 1999), pp. 56-76.

Robinson, Eric, Review of Todd (1973), Barrell (1972), Storey (1973 and 1974), *The Wordsworth Circle*, 6 (Summer), 221-3.

Swingle, L. J. 'Stalking the essential John Clare: Clare in relation to his Romantic Contemporaries', *Studies in Romanticism*, 14 (Summer), 273-84.

(c)

Crossan, Greg, '"A Relish for Eternity": the process of divinization in the poetry of John Clare', PhD dissertation, University of Canterbury, New Zealand (published as a book in 1976).

James, A. W. P., 'John Clare's Art: Development and Disintegration in the Later Poetry', MPhil dissertation, University of London, Birkbeck College.

1976

(a)

Crossan, Greg, *A Relish for Eternity: the process of divinization in the poetry of John Clare* (Saltzburg: Universität Salzburg), Saltzburg Studies in English Literature, Romantic Reassessment 53, reviewed in *Yearbook of English Studies*, 10 (1980), 303.

(b)

Bond, Edward, 'An Introduction to "The Fool"', *Theatre Quarterly*, 6 (Spring), 33-8 See also the materials by Walter Donohue and Peter Gill on pp. 12-32 of this number, Tony Coult's interview with Bond, 'Creating What is Normal', *Plays and Players*, 23 (Dec 1975), 9-13, and Benedict Nightingale's review of this play about Clare, 'Compassionate Scribler', *New Statesman*, 28 Nov 1975, p. 689.

Esslin, Martin, 'Nor Yet a "Fool" to Fame...', *Theatre Quarterly*, 6 (Spring), 39-44.

Haynes, John, 'Clare's Description', *Stand*, 17 (2), 9-14.

Pinsky, Robert, *The Situation of Poetry: Contemporary Poetry and its Traditions* (Princeton: Princeton University Press), pp. 118-33, 181-2, comparative discussing of Clare's badger poem.

(c)

Al-Wasiti, S. D., 'The Poetry of John Clare', PhD dissertation, Leicester University.

Brownlow, David Timothy, 'John Clare and Picturesque Landscape', PhD dissertation, University of York (Canada); *Dissertation Abstracts International*, 37, 5842A-3A (published as a book in 1983).

Link, Ronald W., 'Towards the Abyss: modern elements in the poetry of John Clare', PhD dissertation, Miami University; *Dissertation Abstracts International*, 37, 2897A-8A.

1977

(b)

Bailey, Brian J., 'Clare's Ruined Village: Pickworth, Leicestershire', *Country Life*, 161 (21 April), 996.

Wade, Stephen P., 'John Clare's "The Parish": A Transition in Verse Satire', *Stand*, 18 (3), 51-5.

Wagner, Mary, 'The Enclosed World of John Clare', *Farmer's Weekly*, 29 April, pp. 110-11.

(c)

Jillings, M., 'Time and Related Themes in the Poetry of John Clare', MLitt dissertation, University of Stirling.

1978

(a)

Crowson, Daniel, *Rambles with John Clare* (Helpston: C.E. Cutforth)

Washington, Peter, *Brodie's Notes on Selected Poetry and Prose of John Clare* (London: Pan Books).

(b)

Brownlow, Timothy, 'A Molehill for Parnassus: John Clare and Prospect Poetry', *University of Toronto Quarterly*, 48 (1) (Fall), 23-40.

Riga, Frank P., and Claud A. Prance, *Index to the London Magazine* (New York: Garland), Garland Reference Library of the Humanities, Vol. 103, identifies Clare's contributions and indexes his poems in the *London*.

Tomlinson, Steven, 'The Antiquary and the Poet: Edmund Artis and John Clare', *Durobrivae*, 6, 6-8.

White, Norman, 'John Clare and Gerard Manley Hopkins', *American Notes and Queries*, Supp. 1, 203-4.

1979

(b)

Beer, Patricia, Review of *The Midsummer Cushion*, *The Listener*, 15 Feb, pp. 261-6.

Collier, Ray, 'John Clare: a Memory Lost?', *Birds*, 7 (Autumn), 27-9, reprinted as 'The finest naturalist...' in *JCSN*, 46 (Dec 1994), 2-3, and 47 (March 1995), 2-3.

Collins, Bob, 'Poet of the Shires: Bob Collins on the Trail of John Clare', *The Lady*, 8 March, pp. 440-1, 444.

Drabble, Margaret, *A Writer's Britain: Landscape in Literature* (London: Thames and Hudson), esp. 'The Pastoral Vision', pp. 60-6.

Gilpin, Arthur, 'John Clare: the Birdwatcher's Poet', *Country Life*, 3 Sep, pp. 766-7.

Grainger, Margaret, 'John Clare', *Notes and Queries*, 224 (n.s. 26) (Dec), 562, queries about quotations in the prose.

McNeil, Helen, Review of *The Midsummer Cushion*, *New Statesman*, 15 June, p. 878.

Taplin, Kim, *The English Path* (Ipswich: The Boydell Press), pp. 7-8, 27-30, 85-6 and passim.

Thatcher, David S. and Bryan N.S. Gooch, *Musical Settings of Early and Mid-Victorian Literature: A Catalogue* (New York: Garland), contains Clare material.

Tibble, Anne, *Alone* (London: Peter Owen), an autobiographical volume which includes the story of Tibble's struggle to publish *The Midsummer Cushion* for the first time.

— and Thornton, R.K.R., Introduction to *John Clare, The Midsummer Cushion* (Ashington and Manchester: Mid-Northumberland Arts Group and Carcanet Press), pp. vii-xvi.

(c)

Paira-Pemberton, Jean, 'Poesie et Folie chez John Clare', Dissertation, University of Strasbourg.

1980

(a)

Neumeyer, Peter, *Homage to John Clare: A Poetical and Critical Correspondence* (Salt Lake City: Peregrine Smith, Inc.), reviewed in *Western Humanitities Review*, 35 (1981), 11-16.

(b)

Bond, Edward, 'The Blackbird in the Bush', *The Guardian*, 23 Oct, a review of Tibble (ed.), *The Journal, Essays...*

Campbell, Bruce, 'The Birds of John Clare', *Folio*, Summer, pp. 3-5.

Gilpin, Arthur, 'Identifying John Clare's Birds', *Country Life*, 25 Sep, pp. 1020-2.

Keith, W. J., *The Poetry of Nature* (Toronto: Toronto University Press), pp. 43-80.

Levi, Peter, Introduction to *John Clare: Bird Poems* (London: Folio Society), pp. 9-18.

Minor, Mark, 'Clare and the Methodists: a Reconsideration', *Studies in Romanticism*, 19 (1) (Spring), 31-50.

Pigrome, Stella, Review of *The Midsummer Cushion*, *Charles Lamb Bulletin*, n.s. 31 (July), 140-6.

Tibble, Anne, Introduction to *John Clare: The Journal, Essays and Journey from Essex* (Ashington and Manchester: Mid-Northumberland Arts Group and Carcanet Press), pp. 9-28.

(c)

Chilcott, Tim, '"A real world & doubting mind": A Critical Study of the Poetry of John Clare', PhD dissertation, University of Sussex (published as a book in 1985).

1981

(a)

Howard, William, *John Clare* (Boston: Twayne Publishers), Twayne's English Authors Series, no. 312, reviewed in *Yearbook of English Studies*, 15 (1985), 312-13.

(b)

Geraths, Armin, 'A Frog's Eye View of the Romantics: Clare and Byron as Outcast Observers of Their Times', in *The Hanover Byron Symposium, 1979*, ed. by G Birkner et al (Salzburg: Institut für Anglistik und Amerikanistic, Universität Salzburg), Romantic Reassessment series, no. 80, pp. 152-4.

Hold, Trevor, 'John Clare's Last Journey', *Northamptonshire Past and Present*, 6 (4) (1980-1), 219-22.

Nye, Robert, 'Poetical Prosings of John Clare' *The Scotsman*, 17 Jan, Weekend Section, p. 3, review of Tibble (ed.), *The Journal, Essays...*

Paira-Pemberton, Jean, 'From Anon to a name: the case of John Clare', *Ranam*, 14, 39-59.

Patten, Brian, 'The Accessible Eden', Introduction to *Clare's Countryside: Natural History Poetry and Prose of John Clare*, selected and introduced by Brian Patten (London: Heinemann / Quixote Press), pp. [xi-xiv].

Raimond, Rosine, 'John Clare et la hantise de l'ailleurs', in *Images de L'ailleurs dans la littérature Anglo-Americaine* (Reims), pp. 49-63.

Scott-James, Anne, *The Cottage Garden* (London: Allen Lane), esp. pp. 42-5.

Spufford, Margaret, *Small Books and Pleasant Histories: Popular Fiction and Its Readership in Seventeenth-Century England* (London: Methuen), esp. pp. 1-6.

Storey, Mark, 'John Clare', in Justin Wintle (ed.), *Makers of Modern Culture* (London: Routledge & Kegan Paul).

Vincent, David, *Bread, Knowledge and Freedom: A Study of Nineteenth-Century Working Class Autobiography* (London: Europa Publications), a very important book, with references to Clare throughout.

Williams, Anne, 'Clare's Gypsies', *The Explicator*, 39 (3), 9-11.

1982

(a)

Storey, Edward, *A Right To Song: The Life of John Clare* (London: Methuen), reviewed by Peter Levi in the *Spectator*, 13 Nov, pp. 24-6; *New Statesman*, 17-24 Dec, p. 47; by Norman Nicholson in *Church Times*, 24 Dec, p. 5; *Daily Telegraph*, 29 Jan 1983; *Critical Quarterly*, 25 (3) (1983), 93;

Review of English Studies, 36 (1985), 283-4; *The Wordsworth Circle*, 16 (1985), 207-9; *Keats-Shelley Journal*, 34 (1985), 194-6; *Studies in Romanticism*, 25 (1986), 154-7.

(b)

Barrell, John, 'John Clare, William Cobbett and the Changing Landscape', in *The New Pelican Guide to English Literature 5. From Blake to Byron*, ed. by Boris Ford (Harmondsworth: Penguin), pp. 226-43.

Blythe, Ronald, 'An Inherited Perspective', and 'The Dangerous Idyll' in his *From the Headlands* (London: Chatto and Windus; New York: Harcourt Brace Jovanovich as *Characters and Their Landscapes*). See also 1975 and 1999.

Franklin, Mark, Introduction to *Nature Poetry from John Clare* (Sutton Mandeville, Salisbury, Wilts.: Perdix Press, 1982), pp. 7-17.

Grigson, Geoffrey, *The Private Art: A Poetry Notebook* (London: Allison and Busby) makes reference to Clare.

Höhne, Horst, 'John Clare's Rural Poetry and the Romantic Concept of Nature', *Wissenschaftliche Zeitschrift der Wilhelm-Pieck-Universität Rostock,* 31, 57-61.

Lessa, Richard, 'Time and John Clare's Calendar', *Critical Quarterly*, 24 (1) (Spring) 59-71, reviewed in *JCSN*, 2 (June), 3.

Minor, Mark, 'Clare, Byron and the Bible: Additional Evidence from the Asylum Manuscripts', *Bulletin of Research in the Humanities*, 85 (1), 104-26.

Purkiss, John, *The World of the English Romantic Poets: A Visual Approach* (London: Heinemann), pp. 122-7.

Robinson, Eric and Richard Fitter, Introduction to *John Clare's Birds* (Oxford: Oxford University Press), pp. vii-xx.

Sales, Roger, 'The Politics of Pastoral', in Kathleen Parkinson and Martin Priestman (eds), *Peasants and Countrymen in Literature* (London: English Department, Roehampton Institute of Higher Education), pp. 91-104 (see also 1983).

Smith, Hammond, *Peter DeWint* (London: F. Lewis), pp. 26-37.

Strang, Barbara M, 'John Clare's Language', in *The Rural Muse*, second edition, ed. by R. K. R. Thornton (Ashington and Manchester: Mid-Northumberland Arts Group and Carcanet Press), pp. 59-73.

Strickland, Edward, 'Conventions and Their Subversion in John Clare's "An Invite to Eternity"', *Criticism*, 24 (1), 1-15.

Thornton, R.K.R., Introduction to *John Clare, The Rural Muse* (Ashington and Manchester: Mid-Northumberland Arts Group and Carcanet Press), pp. 11-22.

(c)

Clare, Johanne Pierce, 'Social Identity and Experience in the Poetry of John Clare', Dissertation, University of Toronto; *Dissertation Abstracts International*, 42 (10), 4456A.

(d) *JCSJ*, 1 (1982)

Dixon, George E., 'Clare and Religion', 47-50.

Hold, Trevor, 'The Composer's Debt to John Clare', 25-9.

Lines, Rodney, 'John Clare's "The Skylark"', 53-6.

Robinson, Eric, 'Clare and Nature', 7-24.

Thornton, R. K. R., 'The Flower and the Book: The Gardens of John Clare', 31-45.

1983

(a)

Brownlow, Timothy, *John Clare and Picturesque Landscape* (Oxford: Oxford University Press), reviewed in *Notes and Queries*, 230 (n.s. 32) (June 1985), 278-9; *New Statesman*, 22 July, p. 27; *Keats-Shelley Journal*, 34 (1985), 194-6; *Modern Language Review*, 81 (1986), 178-81; *Studies in Romanticism*, 26 (1987), 179-82.

Deacon, George, *John Clare and the Folk Tradition* (London: Sinclair Browne; New York: State Mutual Book and Periodical Service), reviewed in *Times Literary Supplement*, 27 July 1984, pp. 845-6; *Victorian Studies*, 28 (1985), 538-9.

(b)

Constantine, David, 'Outside Eden: John Clare's Descriptive Poetry', in J.R. Watson (ed.), *An Infinite Complexity: Essays in Romanticism* (Edinburgh: Edinburgh University Press for the University of Durham), pp. 181-201.

Dawson, P.M.S., Review of *The Rural Muse* and *John Clare's Birds*, *Critical Quarterly*, 25 (2), 90-4.

Essex, Alice, 'My Clare Summer', *JCSN*, 6 (Nov), 3-4, reminiscences of Clare descendants, etc.

Grainger, Margaret, General Introduction to *Natural History*, pp. xxxiii-l.

Hatley, Victor A. and Brian G. Statham, 'Nassaburgh Militia Lists 1762', in *A Northamptonshire Miscellany*, ed. by Edmund King (Northampton: Northamptonshire Record Society), pp. 109-46.

Motion, Andrew, 'Sublimely Humble', *Times Literary Supplement*, 25 Nov, p. 1306, a review of *John Clare's Autobiographical Writings*.

Philip, Neil, 'In search of an ideal landscape', *Times Educational Supplement*, 18 March, p. 31, a review of Storey (1982), the first *Clare Journal*, and *John Clare's Birds*, ed. by Robinson and Fitter.

Raimond, Rosine, 'Le moi et l'autre ou la quête de soi chez John Clare', in *L'Autre dans la sensibilité Anglo-Saxonne* (Reims), pp. 63-75.

Robinson, Eric, Introduction to *John Clare's Autobiographical Writings* (Oxford: Oxford University Press), pp. vii-xiv.

Rush, Phil, 'John Clare: Village Fiddler', *English Dance and Song*, 45 (3), 10-12.

Sales, Roger, 'John Clare and the Politics of Pastoral', in *English Literature in History 1780-1830: Pastoral and Politics* (London: Hutchinson), pp. 88-109, developed from his 1981 essay, listed above.

Tate, Ann, 'In Search of Clare's Birds', *Camping and Caravanning*, 78 (6) (June), 36-40.

(d) *JCSJ*, 2 (1983)

Barrell, John, 'John Clare's "The Lane"', 3-8.

Dean, E. Barbara, 'John Clare at Lolham Bridges', 24-7.

Robinson, Eric, 'Editorial Problems in John Clare', 9-23.

Scrimgeour, Cecil, 'John Clare and the Price of Experience', 28-39.

1984

(b)

Crossan, Greg, 'Three "lost" Epitaphs Recovered', *JCSN*, 8 (June), [3-4].

Hayward, Joan, [a short piece on memories of Helpston in the 1920s], *JCSN*, 8 (June), [2-3].

Hunnikin-Lepper, Philip, 'Memories of St Andrews Hospital', *JCSN*, 7 (April), 4.

Lucas, John, 'More Poet than Peasant', *Times Literary Supplement*, 27 July, pp. 845-6, a review of *Later Poems* and Deacon (1983).

Pigrome, Stella, 'John Clare Books', *Charles Lamb Bulletin*, n.s. 46 (April), 114-24, a review of *Journal, Essays...*, *Midsummer Cushion*, *Rural Muse, John Clare's Birds*, the Dendurent bibliography and the first *Clare Journal*.

Robinson, Eric and David Powell, Introduction to *John Clare* (Oxford: Oxford University Press), Oxford Authros series, pp. xv-xxvi.

— Introduction to *Later Poems*, pp. ix-xviii.

Shurey, Richard, *Walking Through Literary Landscapes* (Newton Abbott: David and Charles), pp. 64-71.

Storey, Mark, 'John Clare', *Times Literary Supplement*, 24 Aug, p. 943.

Strickland, Edward, 'Approaching "A Vision"', *Victorian Poetry*, 22 (3), 229-45.

Summerfield, Geoffrey, *Fantasy and Reason: Children's Literature in the Eighteenth Century* (London: Methuen), esp. pp. 58-63.

Wilson, Dudley, 'Peasant-Poet or King?', *In Britain*, May, pp. 26-7.

Young, L.S.H., 'John Clare and High Beech', *JCSN*, 7 (April), 1-4.

(c)

Rankin, Paula Clark, 'John Clare's Quest for Identity', Dissertation; *Dissertation Abstracts International*, 45 (5), 1410A; Ann Arbor, Michigan: University Microfilms International, 1984.

Spencer, C. M., 'Artifice in the Poetry of John Clare: a Study of Formal Devices and their Reception by the Reader', PhD dissertation, University of Wales, Cardiff.

(d) *JCSJ*, 3 (1984)

Banfield-Pearce, Lynne, 'John Clare and Peter De Wint', 40-8.

Brownlow, Timothy, 'A Moment's Monument', 34-7.

Crossan, Greg, 'The Godfrey Collection of Clare Items in the Peterborough Museum', 17-25.

Goddard, Joe, 'A Formative Influence of John Clare', 49-52.

Lessa, Richard, 'John Clare's Voice, and Two Sonnets', 26-33.

Storey, Mark, 'Clare in His Letters', 5-16.

1985

(a)

Chilcott, Tim, '*A real world & doubting mind*': *A Critical Study of the Poetry of John Clare* (Hull: Hull University Press), reviewed in *Romantic Movement Bibliography* (1985), 14-15; with *The Parish* in *Notes and Queries*, 232 (n.s. 34) (March 1987), 98-9; *Keats-Shelley Journal*, 36 (1987), 203-5.

(b)

Barker, Jonathan, 'The Songs of Our Land Are Like Ancient Landmarks: The Poetry of John Clare', *Agenda*, 22 (3-4) (1984-5), 78-89, a review of *Oxford Authors*, *Natural History*, and *Later Poems*.

Crossan, Greg, 'John Clare's Poetry: an Examination of the Textual Accuracy of Some Recent Editions', *Studies in Romanticism*, 24 (Spring), 581-98.

— 'Putting Some More Foliage on the Clare Family Tree', *JCSN*, 10 (April), [1-3].

Dawson, P.M.S., Review of *Later Poems, Natural History*, and *Oxford Authors*, *Critical Quarterly*, 27 (2), 86-7.

Groves, David, 'John Clare: "To a Lair at Noon"', *Notes and Queries*, 230 (n.s. 32) (Sep), 356; see also correction, 231 (Sep 1986), 402.

Lucas, John, Review of Brownlow (1983), Deacon (1983), and Storey (1982), *Victorian Studies*, 28, 538-9.

Powell, Margaret, [note on Parker Clare's marriage], *JCSN*, 11 (June), [2].

Robinson, Eric, Introduction to *The Parish* (Harmondsworth and New York: Viking), pp. 9-25.

Schultz, Max F., 'Crabbe's and Clare's Enclosured Vales', in *Paradise Preserved: Recreations of Eden in Eighteenth and Nineteenth-Century England* (Cambridge: Cambridge University Press), pp. 137-51.

Shurey, Richard, 'In the Footsteps of John Clare', *Evergreen*, Autumn, 44-50.

Strickland, Edward, Review of *Later Poems, Oxford Authors*, *Autobiographical Writings*, and *Natural History*, *The Wordsworth Circle*, 16, 204-7.

Thomas, Edward, 'John Clare', in *Selected Prose: a language not to be betrayed*, ed. by Edna Longley (Manchester: Carcanet), pp. 24-30. Thomas's essay on Clare was first published in 1917.

Watson, J. R., 'The Minor Poets', *English Poetry of the Romantic Period 1789-1830* (London: Longman), pp. 303-13.

— Review of *The Rural Muse*, and Brownlow (1983), *Durham University Journal*, n.s. 46, 127-8.

Weedon, Margaret, 'John Clare's Early Acquaintance with Literature', *Notes and Queries*, 230 (n.s. 32) (Sep), 356-7.

(d) *JCSJ*, 4 (1985)

Chilcott, Tim, 'Indeterminacy in Clare's "The Landrail"', 5-11.

Heyes, Bob, 'John Clare and the Militia', 48-54.

Howard, William, 'John Clare's Passionate Shepherd', 12-22.

Robinson, Eric, 'Early Poems: the Biographical Evidence', 31-47.

Schechter, Harriet, 'The Limitations of Imitation: Byron, Clare and the "Hebrew Melodies"', 24-30.

Thomas, Denis, 'John Clare and the Private Press', 55-8.

1986

(a) Aldritch, Arthur, *The Road to Northborough: A Play* (London and New York: S. French).

(b)

Blackmore, Evan, 'Clare's Psychiatric Disorder and Its Influence on His Poetry', *Victorian Poetry*, 24 (3) 209-28.

Bowman, Ian, 'Aiblins—John Clare?', *Lallans*, 26 (Whitsuntid), 10-24.

Chilcott, Tim, 'The rest is silence', *Times Higher Education Supplement*, 16 May, p. 17, a review of *Letters*.

Counsel, June, 'Dickens and Clare', *JCSN*, 14 (June), [3-4].

Fletcher, Angus, 'Style and the Extreme Situation', in *Textual Analysis: Some Readers Reading*, ed. by Mary Ann Caws (New York: Modern Language Association), pp. 289-305, on Clare and John Aubrey as outsiderly writers.

Jennings, Elizabeth, 'Written Amid Bustle', *Daily Telegraph*, 21 March, a review of *Letters*.

Lines, Rodney, [note and query on William Gilbert and High Beech], *JCSN*, 14 (June), [3].

Meyer, Richard, *The Fate of the Badger* (London: Batsford), esp. pp. 107-10.

Paulin, Tom, 'Clare in Babylon', *Times Literary Supplement*, 20 June, pp. 675-6, a review of *Letters*, reprinted in his *Minotaur: Poetry and the Nation State* (London: Faber, 1992), pp. 47-55.

Pearce, Lynne, Review of *Later Poems* and *Oxford Authors*, *Notes and Queries*, 231 (n.s. 33) (March), 122-3.

Sale, Roger, *Closer to Home: Writers and Places in England, 1780-1830* (Cambridge, MA: Harvard University Press), pp. 87-111.

Seeber, Hans Ulrich, 'The English Pastoral in the Nineteenth Century', *Yearbook of Research in English and American Literature*, 4, 67-96, includes brief but acute comment on Clare.

Storey, Mark, Introduction to *Letters*, pp. xvii-xxx.

Wagner, Mary, 'On a Clare Day', *Farmer's Weekly*, 15 Aug, pp. 62-3.

Williams, Merryn and Raymond, Introduction to *John Clare, Selected Poems* (London: Methuen), pp. 1-20.

Williams, Raymond, 'Clare's Voices', *The Guardian*, 13 Feb, a review of *Letters*.

(d) *JCSJ*, 5 (1986)

Counsel, June, 'Coming to Clare', 5-8.

Crossan, Greg, 'The Nine *Lives* of John Clare', 37-46.

Gillin, Richard L., 'Minute Particulars and Imaginative Forms', 22-9.

Lines, Rodney, 'John Clare and Herbal Medicine', 16-21.

Lucas, John, 'The Flitting', 9-13.

Thornton, R.K.R., 'The Nature of *The Parish*', 30-5.

1987

(a)

Clare, Johanne, *John Clare and the Bounds of Circumstance* (Kingston and Montreal: McGill-Queens University Press), reviewed in *Studies in Romanticism*, 28 (Winter 1989), 660-5.

(b)

Crossan, Greg, 'Clare and Enfield's *Speaker*', *Notes and Queries*, 232 (n.s 34) (March), 27-8.

Grainger, Margaret, [note on John Clare's cravat], *JCSN*, 16 (May), [3].

Groves, David, 'John Clare and James Hogg: Two Poets in the Athenaeum', *Bulletin of Research in the Humanities*, 87 (2-3) (1986-7), 225-9.

Helsinger, Elizabeth, 'Clare and the Place of the Peasant Poet', *Critical Inquiry*, 13 (3), 509-31, reprinted in her *Rural Scenes and National Representation: Britain, 1815-1850* (Princeton, New Jersey: Princeton University Press, 1997), pp. 141-61.

Herman, Vimala, 'How to See Things with Words: Language Use and Descriptive Art in John Clare's "Signs of Winter"', *Language and Style*, 20 (2), 91-109.

Porter, Roy, *A Social History of Madness: Stories of the Insane* (London: Weidenfeld and Nicolson), pp. 76-81.

Powell, David, and Eric Robinson, 'John Clare', *Notes and Queries*, 232 (n.s. 34) (June), 244-5, a query about missing texts.

Robinson, Eric, '"To an Oaken Stem": John Clare's Poem Recovered and Reconstructed', *Review of English Studies*, 38, 483-91.

— 'A French Admirer of John Clare', *JCSN*, 17 (June), [2], summarises and recommends Rosine Raimond's two essays (listed above, 1981 and 1983).

— Review of Estermann (1985), Chilcott (1985), and *Letters*, *Keats-Shelley Journal*, 36, 203-5.

Storey, Mark, 'Byron and Clare: "Childe Harold" and "Child Harold"', in *Byron: Byronism—Liberalism—Philhellenism,* Proceedings of the 14th International Symposium, Athens, 6-8 July 1987, pp. 42-52.

Strickland, Edward, 'John Clare and the Sublime', *Criticism*, 29 (2), 141-61.

(c)

Pearce, Lynne, 'John Clare and Mikhail Bakhtin: The Dialogic Principle. Readings from John Clare's Manuscripts 1832-1845', PhD dissertation, University of Birmingham, an important and influential study.

Staples, Nöel, 'John Clare's "To the Rural Muse": a Textual Criticism and Commentary', BA dissertation, Cambridge College of Arts and Technology.

(d) *JCSJ*, 6 (1987)

Carr, J.L., 'Summer of '64', 34-5.

Clare, Johanne, 'The "English Truth" of John Clare', 21-33.

Heyes, Bob, 'John Clare and Enclosure', 10-19.

Powell, Margaret A., 'Clare and His Patrons in 1820: Some Unpublished Papers' 4-9.

Robinson, Eric, 'John Clare and the Newspapers: Reader and Contributor', 37-47.

1988

(b)

Barrell, John, 'Being is Perceiving: James Thomson and John Clare', in his *Poetry, Language and Politics* (Manchester: Manchester University Press, 1988), pp. 100-35; developed from his 1984 *JCSJ* essay.

Bowman, A. I., 'John Clare—The Scottish Connection', *Scots Magazine*, March, pp. 580-5.

Cronin, Richard, *Colour and Experience in Nineteenth-Century Poetry* (Basingstoke: Macmillan Press), pp. 1-4.

Crossan, Greg, 'The Helpston Clare Memorial', *JCSN*, 22 (Nov), [2-3].

Foss, Arthur and Kerith Trick, 'John Clare (1793-1864)', in *St Andrews Hospital Northampton, the first 150 years (1838-1988)* (Cambridge: Granta Editions), pp. 121-44.

Grainger, Margaret, 'The Nightjar and John Clare', in *The Nightjar: Yesterday and Today*, by Margaret Grainger and Richard Williamson (Chichester: West Sussex Institute of Higher Education), Otter Memorial Paper Number 3, pp. 30-2.

Lucas, John, 'Places and Dwellings: Wordsworth, Clare and the anti-picturesque', in Denis Cosgrove and Stephen Daniel (eds), *The Iconography of Landscape: Essays on the Symbolic Representation, Design and Use of Past Environments* (Cambridge: Cambridge University Press), pp. 83-97.

Thornton, R.K.R., 'The John Clare exhibition of 1893', *Peterborough's Past*, 3, 40-4.

(d) *JCSJ*, 7 (1988)

Caddel, Richard, 'Things Held in Common', 41-8.

Chilcott, Tim, 'The Circumference of Knowledge: Clare's "Stone Pit"', 4-9.

Crossan, Greg, 'Note: Clare's "Aching(?) Sight"', 50-1.

Grainger, Margaret and John Chandler, 'From Helpston to Burghley: a Reading of Clare's "Narrative Verses"', 26-40.

Groves, David, 'Note: A Poem in *The Englishman's Magazine*', 51-2.

Robinson, Eric, 'John Clare's Learning', 10-25.

1989

(b)

Buttery, Pauline, 'Pictures in Poetry', *Home and Country*, June, pp. 14-15.

Crossan, Greg; Evans, Dulcie, [information on the Clare cottage plaque], *JCSN*, 23 (Feb), [1-3].

Hand, R.J., 'Anthologised Clare and the Problem of Death Date', *Notes and Queries*, 234 (n.s. 36) (June), 181-2.

Paulin, Tom, 'The clown's last laugh', *Observer*, 11 June.

Pringle-Wilson, Douglas, [brief note on Clare and Haiku], *JCSN*, 26 (Dec), [2].

Pearce, Lynne, 'John Clare's "Child Harold": a Polyphonic Reading', *Criticism*, 31(2), 139-57.

Robinson, Eric and David Powell, Introduction to *Early Poems*, I, pp. ix-xxiv.

— '"A Second Edition of Imbecility": or, the Triumphs, Trials and Aspirations of an Editor' (Boston, MA: University of Massachusetts at Boston), pamphlet.

Strickland, Edward, 'Boxer Byron: A Clare Obsession', *Byron Journal*, 17, 57-76.

Sychrava, Juliet, *Schiller to Derrida: Idealism in Aesthetics* (Cambridge: Cambridge University Press), esp. ch. 6 (pp. 196-219).

Taplin, Kim, *Tongues in Trees: Studies in Literature and Ecology* (Bideford: Green Books), esp. pp. 41-55.

(d) *JCSJ*, 8 (1989)

Crossan, Greg, [note on Butterworth's version of the Scriven Engraving], 55.

Goodridge, John, 'Some Predecessors of Clare: "Honest Duck"', 5-10.
Moyse, Mary, 'John Clare's Family Tree', 24-30.
Pedlar, Valerie, 'John Clare's *Child Harold*', 11-16.
Powell, David, 'The John Clare Collection in Northampton Public Library', 37-43.
Robinson, Eric, 'Note: John Clare: "Bud of the Waste" in *Child Harold*', 53-4.
Strickland, Edward, 'The Shipwreck Metaphor in Clare', 17-23.

1990

(b)
Carter, Russell, 'Mary Joyce's Grave', *JCSN*, 29 (Sep), 6.
Grainger, Margaret, 'The Decipherment of John Clare (1793-1864)', *Archives of Natural History*, 17 (3), 283-98.
Hillier, Richard, 'John Clare's Doctors', *JCSN*, 28 (June), 4.
Landry, Donna, *The Muses of Resistance: Laboring-class Women's Poetry in Britain, 1739-1796* (Cambridge: Cambridge University Press), esp. pp. 133-5, comparing Clare and Anne Yearsley.
Lucas, John, 'Peasants and Outlaws: John Clare', in his *England and Englishness: Ideas of Nationhood in English Poetry 1688-1900* (London: Hogarth), pp. 135-60; the Clare content is reviewed in *JCSN*, 27 (March), pp. 3-4.
Pyecroft, Beryl, 'John Clare Country', *Heritage*, 30 (Dec 1989/Jan 1990), 26-33.
Rayment, Nigel, 'The Failure of John Clare's Natural History of Helpstone: a Problem of Privilege', *Critical Survey*, 2 (1), 36-41.
Robinson, Eric, 'John Clare: Selections from the Northborough Poems', *Antaeus*, 64/5, 396-403.
— 'Vowel Play', *JCSN*, 27 (March), [1].
Staples, Noël, 'Pickworth Lime Kiln', *JCSN*, 30 (Dec), 1-2.
Storey, Mark, Introduction to *John Clare, Selected Letters* (Oxford: Oxford University Press), pp. vii-xiii.
Summerfield, Geoffrey, Introduction to *John Clare, Selected Poetry* (London: Penguin Books, Penguin Poetry Library, reprinted in the Penguin Classics series, 2000), pp. 13-22. Summerfield's section introductions are also valuable.

Thornton, Kelsey, 'Ivor Gurney and John Clare', *JCSN*, 29 (Sep), 3.
— 'John Turnill Sketches' *JCSN*, 30 (Dec), 3-4.

(c)

Rayment, Nigel, 'Empiricism and the Nature Tradition', Dissertation; *Dissertation Abstracts International*, 51 (2), 506A.

(d) *JCSJ*, 9 (1990)
Chilcott, Tim, 'An Article on Articles', 31-43.
Goodridge, John, 'Some Predecessors of Clare: 2. The Response to Duck', 17-26.
Moyse, Mary, 'Richard Clare: Settlement Bond, 1670', 27-9.
Smith, J. B., 'John Clare's Constellations', 5-13.

1991

(b)

Crossan, Greg, 'John Clare's Last Letter', *Notes and Queries*, 236 (n.s. 38) (Sep), 319.
— 'Joyce Family', *JCSN*, 34 (Dec), 4-5.
Dawson, Paul, 'Parker Clare's Scarborough Health Cure', *JCSN*, 31 (March [1991]), 2.
Grimes, Dorothy A., *Like Dew Before the Sun: Life and Language in Northamptonshire* (Northampton: privately published; reprinted 1992 and 1993), esp. pp. 271-88.
Hopkins, Chris, *John Clare: A Natural Poet?* (Sheffield: PAVIC Publications), pamphlet.
Jarvis, Frederick, *Burning Bright: Poets of the Industrial Revolution* (Upton-upon-Severn: The Self-Publishing Association), pp. 49-87.
Lines, Rodney 'Patty's Cottage', *JCSN*, 33 (Oct), 2.
McKusick, James, '"A language that is ever green": The Ecological Vision of John Clare', *University of Toronto Quarterly*, 61 (Winter 1991-2), 30-52.
Pearce, Lynne, 'John Clare's *Child Harold*: the road not taken', in Susan Sellers, Linda Hutcheon and Paul Perron (eds), *Feminist Criticism: Theory and Practice* (Toronto: University of Toronto Press, 1991), pp. 143-56.

Robinson, Eric, 'Joyce Family', *JCSN*, 33 (Oct), 2.

Staples, Noël, 'John Clare Symposium—10th Essex Festival', *JCSN*, 44 (Dec), 5-6, a useful report on the six papers, not all of which have been published.

Staples, Noël; Robinson, Eric, 'Clare's Flowers and Herbs', *JCSN*, 33 (Oct), 3.

Storey, Mark, 'Creeping into Print: Editing the Letters of John Clare', in *The Theory and Practice of Text Editing*, ed. by Ian Small and Marcus Walsh (Cambridge: Cambridge University Press), pp. 62-89

Thompson, E.P., *Customs in Common* (London: Merlin Press), pp. 179-84.

Ward, John Powell, *The English Line: Poetry of the Unpoetic from Wordsworth to Larkin* (London: Macmillan), esp. pp. 57-60.

Wordsworth, Jonathan, Introduction to *John Clare, The Shepherd's Calendar [1827]* (Oxford and New York: Woodstock Books), 5 pp., unpaginated.

(d) *JCSJ*, 10 (1991)

Bates, Tom, 'Notes on "Maying or Love & Flowers"', 43-6.

Crossan, Greg, 'Clare's Debt to the Poets in His Library', 27-41.

Robinson, Eric, 'John Clare: Passing the Time of Day', 17-26.

Storey, Mark, 'The Poet Overheard: John Clare and His Audience', 5-16.

1992

(a)

Martin, Frederick, *The Life of John Clare* (Temecula, CA: Reprint Services Corporation), a reprint of the 1865 biography.

(b)

Harrison, Robert Pogue, 'London Versus Epping Forest', in his *Forests: The Shadow of Civilisation* (Chicago and London: University of Chicago Press), pp. 211-20, on Clare and place.

Lucas, John, 'England in 1830—Wordsworth, Clare and the Question of Poetic Authority', *Critical Survey*, 4 (1), 62-6.

MacLennan, George, 'Clare', in his *Lucid Intervals: Subjective Writing and Madness in History* (Leicester and London: Leicester University Press), pp. 120-52.

McKusick, James, 'John Clare's London Journal: A Peasant Poet Encounters the Metropolis', *The Wordsworth Circle*, 23, 172-5.

Milne, Kirsty, 'Lines to a Lost Village Green', *New Statesman and Society*, 14 Aug, pp. 18-19.

Paulin, Tom, 'John Clare in Babylon', in his *Minotaur: Poetry and the Nation State* (London: Faber), pp. 47-55 (based on his 1986 review essay, listed above).

Robinson, Eric, 'Clare in the USA', *JCSN*, 36 (June), 5.

Wallace, Anne D., 'Farming on Foot: tracking georgic in Clare and Wordsworth', *Texas Studies in Language and Literature*, 34 (4), 509-40. See also 1993.

Yamakage, Takashi, 'The Vocation and the Poetic Structure in the Early Poems of John Clare', *Studies in Humanities* (Niigata University, Japan), 80.

— 'The Poetic Consciousness and Structure in John Clare's *The Shepherd's Calendar*', *Studies in Humanities* (Niigata University, Japan), 82.

(c)

Zimmerman, Sarah Mackenzie, 'Romantic Lyricism and the Rhetoric of Actuality: Charlotte Smith, Dorothy Wordsworth, and John Clare', PhD dissertation, Princeton University.

(d) *JCSJ*, 11 (1992)

Boden, Helen, 'Clare, Wordsworth's Pedlar, and the Fate of Genius', 30-42.

Blythe, Ronald, 'Some Fragments from the President's Addresses', 5-13.

Brewer, William D., 'John Clare and Lord Byron', 43-56.

Crossan, Greg, 'Another Version of the Scriven Engraving', 28-9.

— [An illustration of the interior of Clare's cottage], 27.

Dawson, P.M.S., 'John Clare—Radical?', 17-27.

Storey, Mark, 'Edward Drury's "Memoir" of Clare', 14-16.

Thomas, Denis, 'John Clare: Blunden's "Unseen Friend"', 57-60.

1993

(a)

McKenna, John, *Clare: A Novel* (Belfast: Blackstaff Press).

Moyse, Peter, *John Clare: The Poet and the Place* (Helpston, Peterborough: The Crossberry Press), monochrome photogarphs of Clare country, with texts; corrected second edition pub. 1999.

Powell, David, *The Life and Times of John Clare* (Northampton: Northamptonshire County Council, Libraries and Information Service), illustrated introductory account of Clare.

(b)

Cobb, David, 'Clare', *Blythe Spirit*, 3 (3) (July), 17-19.

Goodridge, John, 'Identity, Authenticity, Class: John Clare and the Mask of Chatterton', *Angelaki*, 1 (2) (Winter 1993-94), 131-48.

— (ed.), *The Poet John Clare, 1793-1864* (Helpston: The John Clare Society), loose-leaf information pack.

Kizer, Caroline, Introduction to *The Essential Clare* (Hopewell, NJ: The Ecco Press), pp. 3-19.

Lessa, Richard, 'A Clare Autograph in Hawaii', *JCSN*, 42 (Dec), 6-7.

Lines, Rodney, 'John Clare's Rutland', *Rutland Record*, 13, 104-7.

Mabey, Richard, *Whistling in the Dark: In Search of the Nightingale* (London: Sinclair-Stevenson); Clare material reviewed in *JCSJ*, 13 (1994), 94; see also his *The Book of Nightingales* (listed under 1997).

Neeson, J.M., *Commoners: Common Right, Enclosure and Social Change in England, 1700-1820* (Cambridge: Cambridge University Press).

Nye, Robert, 'Ploughing a Lonely Furrow', *The Times*, 5 Aug, p. 32, review of *The Shepherd's Calendar* and *The New Oxford Book of Romantic Period Verse*.

Paira-Pemberton, Jean, 'Transmission Orale, Consigne écrité', *Littoral*, 33 (1992-3), 61-76.

— 'John Clare: Nom et Renom', *Revue du Littoral*, 38 (Nov), 43-61; translated as: 'John Clare: Name and Fame', *Ranam*, 37 (1994), 115-35.

Robinson, Eric, Introduction to *Shepherd's Calendar*, pp. ix-xxi.
—, David Powell and P.M.S. Dawson, Introduction to *John Clare, Cottage Tales* (Ashington and Manchester: Mid-Northumberland Arts Group and Carcanet Press), pp. ix-xlviii.
Staples, Nöel, 'Clare and Mary Queen of Scots', *JCSN*, 40 (June), 14.
Suzuki, Renichi, 'Lubin of "The Village Minstrel" and Clare' (Memoir of The Faculty of General Education, Kumamoto University, Foreign Language and Literature, no. 28), in Japanese.
Wallace, Anne D., *Walking, Literature, and English Culture: The Origins and Uses of Peripatetic in the Nineteenth Century* (Oxford: Clarendon Press), reworks and extends material from her essay listed under 1992 (b).

The following press and magazine articles, listed chronologically, celebrate Clare's 1993 bicentenary:
'John Who?', *Northampton Chronicle and Echo*, 15 Jan.
Tate, Ann, 'The Countryside in February', *Camping and Caravanning*, 88 (2) (Feb), 24.
Rogers, Byron, 'A long walk with Clare', *The Guardian*, 18 May.
Stuttaford, Dr Thomas, 'Medical Briefing: Poet in a Corner', *The Times*, 17 June.
'Genius wordsmith who was born poor, lived poor and died in an asylum', *Peterborough Evening Telegraph*, 26 June, pp. 28-9.
Nicholson, Christopher, 'The Rural Muse', *BBC Worldwide*, July, pp. 74-5.
Burton, Rosemary, 'Verse things first', *The Guardian*, 3 July, Weekend section, p. 47.
Somerville, Christopher, 'Under a cloud with the peasant poet', *Daily Telegraph*, 3 July, p. xxvii.
Paulin, Tom, 'Northamptonshire Visionary', *Independent on Sunday*, 11 July.
Cripps, Jennifer, 'Clare: the legacy no evil can destroy', *Peterborough Evening Telegraph*, 13 July, pp. 8-9.
Woollard, Ron, 'John Clare: A Born Poet', *The Lady*, 13-19 July, p. 45.
Glover, Michael, 'Romantic whose roots reached deep into the stony soil', *Financial Times Weekend*, 17-18 July, a review of *Cottage Tales* and Peter Moyse, *John Clare: the Poet and the Place.*
Taplin, Kim, 'Through John Clare's injur'd fields', *Countryman*, 98 (4) (High Summer), 100-4.

Brandon, David, 'Lunatic Poet', *Nursing Times*, 89 (34) (25 Aug), 71.
Motion, Andrew, 'Find enclosed: John Clare', *Observer*, 5 Sep, pp. 51-2.
Mabey, Richard, 'On the Sidelines', *BBC Wildlife*, Oct, p. 16.
Goodridge, John, 'John Clare at Two Hundred: A Memory Lost?', *BARS Bulletin*, no. 5 (Nov), 11-12.
Holloway, John, 'Neglected Greenness: Bicentenary Thoughts on John Clare', *Cambridge Review*, 114, 129.

(c)
Adams, Linden E., 'John Clare: Poet of Art or Poet of Nature?', MA dissertation, University of Liverpool.
Keegan, Bridget Mary, 'Sordid Melpomene: poetry and poverty in the work of Wordsworth, Clare, Hugo and Baudelaire', PhD dissertation, New York State University, Buffalo.

(d) *JCSJ*, 12 (1993)
Barrell, John, 'Bicentenary Thoughts', 52-3.
Bates, Tom, 'Sculpting Clare', 64-8.
Blade, Brian, 'Bicentenary Thoughts', 16.
Blythe, Ronald, 'Bicentenary Thoughts' 5-6.
Brownjohn, Alan, 'Bicentenary Thoughts', 54-5.
Crossan, Greg, 'Celebrating John Clare', 18-25.
Dixon, George E., 'Bicentenary Thoughts', 16-17.
Foster, Paul, 'Margaret Grainger (31 January 1936-2 August 1992)', 9-14.
Goodridge, John, 'The Writings of Margaret Grainger 1959-1992', 14.
Hand, Richard J., 'John Clare on Stage: Edward Bond's "The Fool" and the Issue of Faction', 57-61.
Heaney, Seamus, 'Bicentenary Thoughts', 28.
Heyes, Bob, 'Little Hills of Cushioned Thyme ', 32-6.
Hold, Trevor, 'Bicentenary Thoughts', 29-30.
Leatham, Lady Victoria, 'Bicentenary Thoughts', 6.
Mabey, Richard, 'John Clare: Knowing his Place', 28-9.
Motion, Andrew, 'Bicentenary Thoughts', 30.
Rae, Simon, 'Bicentenary Thoughts', 53.
Robinson, Eric, 'Bicentenary Thoughts', 30-1.
Storey, Edward, 'Bicentenary Thoughts', 17.
Storey, Mark (ed.), 'Past Thoughts', 37-9.

Street, Sean, 'Bicentenary Thoughts', 54.

Strickland, Edward, 'A Reading of "Song Last Day"', 40-50.

Thomas, R.S., 'Lunar', 62, poem, collected in his *No Truce with the Furies* (Newcastle upon Tyne: Bloodaxe Books, 1995), p. 12.

Thompson, E. P., 'Bicentenary Thoughts', 31.

Wain, John, 'Bicentenary Thoughts', 55.

Westwood, William, The Lord Bishop of Peterborough, 'Bicentenary Thoughts', 7.

1994

(a)

Foulkes, Richard (ed.), *John Clare: a Bicentenary Celebration* (Northampton: University of Leicester, Department of Adult Education), reviewed by Philip Martin in *Byron Journal*, 23 (1995), 99-100; contains the following:

> Crossan, Greg, 'John Clare: Our Contemporary', pp. 57-68.
> Paulin, Tom, 'John Clare: A Bicentennial Celebration', pp. 69-78.
> Powell, David, 'John Clare: Getting Into Print', pp. 1-26.
> Street, Sean, 'The Making of *Honest John*', pp. 79-96.
> Thornton, Kelsey, 'The Complexity of Clare', pp. 41-56.
> Trick, Kerith, 'Clare's Asylum Experience', pp. 27-40.

Goodridge, John (ed.), *The Independent Spirit: John Clare and the Self-Taught Tradition* (Helpston: The John Clare Society and the Margaret Grainger Memorial Trust), reviewed in *Bibliography of the Romantic Movement* (1994), 55; *Countryman*, 100 (2) (Spring 1995), 110; *English*, 45 (Spring 1996), 79-84; *Review of English Studies*, 47 (1996), 306; *Romanticism*, 2 (1) (1996), 113-17. Contains the following:

> Blythe, Ronald, '"The Best Of Thee Is Still Unknown": Kindred Spirits', pp. 181-92; reprinted in his *Talking About John Clare* (1999, listed below).
> Boden, Helen, 'Review Essay: Clare, Gender And Art', pp. 198-208.
> Bold, Valentina, 'James Hogg and the Scottish Self-Taught Tradition', pp. 69-86.
> Cannell, Mary, 'John Clare and George Green', pp. 193-7.

Chirico, Paul, 'Writing Misreadings: Clare and the Real World', pp. 125-38; reprinted in Laurie Lanzen Harris (ed.), *Nineteenth-Century Literature Criticism*, Vol. 86 (Detroit and New York: Gale Group, 2000).

Ellis, R.J., 'Plodding Plowmen: Issues of Labour and Literacy in Gray's "Elegy"', pp. 27-43; reprinted in Ira Mark Milne (ed.), *Poetry for Students*, Vol. 9 (Detroit and New York: Gale Group, 2000), pp. 87-94.

Goodridge, John, Introduction, pp. 13-24.

— 'Pastoral and Popular Modes in Clare's Enclosure Elegies', pp. 139-55.

— Further Reading, pp. 209-21.

Lines, Rodney, 'Clare's "Rough Country Sonnets"', pp. 156-63.

Lucas, John, 'Bloomfield and Clare', pp. 55-68.

MacDonald Shaw, Clare, 'Some Contemporary Women Poets in Clare's Library', pp. 87-122.

Nattrass, Leonora, 'John Clare and William Cobbett: The Personal and the Political', pp. 44-54.

Rowbotham, Judith, 'An Exercise in Nostalgia?: Clare and Enclosure', pp. 164-77.

Haughton, Hugh, Adam Phillips and Geoffrey Summerfield (eds), *John Clare in Context* (Cambridge: Cambridge University Press), reviewed in *Times Literary Supplement*, 8 July, pp. 5-6; *Bibliography of the Romantic Movement* (1994), 55-6; *Essays in Criticism*, 45 (1) (Jan 1995), 62-9; *Romanticism*, 1 (1) (Spring 1995), 152-8; *English*, 44 (Spring 1995), 87-91; *Times Higher*, 21 April 1995, p. 18; *The Wordsworth Circle*, 26 (2) (1995), 229-30; *Literature and History*, 3rd ser., 5 (2) (Autumn 1996), 68-72; *Keats-Shelley Review*, 11 (1997), 207-11. Contains the following:

Birns, Nicholas, '"The Riddle Nature Could Not Prove": Hidden Landscapes in Clare's Poetry', pp. 189-220.

Chambers, Douglas, '"A Love for Every Simple Weed": Clare, Botany and the Poetic Language of Lost Eden', pp. 238-58.

Gaull, Marilyn, 'Clare and the "Dark System"', pp. 279-94.

Haughton, Hugh, 'Progress and Rhyme: "The Nightingale's Nest" and Romantic Poetry', pp. 51-86.

— and Adam Phillips, 'Introduction: Relocating John Clare', pp. 1-27.

Heaney, Seamus, 'John Clare: A Bi-centenary Lecture', pp. 130-47; reprinted in his *The Redress of Poetry* (London: Faber, 1995), pp. 63-82, as 'John Clare's Prog'.

Lucas, John, 'Clare's Politics', pp. 148-77.

McKusick, James, 'Beyond the Visionary Company: John Clare's Resistance to Romanticism', pp. 221-37.

Phillips, Adam, 'The Exposure of John Clare', pp. 178-88, also published in his *On Flirtation* (London: Faber, 1994, 1995), pp. 206-17.

Porter, Roy, '"All Madness for Writing": John Clare and the Asylum', pp. 259-78.

Storey, Mark, 'Clare and the Critics', pp. 28-50.

Selected Further Reading, pp. 295-301.

Lucas, John, *John Clare* (Plymouth: Northcote House), Writers and Their Work series.

(b)

Heinzelman, Kurt, 'The Uneducated Imagination: Romantic Representations of Labor', in *At the Limits of Romanticism: Essays in Cultural, Feminist, and Materialist Criticism*, ed. by Mary A. Favret and Nicola J. Watson (Bloomington, Indiana: Indiana University Press, 1994), pp. 101-24, indirectly relevant to the study of Clare, who is mentioned once or twice in the essay.

Hutchings, Geoffrey, 'The Containment of John Clare: a Case-Study in Literary Enclosure', *English Studies in Africa*, 37 (1), 1-17.

Jurgis, Andy, 'Edward Thomas at High Beech', *JCSN*, 46 (Dec), 4-5.

Lucas, John, 'Revising Clare', in *Romantic Revisions*, ed. by Robert Brinkley and Keith Hanley (Cambridge: Cambridge University Press).

McKusick, James, 'John Clare and the Tyranny of Grammar', *Studies in Romanticism*, 33 (Summer), 255-77.

Moss, Stephen, 'A Poet for All Seasons', *The Guardian*, 3 March.

Olsen, William, 'Poetry and Vision', *Chicago Review*, 40, 33-50.

Phillips, W.C., 'Loose Notes in the Waste of Air: The Skylark According to Shelley, Wordsworth and John Clare', *Revista Canaria de Estudios Ingleses* [Universidad de La Laguna, Tenerife], 29 (Nov), 179-186.

Powell, David, 'More Clare Manuscripts at Northampton', *JCSN*, 44 (June), 6.

Richardson, Alan, *Literature, Education and Romanticism: Reading as Social Practice, 1780-1832* (Cambridge: Cambridge University Press), esp. pp. 254-7.

Sales, Roger, 'Poor Relations: Writing in the Working Class 1770-1835', in David B. Pirie (ed.), *Penguin History of Literature 5. The Romantic Period* (London: Penguin), pp. 257-88.

Shepherd, Valerie, Review of *Cottage Tales*, *Spoken English*, 27 (1) (Jan).

(d) *JCSJ*, 13 (1994)

Bates, Tom, 'John Clare and "Boximania"', 5-17.

Brewer, William D., 'Clare's Struggle for Poetic Identity in *The Village Minstrel*', 73-80.

Cox, Peter, '"The Hearts Hid Anguish": Clare and Tennyson in Epping Forest', 33-9.

Dawson, P.M.S., 'Review Essay: History and Natural History', 92-4.

Heyes, Bob, 'A Neglected Account of Clare in the Asylum', 59-60.

Kossick, Kaye, 'Review Essay: Starting Points', 81-4.

Lamont, Claire, 'John Clare and the Gypsies', 19-31.

Lessa, Richard, '"Disdaining Bounds of Place and Time": John Clare in Hawaii', 61-72.

Lincoln, John, 'Review Essay: Clare and the Modern Artist', 84-5.

Pedlar, Valerie, '"No Place Like Home": Reconsidering Matthew Allen and His "Mild System" of Treatment', 41-57.

Powell, David, Review Essay: 'Northamptonshire Prodigies', 89-92.

Storey, Edward, Review Essay: 'Clare's Influence on the Writer's Imagination', 85-9.

1995

(b)

Adams, Anna, 'Born not made? largely about John Clare', *Acumen*, 23 (Sep), 29-34.

Cafarelli, Annette Wheeler, 'The Romantic "Peasant" Poets and their Patrons', *The Wordsworth Circle*, 26, 77-87, a survey of Clare's 'self-taught' predecessors.

Goodridge, John, 'Clare Should Belong to Us All', *Independent on Sunday*, 23 July), letter to the editor about the copyright issue.

— Introduction to *The Works of John Clare* (Ware, Herts: Wordsworth Editions), pp. ix-xiv.

Green, Jenny, 'John Clare (1793-1864)' in *Key Poets: Classic Poetry for the National Curriculum Key Stages 3 and 4* (London: Penguin, 1995), pp. 336-49, an introduction and selection for secondary school children.

Martin, Philip, 'Authorial Identity and the Critical Act: John Clare and Lord Byron', in *Questioning Romanticism*, ed. by John Beer (Baltimore and London: Johns Hopkins University Press), pp. 71-91 and 278-80.

Martin, R.A., 'The Geology and Scenery of Clare's Parish', *JCSN*, 50 (Dec), 2-5 (first publication cited as *Journal of the Northamptonshire Natural History Society*, 41, no. 2 (1993), unseen).

Paulin, Tom, 'John Clare: a Northamptonshire Visionary', *English Review*, 5 (4) (April), 6-8.

Powell, David, 'A Day at Colindale', *JCSN*, 49 (Sep), 4-6.

Robinson, Eric, David Powell and P.M.S Dawson, Introduction to *John Clare, Northborough Sonnets* (Ashington and Manchester: Mid-Northumberland Arts Group and Carcanet Press), pp. vii-xxii.

Stummer, Robin and Nick Curwin, 'John Clare's Lost Poems Revealed', *Independent on Sunday*, 16 July, news story.

Tate, Ann, 'Fields of Dreams', *The Lady*, 14-20 March 1995, p. 64, reprinted as 'The Northamptonshire Flora' in *JCSN*, 49 (Sep), pp. 8-9.

Wareham, John, 'Clare's "The Awthorn"', *The Explicator,* 53 (4), 197-200.

Yamakage, Takashi, 'The Transformation of John Clare's Muse', in *Centre and Circumference: Essays in English Romanticism* (Tokyo: Kirihawa Shoten), Association of English Romanticism in Japan.

Young, Robin, 'At the margins: outsider-figures in nineteenth-century poetry', in *Poetry in the British Isles: Non-Metropolitan Perspectives*, ed. by Hans-Werner Ludwig and Lothar Fietz (Cardiff: University of Wales Press), pp. 31-45.

(d) *JCSJ*, 14 (1995), 'Clare and Ecology'

Bate, Jonathan, 'The Rights of Nature', 7-15.

Blythe, Ronald, '*Solvitur Ambulando*: John Clare and Footpath Walking', 17-27.

Coletta, W. John, 'Ecological Aesthetics and the Natural History Poetry of John Clare', 29-46.

Crossan, Greg, 'Review Essay: Bicentenary Essays', 89-91.

Fulford, Tim, 'Cowper, Wordsworth, Clare: the Politics of Trees', 47-59.

Mabey, Richard, 'Guest Editorial: Clare and Ecology', 5-6.

Robinson, Eric, 'John Clare and Weather-Lore', 61-79.

Swingle, L.J., 'John Clare and the Heedless Beetle', 81-7.

Thornton, Kelsey, 'Review Essay: Shepherd's Calendars', 91-2.

1996

(b)

Barton, Anne, 'John Clare reads Lord Byron', *Romanticism*, 2 (2), 127-48.

— 'The Village Genius', *New York Review of Books*, 43 (20) (19 Dec), 42-8, a review of *Middle Poems I-II*.

Blythe, Ronald, 'Thomas Hardy and John Clare: a Soil Observed, a Soil Ploughed', in Charles P.C. Pettit (ed.), *Celebrating Thomas Hardy: Insights and Appreciations* (London: Macmillan; New York: St. Martin's Press), pp. 54-67, reprinted in his *Talking About John Clare*, 1999, listed below.

Burwick, Frederick, 'Clare's "Child Harold", in his *Poetic Madness and the Romantic Imagination* (University park, PA: Pennsylvania State University Press), pp. 254-75.

Bygrave, Stephen, 'Romantic Poets and Contexts' in *Approaching Literature: Romantic Writings,* ed. by Stephen Bygrave (London: Routledge, in association with the Open University), pp. 3-7, critical discussion of 'I Am'.

Crossan, Greg, 'Another Tale of Two Clares', *JCSN*, 53 (Sep), 9.

Dawson, P.M.S., 'Common Sense or Radicalism? Some Reflections on Clare's Politics', *Romanticism*, 2 (1), 81-97.

Doyle, Dennis, 'John Clare's Gardens', faculty publication, Shukutoku University, Japan.

Erickson, Lee, *The Economy of Literary Form: English Literature and the Industrialization of Publishing, 1800-1850* (Baltimore: Johns Hopkins University Press), makes several references to Clare.

Goodridge, John, 'John Clare, 1793-1864; English poet', *Reader's Guide to Literature in English*, ed. by Mark Hawkins-Dady (Chicago and London: Fitzroy Dearborn), a survey of major critical work.

Heyes, Bob, 'Some Friends of John Clare: the Poet and the Scientists', *Romanticism*, 2 (1), 98-109.

— 'A Tale of Two Clares', *JCSN*, 51 (March), 4-6.

Hill, Christopher, *Liberty Against the Law: Some Sevententh-Century Controversies* (London: Penguin/Allen Lane), pp. 311-24.

Leader, Zachary, 'John Taylor and the Poems of Clare', in his *Revision and Romantic Authorship* (Oxford: Clarendon Press), pp. 206-61.

Mabey, Richard, *Flora Britannica* (London: Sinclair-Stevenson), contains a dozen or more citations to Clare as a botanical witness.

McEathron, Scott, 'John Clare and Charles Lamb: Friends in the Past', *Charles Lamb Bulletin*, n.s. 95 (July), 98-109.

Nye, Robert, 'Spirit and Stink Bombs', *The Times*, 4 Jan, a review of *Northborough Sonnets* and Michael Hamburger's poems.

Peterfreund, Stuart, 'Clare, White, the Poets and the modalities of mediation', *The Wordsworth Circle*, 27 (3) (Summer), 145-51.

Pratt, Jean and Geoff, *Short Walks from Cambridgeshire Pubs* (Newbury: Countryside).

Robinson, Eric H., 'John Clare (1793-1864) and James Plumtre (1771-1832), "a methodistical parson"', *Trans. Cambridge Bibliographical Society*, XI, 59-88.

— and David Powell, Introduction to *John Clare By Himself* (Ashington and Manchester: Mid-Northumberland Arts Group and Carcanet Press), pp. vii-xxi.

—, David Powell and P.M.S. Dawson, Introduction to *John Clare, Poems of the Middle Period*, I-II (Oxford: Clarendon Press), pp. ix-xxii.

Sales, Roger, 'The John Clare Revival', *Literature and History*, 3rd ser., 5, no. 2 (Autumn), 68-72, review of Haughton, *Context* and Lucas (1994).

Sanada, Simon, 'Landscape in John Clare and Peter de Wint', *Aichi University Eibunkai Essays*, Japan, pp. 145-54.

Smith, J.B., 'Towards a Demystification of Lawrence Lazy', *Folklore,* 107, 101-5.

Wareham, John, 'Clare's "Mouse's Nest"', *The Explicator*, 55, no. 1, 17-19.

(c)

Colclough, Stephen M., 'Voicing Loss: Versions of Pastoral in the Poetry of John Clare, 1817-1832', PhD dissertation, University of Keele.

Phillips, William Charles, 'John Clare: A Critical Reassessment', PhD dissertation, Universitat Autònoma de Barcelona.

(d) *JCSJ*, 15 (1996)

Blamires, David, 'Chapbooks, Fairytales and Children's Books in the Writings of John Clare: Part I', 27-53.

Blunden, Edmund, 'Beginner's Luck', 5-10 (see also 1971(a)).

Engels, William C., 'Clare's Mocking Tone in "An Invite to Eternity"', 57-67.

Keegan, Bridget, 'Broadsides, Ballads and Books: the Landscape of Cultural Literacy in "The Village Minstrel"', 11-19.

Shepherd, Valerie, 'Review Essay: Anne Elizabeth Baker's *Glossary of Northamptonshire Words and Phrases* and John Clare's "Rustic Idiom"', 69-75.

Smith, Matthew, 'The "Peasant Poet" Replies: *Sketches in the Life of John Clare* as a Response to Taylor's Introduction to *Poems Descriptive'*, 21-5.

1997

(a)

Lucas, John (ed.), *For John Clare: an Anthology of Verse* (Helpston: The John Clare Society), reviewed in *Other Poetry*, II (9) (Nov), 75-6.

(b)

Camaiora, Luisa Conti, 'Poetical Inspiration and Editorial Intervention in John Clare's Sonnet to the Memory of John Keats', *Quaderni di Lingue e Letterature* (Verona, Italy), 22, 61-70, discusses the editing and text of this sonnet.

Coletta, W. John, '"Writing Larks": John Clare's Semiosis of Nature', *The Wordsworth Circle*, 28 (3), 192-200.

Jarvis, Robin, *Romantic Writing and Pedestrian Travel* (London: Macmillan), esp. ch. 6, 'Gender, Class, and Walking: Dorothy Wordsworth and John Clare'.

Kavanagh, P.J., 'Bywords', *Times Literary Supplement*, 7 Feb, p. 16, on Clare's love poems.

Lines, Rodney, 'John Clare's Pubs', *Peterborough Pub History Journal 1997*.

Mabey, Richard, 'Hidden as a Thought Unborn' in *The Book of Nightingales* (London: Sinclair-Stevenson), pp. 93-105, based on his 1993 book, listed above.

Phillips, W.C. 'Clare's Sonnets', *Proceedings of the 18th Asociación de estudios anglo-norteamericanos (AEDEAN) Congress at Alcalá de Henares, 1994* (Alcalá de Henares: Universidad de Alcalá), pp. 615-22.

Suzuki, Renichi, 'Clare and the Religion in "The Parish"' (Memoir of The Faculty of General Education, Kumamoto University, Foreign Language and Literature, no. 32), in Japanese.

Thornton, R.K.R., Introduction to *John Clare, Selected Poems* (London: J.M. Dent), Everyman's Poetry series, pp. xi-xvi.

Wareham, John, *The Poetry of John Clare* (Leicester: English Association, Bookmark Series), pamphlet.

Wells, Robert, 'The waking dream of fact', *Times Literary Supplement*, 13 June, pp. 3-4, review of *Middle Poems*, I-II.

Zimmer, Paul, 'John Clare's "I Am"', in *Touchstones: American Poets on a Favorite Poem*, ed. by Robert Park and Say Parini (Hanover, NH: University Press of New England Press), pp. 315-18.

JOHN GOODRIDGE

(c)

Miller, Eric Anderson Campbell, 'System and Nemesis: Christopher Smart, Jean-Jacques Rousseau, John Clare and the Legacy of Linnaeus', PhD dissertation, University of Virginia; *Dissertation Abstracts International*, 58 (7), 2640.

(d) *JCSJ*, 16 (1997)

Blamires, David, 'Chapbooks, Fairytales and Children's Books in the Writings of John Clare: Part II', 43-70.

Dawson, P.M.S., 'Clare and the Ideology of "Common Sense"', 71-8.

Heyes, Bob, '"Triumphs of Time": John Clare and the Uses of Antiquity', 5-17.

Lamont, Claire, '"The essence and simplicity of true poetry": John Clare and Folk-song', 19-33.

Rippingille, E.V., 'Rippingille's Memoir of Burlowe the Sculptor', 35-41.

1998

(b)

Burwick, Frederick, 'Romantic Madness: Holderlin, Nerval, Clare', in *Cultural Interactions in the Romantic Age: Critical Essays in Comparative Literature,* ed. by Gregory Maertz (New York, NY: State University of New York, Albany, 1998), pp. 29-51.

Goodridge, John, 'Out There in the Night: Rituals of Nurture and Exclusion in Clare's "St. Martin's Eve"', *Romanticism*, 4 (1), 202-11.

— 'Telling Stories: Clare, Folk Culture, and Narrative Techniques', *The Wordsworth Circle*, 29 (3) (Summer), 164-7.

Janowitz, Anne, *Lyric and Labour in the Romantic Tradition* (Cambridge: Cambridge University Press), pp. 33-4, 108-12.

— 'Clare Among the Gipsies', *The Wordsworth Circle*, 29 (3) (Summer), 167-70.

Kelley, Theresa M., 'Postmodernism, Romanticism, and John Clare', in Thomas Pfau and Robert F. Gleckner (eds), *Lessons of Romanticism: a Critical Companion* (Durham, NC and London: Duke University Press), pp. 157-70.

Lewis, Stephen, 'John Clare and the Bees', *JCSN*, 62 (Dec), 4-5.

242

Lincoln, John, 'John Clare: Poet—or Stonemason', *JCSN*, 62 (Dec), 6-7.

Lodge, Sara, 'Hood, Clare, and the "Mary" chain', *Notes and Queries*, n.s. 45, 205-8.

Lucas, John, 'Crabbe's Disorderly Nature', in *Writing the Environment: Ecocriticism and Literature*, ed. by Richard Kerridge and Neil Sammells (London: Zed Books), pp. 110-23, compares Crabbe and Clare.

Mahood, M. M., 'John Clare: The Poet as Raptor', *Essays in Criticism*, 48 (3), 201-23.

Preen, David, 'John Clare's Claims in the National Curriculum', *The Use of English*, 50 (1) (Autumn), 1-11

Rattenbury, Arnold, 'John Clare and the Bikers', *London Magazine*, n.s. 38, nos. 9-10 (Dec 1998/Jan 1999), 33-42, critiques 'heritage' Clare.

Robinson, Eric, David Powell and P.M.S. Dawson, Introduction to *John Clare, Poems of the Middle Period*, III-IV (Oxford: Clarendon Press), pp. ix-xl.

Rogers, Byron, 'Hospital Story', *Saga Magazine*, June, pp. 62-7, on St. Andrews Hospital, Northampton, and its history.

Sail, Lawrence, 'Dens and Displays', *PN Review*, 119 (Jan-Feb), 4-5, includes an account of a trip to Helpston in search of Clare.

Stillinger, Jack, Review of John Clare, *Poems of the Middle Period*, I-II, *Keats-Shelley Journal*, 47, 201-2.

Swartz, Richard G., '"Their terror came upon me tenfold": Literacy and ghosts in John Clare's *Autobiography*', in Thomas Pfau and Robert F. Gleckner (eds), *Lessons of Romanticism: a Critical Companion* (Durham, NC and London: Duke University Press), pp. 328-46.

Traynar, H. Keith, 'The Joyces of Glinton', *JCSN*, 60 (June), 4.

(c)

Taylor, Cathy, 'The Resurrection of *Child Harold*: A Transcription of Nor, MS6 and a Reconsideration of John Clare's *Child Harold* and Related Writings', PhD dissertation, University of York.

(d) *JCSJ*, 17 (1998)

Cox, Peter, '"A Liking to Use the Pen": Edward Villiers Rippingille and John Clare', 17-33.

Harrison, Gary, '"Ambition's Projects": Peasant and Poet in John Clare's "The Wish" and "Helpstone"', 41-58.

Haughton, Hugh, 'Review Essay: Revision and Romantic authorship: the case of Clare', 65-73.

Keegan, Bridget, 'Review Essay: "A sun in songs posterity": recent publications on John Clare and self-taught poets', 73-7.

Moyse, Mary, 'New Light On Clare's Eldest Surviving Son', 59-63.

Paulin, Tom, 'The Writing Lark: A Letter to John Clare', 5-15, poem.

Sylvester, Louise, '"The Misterys of His Art": A Moment of Ambiguity in Clare's "Autobiography"', 35-40.

1999

(a)

Blythe, Ronald, *Talking About John Clare* (Nottingham: Trent Books).

Hold, Trevor, *A John Clare Songbook, for high voice and piano* (London: Thames Publishing [1999]), distributed by William Elkin Music Services, Norwich.

(b)

Chilcott, Tim, Introduction to *John Clare, The Living Year 1841* (Nottingham: Trent Editions), pp. [vii]-xvii.

Clay, Arnold, *John Clare, The Peasant Poet* (no publisher named), pamphlet.

Colclough, Stephen, 'Clare and the Annuals: A Previously Unpublished Letter from John Clare to L. T. Ventouillac, Editor of "The Iris"', *Notes and Queries*, n.s. 46, 468-70.

Coletta, W. John, 'Literary Biosemiotics and the Postmodern Ecology of John Clare', *Semiotica*, 127 (1-4), 239-71.

Fitter, Richard, 'Clare's Birds and Wild Flowers', *JCSN*, 66 (Dec 1999), 2-5, and 67 (March 2000), 3-4.

Harvey, A.D., 'Working-Class Poets and Self-Education', *Contemporary Review*, 274 (May), 252.

Heyes, Bob, Review of *Poems of the Middle Period*, III-IV, *English*, 48 (Spring), 65-6.

Hurtrez, Lionel, 'Nature and God: Clare's "The Progress of rhyme" and Hölderlin's "Da ich ein Knabe war"', *JCSN*, 64 (June), 8-9.

Keegan, Bridget, Review of *Poems of the Middle Period*, III-IV and Robert Bloomfield, *Selected Poems*, *The Wordsworth Circle*, 30 (4) (Fall), 232.

Keith, W.J., Review of *Poems of the Middle Period*, I-II, *JEGP*, 98 (1), 127-9.

Kelley, Theresa M., 'Romantic Interiority and Cultural Objects', *Romantic Circles Praxis Series*, number on Romanticism and Philosophy in an Historical Age

(Aug), published online at: <http://www.rc.umd.edu/praxis/philosophy/kelley1/tk1.html>.

Kövesi, Simon, Introduction to *John Clare, Love Poems* (Bangkok: M & C Services Co.), pp. ix-xvi.

Larissy, Edward (ed.), *Postmodernism and Romanticism* (Cambridge: Cambridge University Press), contains two essays which refer briefly to Clare: Paul Hamilton, 'From Sublimity to Indeterminacy: New World Order or Aftermath of Romantic Ideology', pp. 13-28 (p. 18); and Fred Botting, 'Virtual Romanticism', pp. 98-112 (p. 112).

Mabey, Richard, *Selected Writings 1974-1999* (London: Chatto and Windus, 1999), pp. 52, 123, 127, 203, 261, brief but valuable comments on Clare.

Mahood, Molly, 'Problems about Clare's Plants', *JCSN*, 63 (March), 7.

McEathron, Scott, 'Wordsworth, Lyrical Ballads and the Problem of Peasant Poetry', *Nineteenth-Century Literature*, 54 (1), 1-26, a valuable contextualising essay which mentions Clare briefly.

McKusick, James C., 'John Clare's Version of Pastoral', *The Wordsworth Circle*, 30 (2), 80-4.

Perkins, David, 'Sweet Helpston! John Clare on Badger Baiting', *Studies in Romanticism*, 38 (3), 387-407.

Russett, Margaret, 'Like "Wedding Gowns or Money from the Mint": Clare's Borrowed Inheritance', *Romantic Circles Praxis Series*, number on Romanticism and the Law (March 1999), published online at: <http://www.rc.umd.edu/praxis/law/russett/mruss.htm>.

Zimmerman, Sarah M., *Romanticism, Lyricism, and History* (Albany, NY: State University of New York Press), esp. ch. 5, 'John Clare's Poetics and Politics of Loss', pp. 147-84.

The following press articles, listed chronologically, cover the dispute over Clare's copyright (see also items under 2000 (b) and (d):

Tonkin, Boyd, 'The People's Poet Must Be Set Free', *Independent on Sunday*, 10 July, Weekend Review section.

Jarvis, Edward, 'Clare Advantage', *Nottingham Evening Post*, 21 July, p. 19.

Pavitt, Analise, 'Academics in War of Words', *Peterborough Evening Telegraph*, 6 Aug, pp. 2, 8-9.

Wallace, Jennifer, 'Dead Poet's Propriety', *Times Higher*, 13 Aug, p. 15.

Phelps, Humphrey, 'People's Poet', *Countryman,* 104 (Summer), 104-6.

Nicolson, Stuart, 'Academic's Quest for Poetic Justice', *The Scotsman*, 16 Nov, p. 3.

(c)

Cooper, Mike, '"Where castles stood and grandeur died": John Clare in the City', MA dissertation, Open University.

Heyes, Robert, '"Looking to Futurity": John Clare and Provincial Culture', PhD dissertation, Birkbeck College, University of London.

Kövesi, Simon, 'Sexuality, Agency and Intertextuality in the Later Poetry of John Clare', PhD dissertation, The Nottingham Trent University.

(d)

JCSJ, 18 (1999)

Barton, Anne, 'Clare's Animals: The Wild and the Tame', 5-21.

Crossan, Greg, 'Samuel Williams' Illustrations of Clare's *The Shepherd's Calendar*,' 23-[36].

Dawson, P.M.S. and David Powell, 'Clare and His Publishers: an Unpublished Prose Work', 65-9.

Kövesi, Simon, '"Her Curious House Is Hidden": Secrecy and Femininity in John Clare's Nest Poems', 51-63.

Simpson, David, 'Is the Academy Ready for John Clare?', 70-8.

Vardy, Alan, 'Clare and Political Equivocation', 37-48.

2000

(a)

Clay, Arnold, *'Itching After Rhyme': A Life of John Clare* (Tunbridge Wells: Para Press), reviewed in *JCSN*, 69 (Sep), 12.

Goodridge, John, and Simon Kövesi (eds), *John Clare: New Approaches and New Voices* (Helpston: The John Clare Society).

(b)

Ashbery, John, *Other Traditions: The Charles Eliot Norton Lectures* (Cambridge, MA: Harvard University Press), Clare is one of six writers the poet discusses.

Barry, Peter, 'The Editorial Commentary', *English,* 49 (195), pp. 301-7. Review of small presses, Clare editing and the copyright controversy.

Bate, Jonathan, *The Song of the Earth* (London: Picador). Clare is a key figure in this study of poetry and ecology: see the review of it by Grevel Lindop, *Times Literary Supplement*, 2 June, p. 12.

— 'Work in Progress', *JCSN*, 68 (June), 5-6, notes on his Clare biography.

Chirico, Paul, 'Writing for Money: The Correspondence of John Clare and Earl Spencer', *Times Literary Supplement*, 17 Nov, pp. 14-15.

Crawford, P., 'The Madness of John Clare', *Mental Health Care*, 3 (6), 182-7.

Crossan, Greg, Review of *Middle Poems*, III-IV, *Notes and Queries*, n.s. 47 (March), 1324-5.

Gaull, Marilyn, 'From the Editor', *The Wordsworth Circle*, 31 (3), (Summer) 109-111. On Eric Robinson, Simon Kövesi and the Clare copyright.

Goodridge, John, '"Three Cheers for Mute Ingloriousness!": Gray's *Elegy* in the Poetry of John Clare', *Critical Survey*, 11 (3), 11-20.

Griffiths, Jonathan, 'Copyright in English Literature: Denying the Public Domain', *European Intellectual Property Review*, 22 (4), 150-3, a legal perspective on the Clare copyright dispute.

Keegan, Bridget, and James C. McKusick, 'John Clare (1793-1864)', in *Literature and Nature: Four Centuries of English and American Nature Writing* (Upper Saddle River, NJ: Prentice-Hall), pp. 559-85, a useful short introduction and selection of poems.

Kövesi, Simon, Introduction to *John Clare: Flower Poems* (Bangkok: M&C Services).

— 'The John Clare Copyright: 1820-2000', *The Wordsworth Circle*, 31 (3), (Summer), 112-119.

McKusick, James C., *Green Writing: Romanticism and Ecology* (New York: St. Martins Press/Palgrave), ch. 3: The Ecological Vision of John Clare.

Moss, Stephen, 'Mystery Bird Solved', *JCSN*, 68 (June), 7-8.

Robinson, Eric, Introduction to *John Clare, A Champion for the Poor: Political Verse and Prose*, ed. by P.M.S. Dawson, Eric Robinson and David Powell (Ashington and Manchester: Mid-Northumberland Arts Group and Carcanet Press), pp. ix-lxiii.

— 'Scholarly Notes', *John Clare Society of North America Newsletter*, 2 (January), [4], note on Clare's vowel-free writing.

Storey, Mark, *The Problem of Poetry in the Romantic Period* (London: Macmillan), esp. ch. 5, 'Clare: "This sad non-identity"', and ch. 6, 'Byron and Clare; "An indigestion of the mind"'.

Zimmerman, Sarah M., 'Accounting for Clare', *College English*, 62 (4) (Jan), 317-34.

— 'Clare in the Libraries', *John Clare Society of North America Newsletter*, 2 (January), [4], note on private press and early editions in the University of Madison-Wisconsin Memorial Library.

The following press articles, listed chronologically, cover the dispute over Clare's copyright (see also items under 1999 (b) and 2000 (d)):

Goodridge, John, John Barrell, Tim Chilcott, and 25 others, 'John Clare's Copyright' [letter], *Times Literary Supplement*, 14 July, p. 15.

Mendick, Robert, 'Poets Protest as US Scholar Corners Clare', *Independent on Sunday*, 16 July, p. 5.

Bate, Jonathan, 'Commentary: Don't Fence Him In', *Times Literary Supplement*, 21 July, pp. 14-15.

Leader, Zachary, 'Editorial Injustice in the Raw', *Times Higher*, 21 July, p. 16.

Goodridge, John, 'Poor Clare', *The Guardian*, 22 July, Weekend section, p. 3.

Kövesi, Simon, 'Whispers on a Not So Clear-cut Case of Publish and Be Damned', *Times Higher*, 4 Aug, pp. 20-1.

Jarvis, Edward, 'A War of Words to "Free" Poet', *Nottingham Evening Post*, 11 Aug, p. 31.

Groom, Nick, 'Readers' Reactions', *Times Higher*, 11 Aug, p. 16.

Ramsden, Alison, 'Readers' Reactions', *Times Higher*, 11 Aug, p. 16.

Percy, William A., 'John Clare Scholarship and Copyright' [letters], *Times Literary Supplement*, 11 Aug, p. 17.

Powell, David, 'John Clare Scholarship and Copyright' [letter], *Times Literary Supplement*, 11 Aug, p. 17.

Fletcher, C.V., 'Poems Belong to World' [letter], *Nottingham Evening Post*, 17 Aug, p. 26.

Kövesi, Simon, 'John Clare Scholarship and Copyright' [letter], *Times Literary Supplement*, 25 Aug, p. 17.

Burton, Raffell, 'John Clare Scholarship and Copyright' [letter], *Times Literary Supplement*, 25 Aug, p. 17.

Robinson, Eric H., 'John Clare Scholarship and Copyright' [letter], *Times Literary Supplement*, 1 Sep, p. 17.

Goodridge, John, 'John Clare Copyright' [letter], *Times Literary Supplement*, 8 Sep, p. 17.

Wareham, John, 'John Clare Copyright' [letter], *Times Literary Supplement*, 8 Sep, p. 17.

Lloyd, Jonathan, 'John Clare Scholarship and Copyright' [letter], *Times Literary Supplement*, 22 Sep, p. 17.

Kövesi, Simon, 'John Clare Scholarship and Copyright' [letter], *Times Literary Supplement*, 29 Sep, p. 17.

Glover, Michael, 'The Clash of Paper Swords', *Independent on Sunday*, 1 Oct, Review Section, p. 61.

Cripps, Pete, 'Academics Row over Poet's Work', *Peterborough Evening Telegraph*, 6 Oct, p. 19.

Peters, Catherine, 'John Clare and Copyright' [letter], *Times Literary Supplement*, 6 Oct, p. 19.

Wells, Robert, 'John Clare Scholarship and Copyright' [letter], *Times Literary Supplement*, 20 Oct, p. 17.

Price, Matthew, 'Free and Clare', *Lingua Franca* 10 (8) (Nov), pp. 22-5.

Lloyd, Jonathan, 'John Clare copyright' [letter], *Times Literary Supplement*, 3 Nov, p. 21.

(d) *JCSJ*, 19 (2000)

Bate, Jonathan, 'John Clare's Copyright, 1854-1893', 19-32.

Blythe, Ronald, 'John Clare In Scotland', 73-81.

Chilcott, Tim, '*Child Harold* or *Child Harold*s: The Editing of Clare's Texts', 5-17.

Chirico, Paul, '"The Woodman" and the Natural Anthology', 41-51.

Worrall, David, '"Obnoxious Performance": The Plebeian Culture of Theatre, Street, and Stage in Romantic-Period Melodrama', 53-60.

INDEX

British Critic, The, 117
Brown, Charles, 43
Browne, William, *Britannia's Pastorals*, 134
Brownlow, Timothy, 97-8
Bunyan, John, *The Pilgrim's Progress*, 136
Burke, Edmund, 86
Burns, Robert, 56, 119, 120, 174
— 'Cotter's Saturday Night, The', 135
Byron, George Gordon, Lord, xix, 2, 9, 29, 44, 56, 134, 158, 163-84, 187, 191, 197
— father of, 'Mad Jack', 9
— funeral of, 175-6
— grandfather of, 'Foulweather Jack', 9
   works by
— *Childe Harold*, 163-5, 174-7
— 'Corsair, The', 170
— 'Darkness', 176
— *Don Juan*, 29, 39, 89-90n, 163, 166, 174, 176, 187-99
— 'Giaour, The', 175, 176
— 'Lament of Tasso, The', 161-5, 170, 172, 177-8, 180, 181-4
— *Poems on his Domestic Circumstances*, 176
— 'Prisoner of Chillon, The', 171, 180
— 'Prophecy of Dante, The', 171, 173, 180, 184
— 'Sonnet on Chillon', 186n
— 'Stanzas To Florence', 161, 163
— *Works* (Galignani edition of 1828), 176, 179
— *Works* (Murray edition of 1828), 176
Caretti, Lanfranco, 171
Caroline, Queen, 89n
Cary, H.F., 23, 49, 50, 168
— Translation of Dante, 168
Casterton, Lincs., 94
Chalmers, Alexander, *Works of the British Poets*, 57
Chapman, George, 51, 63n
Chatterton, Thomas, 54-5, 56, 69, 70, 72, 74
— Rowley Poems, 56
— 'Resignation, The', 69
Chaucer, Geoffrey, 134
Cherry, J.L., 1
Chilcott, Tim, xviii, 185n

INDEX

INDEX